CW01333085

A 17TH CENTURY KNIGHT

For Nathan

A 17TH CENTURY KNIGHT

THE LIFE AND TIMES OF SIMONDS D'EWES

BEN NORMAN

Pen & Sword
HISTORY

AN IMPRINT OF PEN & SWORD BOOKS LTD.
YORKSHIRE – PHILADELPHIA

First published in Great Britain in 2024 by
PEN AND SWORD HISTORY
An imprint of
Pen & Sword Books Ltd
Yorkshire – Philadelphia

Copyright © Ben Norman, 2024

ISBN 978 1 39904 225 3

The right of Ben Norman to be identified as Author of this work has been asserted by him in accordance with the Copyright, Designs and Patents Act 1988.

A CIP catalogue record for this book is available from the British Library.

All rights reserved. No part of this book may be reproduced or transmitted in any form or by any means, electronic or mechanical including photocopying, recording or by any information storage and retrieval system, without permission from the Publisher in writing.

Typeset in Times New Roman 10/12 by
SJmagic DESIGN SERVICES, India.
Printed and bound in the UK by CPI Group (UK) Ltd.

Pen & Sword Books Limited incorporates the imprints of Atlas, Archaeology, Aviation, Discovery, Family History, Fiction, History, Maritime, Military, Military Classics, Politics, Select, Transport, True Crime, Air World, Frontline Publishing, Leo Cooper, Remember When, Seaforth Publishing, The Praetorian Press, Wharncliffe Local History, Wharncliffe Transport, Wharncliffe True Crime and White Owl.

For a complete list of Pen & Sword titles please contact
PEN & SWORD BOOKS LIMITED
George House, Units 12 & 13, Beevor Street, Off Pontefract Road,
Barnsley, South Yorkshire, S71 1HN, England
E-mail: enquiries@pen-and-sword.co.uk
Website: www.pen-and-sword.co.uk

or

PEN AND SWORD BOOKS
1950 Lawrence Rd, Havertown, PA 19083, USA
E-mail: uspen-and-sword@casematepublishers.com
Website: www.penandswordbooks.com

CONTENTS

Author's Note vii
Image Credits viii
Acknowledgements x
Preface xi
Introduction xiii

PART ONE: PEACE

Chapter 1   In the beginning 2
Chapter 2   Out of Dorset 8
Chapter 3   Stowlangtoft 12
Chapter 4   A universal education 16
Chapter 5   The road to the Temple 22
Chapter 6   Jemima Waldegrave 28
Chapter 7   City living 33
Chapter 8   Anne Clopton 40
Chapter 9   Wolves 43

PART TWO: UNEASE

Chapter 10   New lives and old 50
Chapter 11   The Lavenham brass 55
Chapter 12   Laud 58
Chapter 13   Ship money, the Elector Palatine and the New World 64
Chapter 14   Conflict at home, conflict afar 69
Chapter 15   The Long Parliament meets 78
Chapter 16   Strafford 82
Chapter 17   The storm gathers 87

PART THREE: WAR

Chapter 18 Brother against brother 96
Chapter 19 Edgehill 102
Chapter 20 An unhappy Christmas 107
Chapter 21 Richard's farewell 110
Chapter 22 'These miserable calamities and civil wars of England' 114
Chapter 23 Marston Moor 120
Chapter 24 The wrath of religion 125
Chapter 25 Naseby 129
Chapter 26 1646 135
Chapter 27 The king's escape 140
Chapter 28 Colchester falls 144
Chapter 29 Purged 151
Chapter 30 'A happy hour' 154

Epilogue   In the end 157
Appendix 1 D'Ewes family tree 160
Appendix 2 Barnardiston family tree 161
Appendix 3 The children of Simonds D'Ewes 162
Notes 163
Bibliography 183
Index 191

AUTHOR'S NOTE

The author has, to the best of his ability, checked prior to publication that all facts, dates, names and places mentioned in this book are historically accurate. Any errors or oversights are entirely the fault of the author.

Spelling and grammar within primary material has been modernised at the author's discretion. Any contemporary sources containing peculiar phrasing, spelling, use of punctuation or use of capitalisation have likely kept their original form. All errors or inconsistencies found within amended or unamended sources are entirely the fault of the author.

All dates presented throughout this work (to the best of the author's knowledge) are in line with the Julian calendar, even where primary source material gives the date in the newer Gregorian style. Years are presented as beginning on 1 January, not 25 March.

IMAGE CREDITS

1. Paul D'Ewes's monument in Stowlangtoft church. (*John Salmon/St George, Stowlangtoft – wall monument*)
2. St George's church, Stowlangtoft, Suffolk. (*Author's private collection*)
3. St Peter and St Paul's church, Lavenham, Suffolk. (*Author's private collection*)
4. Jemima Crew (née Waldegrave). (*Cornelis Janssens van Ceulen, public domain, via Wikimedia Commons*)
5. A monument to the Barnardiston family inside Kedington church, Suffolk. (*Author's private collection*)
6. Epitaph fixed to the tomb of Sir William Clopton and his first wife, found inside Long Melford church, Suffolk. (*Author's private collection*)
7. D'Ewes impaling Clopton, Long Melford church. (*Author's private collection*)
8. The 'baby brass' inside Lavenham church. (*Author's private collection*)
9. The grave slab of Cecilia Darcy inside Long Melford church. (*Author's private collection*)
10. Sir Martin Stuteville's wall memorial inside Dalham church, Suffolk. (*Author's private collection*)
11. Archbishop William Laud. (*Workshop of Anthony van Dyck, public domain, via Wikimedia Commons*)
12. King Charles I and Queen Henrietta Maria. (*Wenceslaus Hollar, CC0, via Wikimedia Commons*)
13. William Prynne's *Histrio-Mastix: The players scourge, or, Actors Tragaedie*. (*Published by Michael Sparke, London, public domain, via Wikimedia Commons*)
14. Charles Louis, Elector Palatine. (*Circle of Anthony van Dyck, public domain, via Wikimedia Commons*)
15. Scottish Prayer Book riots. (*Wenceslaus Hollar, public domain, via Wikimedia Commons*)
16. English and Scottish soldiers embracing. (*Unknown author, public domain, via Wikimedia Commons*)
17. The Earl of Strafford. (*Anthony van Dyck, no restrictions, via Wikimedia Commons*)
18. The Earl of Strafford's execution. (*Wenceslaus Hollar, public domain, via Wikimedia Commons*)
19. John Pym. (*Edward Bower, public domain, via Wikimedia Commons*)
20. Oliver Cromwell. (*Author unknown, CC BY 4.0 <https://creativecommons.org/licenses/by/4.0>, via Wikimedia Commons*)

Image Credits

21. The Earl of Essex. (*Wenceslaus Hollar, CC0, via Wikimedia Commons*)
22. Parliamentary pamphlet on the raising of the royal standard in Nottingham. (*Unknown author, public domain, via Wikimedia Commons*)
23. The taking of the Solemn League and Covenant. (*Author unknown, public domain, via Wikimedia Commons*)
24. The shooting of Prince Rupert's dog, Boye, at Marston Moor. (*English Civil War-era woodcut artist, public domain, via Wikimedia Commons*)
25. The battlefield at Naseby. (*Internet Archive Book Images, no restrictions, via Wikimedia Commons*)
26. Plan of the siege of Colchester. (*British Museum, public domain, via Wikimedia Commons*)
27. Portrait of the siege of Colchester. (*Abraham Cooper, public domain, via Wikimedia Commons*)
28. Charles I's execution. (*Unknown author, public domain, via Wikimedia Commons*)
29. William Dugdale. (*Wenceslaus Hollar, CC0, via Wikimedia Commons*)

Cover Artwork

Charles I. (*Anthony van Dyck, public domain, via Wikimedia Commons*)

The Short Parliament in April 1640. (*Anonymous, public domain, via Wikimedia Commons*)

Broadside allegory of the Houses of Commons and Lords and the Westminster Assembly of Divines. (*British Museum, public domain, via Wikimedia Commons*)

'Arraignment of *Mercurius Aulicus*.' (*British Museum, public domain, via Wikimedia Commons*)

ACKNOWLEDGEMENTS

I DON'T LIKE to go on and on in the acknowledgements, but a few words of gratitude are absolutely necessary here.

In the first place, I would like to convey my thanks to Pen & Sword Books for agreeing to publish this book. My particular thanks go to Jon Wright, who saw the potential in combining a biography on Sir Simonds D'Ewes with a wider commentary on the political and military events of the first half of the seventeenth century.

I am also keen to thank my brother, Nathan, for accompanying me on a tour of some Suffolk churches connected with D'Ewes in December 2022, and again in June 2023 – namely those of Stowlangtoft, Lavenham, Long Melford and Dalham. It was great to walk the spaces that Simonds himself would have walked 400 years ago.

Along with the usual suspects (they know who they are), I want to finally pay tribute to each and every researcher – past and present – who has made information and/or primary material on D'Ewes available in printed form. I could not have written this book without it.

Ben Norman,
July 2023

PREFACE

I ALWAYS KNEW I had something of a tenuous link with Sir Simonds D'Ewes of Stowlangtoft. One of the first things that struck me about him, when reading through his autobiography in the very early days, was the amount of places he visited in his lifetime that were instantly familiar to me. He often called in on his friend and spiritual ally, Sir Nathaniel Barnardiston, at Kedington in Suffolk, a small and pretty settlement where some relatives of mine now live. Naturally, I have grown to know the village well: especially the church of St Peter and St Paul, with its remarkable, preserved interior and unrivalled collection of aristocratic monuments to the dead. A wall installation dedicated to the memory of Sir Nathaniel Barnardiston himself, as well as his wife, Jane, numbers among the memorials that can still be viewed inside the fifteenth-century edifice. Simonds also frequented both Cambridge and Bury St Edmunds during his life, at the beginning for educational purposes, but later because he would live near both towns (and, for a time, actually in Bury). I am very well-acquainted with the two, having grown up at the point where Cambridgeshire, Suffolk and Essex meet each other.

This connection alone was enough to satisfy me that, beyond believing the premise of the present work would be an interesting one, there was some justification in me retelling the story of Simonds D'Ewes: antiquary, knight, baronet, lord of the manor and sometime MP for Sudbury. Then, however, I remembered something else during the book's planning stages. Having researched my family history several years ago, I know that my ninth great-grandfather, Henry Norman, was living in Thorncombe, Dorset, in the 1670s. There is a record of another Henry Norman, potentially his father, being buried in the parish in January 1667, which lends itself to the idea that my ancestors, in fact, may have had deep roots in the area, stretching back many decades. But why do I mention this?

Well, Sir Simonds D'Ewes had not always called rural Suffolk home when he was alive. The antiquary hailed from Dorset originally, being born and partially raised at Coxden, the manor of his maternal grandfather, Richard Simonds. The site of this manor was probably less than four miles from Thorncombe, where my ancestors were in residence at least as early as 1672, and likely well before. Therefore, it is not beyond the realms of possibility that Simonds's family and my own came into contact with each other at some point in the distant past, if only fleetingly or inconsequentially, through a local connection or circumstance of no great note. Perhaps they merely passed one another on the road one day, somewhere in the countryside between Coxden and Thorncombe. Perhaps there were more meaningful interactions than this.

We will never know, but this only makes it all the more intriguing to ponder. Such a notion has certainly entered my mind on more than one occasion during the writing up of D'Ewes's life.

INTRODUCTION

STANDING IN THE sleepy churchyard in Stowlangtoft, Suffolk, with its gently creaking trees, carpet of neatly cut grass, and modest patchwork of gravestones marking the final resting places of local men and women, it is hard to imagine that anybody buried within the medieval building itself could ever have been caught up in something like a great historical event. The tiny village of Stowlangtoft gives off a rather nondescript air generally: the few houses are charming and unassuming, straddling lanes that appear to lead nowhere; the farmland surrounding them is temptingly rustic and delightfully untouched, as well as strikingly empty; and the attractive village sign – positioned effectively in the shadow of St George's, at the bottom of a shallow decline – might be counted among the most quaint in the whole county.

Looks can be deceiving, however. On 7 June 1650, probably during daylight hours, Simonds D'Ewes was one such individual laid to rest within the holy walls of Stowlangtoft church. Though no grave marker or visible tomb survives for him today, there is a handsome wall monument dedicated to his father, Paul D'Ewes, that can still be admired over the south door of the chancel. The ornateness of this memorial hints at the former distinction of the recipient's eldest son and heir, Simonds, who can be glimpsed, immortalised in marble, kneeling with his younger brothers at the bottom-left of the handsome installation. Indeed, the whole is an impressive feat of early seventeenth-century craftsmanship. Paul D'Ewes's likeness takes centre stage beneath a veined arch flanked decoratively by a set of darker pillars, the long-dead man dressed in a white ruff and black gown that falls elegantly about his lower body, with his hands cupped piously around a book. He stares straight out of the memorial into the cavernous expanse of the nave, enabling him to watch with perpetually glazed eyes the many thousands of congregants and visitors who have continued to frequent the church since the real Paul's death in 1631.

Kneeling either side of D'Ewes, with pale hands clasped in prayer, are the submissive forms of his two wives. They are looking directly at each other instead of outwards. Both also wear long, black gowns and white ruffs, the creased hems of their skirts spilling across the marble platform upon which the three figures pose with such severity. Beneath this narrow platform, all seven of Paul's children from his first marriage are captured in stone, kneeling and looking inwards at each other, just like his wives above. There are four girls on one side and three boys on the other, one of whom, as we know, represents Simonds. Being the eldest male child, Simonds's likeness is larger than the rest, though still small in comparison to the sizeable depictions of his father, mother and stepmother. Nevertheless, his own attire is easily discernible. He wears a ruff, jerkin, doublet and breeches, finished with a pair of dark stockings. One brother and one sister carry skulls as opposed to praying, symbolising that they died before the monument was erected.

Simonds D'Ewes was no ordinary parishioner of Stowlangtoft, bound to the village and its provincial insularity from birth until the final moments of life. He was a man of notability, standing and some rank; a man well-informed and well-read; and a man who would find himself caught up in, and on the political frontline of, one of the biggest and most catastrophic upheavals ever to befall England. Born in 1602 to parents who gratefully inhabited the lower rungs of the English gentry, and who, combined, were worth thousands of pounds, Simonds's life from the very beginning was destined to be tinged with a certain level of prominence. As a child, he was educated thoroughly and rigorously at a succession of respectable schools, and under a variety of able tutors; as an adolescent, he followed in the footsteps of many an esquire's son by enrolling at the University of Cambridge, specifically St John's College. Later on, he made the leap from East Anglia to London and commenced his study of the common law at the Middle Temple, with a view to becoming a qualified barrister. In fact, he was first admitted here in 1611, at the tender age of just 8.

From his protracted studies onwards, there was only further social, financial and intellectual improvement for Simonds D'Ewes. He married for both love and money in October 1626, finding for his first spouse an attractive heiress who satisfied his carnal desires and – even more importantly – allowed him to shed his legal career and pursue a lifetime of antiquarian research. With this then came a knighthood from Charles I; a young family of his own; a succession of intellectual alliances and friendships; and, finally, when his father died in March 1631, a considerable portfolio of lands in Suffolk.

Alas, such distinction also brought trials aplenty. The aristocratic mission to bear a son and heir to continue the D'Ewes family line would end in tragedy on more than one occasion for Simonds and Anne, his first wife. Stature in the local community would also lead to the Suffolk knight assuming the role of high sheriff of the county in November 1639, at a time when the position demanded complicity with a hugely unpopular tax known as ship money, levied on the people by an equally unpopular king. It was not long before Simonds was returned to the illustrious House of Commons itself as a member of parliament for Sudbury, as part of the convening of the Long Parliament in November 1640. This is when the man truly stared great historical events, on an unprecedented scale, straight in the face; when the fate of the land – of the very future of the kingdom even – was quite literally at his fingertips.

For, soon after taking his seat in Westminster, which had been silenced for eleven long years on the orders of the irascible Charles I, war broke out on English soil. The opposing parties struggling for supremacy were the Stuart king himself, bent on reigning independently and at the direction of God alone, and parliament. As a serving member of the latter camp, Simonds would have a ringside view of the

Introduction

civil calamity unfolding across the country, with the pen being his ultimate choice of weapon. He would see, and sometimes be involved in personally, the making of political decisions that would affect the entire trajectory of the war. Furthermore, he would witness at close proximity, through appearances in the Commons, first-hand accounts that were the privilege of parliament, and petitions read from aggrieved parties, some of the devastation and complexities of the fighting – without ever setting foot on a battlefield himself. Towards the end of the conflict, particularly following the surrender of King Charles to the covenanter army in 1646, Simonds would also consistently put himself in the spotlight to urge a peaceful settlement over further hostilities with the royalist faction. When the infamous purge of parliamentary members committed to reconciling with the imprisoned king took place in late 1648, Simonds was one of those barred from entering the House of Commons and imprisoned.

Even before the civil war, however, an argument can easily be made that Sir Simonds D'Ewes was involving himself in significant historical episodes. He attended the coronation of Charles I in February 1626, albeit by sneaking through the back door to gain entry; ten years later in February 1636, meanwhile, when in Newmarket in Suffolk, he advised the Elector Palatine on how best to recover his lost lands and usurped position on the continent. At the end of the 1630s, as previously mentioned, Simonds was forced to orchestrate the collection of the detested ship money, which constituted another considerable chapter in English history, in that it would be regarded as one of the chief reasons behind the irrevocable breakdown in relations between king and parliament. Immediately prior to the outbreak of armed hostilities in 1642, Simonds was one of those dispatched to Hampton Court Palace to present the Grand Remonstrance to King Charles and his privy council; he then witnessed the monarch strut into the House of Commons in January 1642, in an unparalleled, unconstitutional move that saw him attempt to arrest five of its members for treason.

The aim of this book has always been twofold. It first and foremost seeks to chart the life of an individual who, in his own right, was interesting, dynamic, intelligent, passionate, privileged and socially notable. Simonds's half-century of existence could never justifiably be described as uninspired or lacking in compelling detail; even contemporaries of his who held the eventual baronet in low regard would not dare to make such an incorrect assertion. Second, it looks to use the life and activities of Sir Simonds D'Ewes, much of which has been recorded in letters, diaries, journals and an unfinished autobiography, to piece together a fresh history – through his exacting eyes – of the tumultuous political happenings of early-to-mid-seventeenth-century England. D'Ewes's involvement in much of the overarching chaos up to December 1648 makes this objective highly attainable.

Where Simonds was a direct witness to an incident in the lead-up to civil war, or experienced first-hand an episode that took place during the conflict, this book uses the thoughts, feelings and observations he left in his personal and formal writings to craft a narrative of proceedings. Of course, much of what D'Ewes saw in the 1640s tended to relate to the goings-on within the House of Commons.

A 17th Century Knight: The Life and Times of Simonds D'Ewes

When talking about events that are crucial to an understanding of the political and martial timeline in England in the 1600s, but that Simonds himself did not see with his own eyes or get involved in directly, the focus on him remains, but is approached in a slightly different way. The protagonist of the present volume was a politician, not a soldier. Where key battles, skirmishes and sieges are discussed, therefore, Simonds's offhand comments about them, or the mentions made of them in parliament where he was usually present, act as springboards for more intensive military commentary. The actions of people whom Simonds knew personally, the movements of members of his extended family, and locations that were familiar to the MP for Sudbury similarly lend themselves to discussions of key moments from which he was absent – both in military and non-military contexts.

Richard D'Ewes, Simonds's younger brother, is a particularly useful figure in this regard. At the coming of conflict, he took an altogether different path to that of his older sibling by enlisting in the king's army – a perfect example of the civil war's ability to divide families right down the middle. Richard would see plenty of action as a lieutenant colonel serving in Colonel Richard Bolle's regiment of foot in the early years of the fighting. Sadly, his military career would end rather quickly upon his death during the frenzied and violent siege of Reading in the spring of 1643. Sir Simonds experienced a good deal of personal tragedy over his lifetime, including the loss of a wife and many children, but it would seem the passing of 27-year-old Richard was no less painful for him. While they had been enemies as far as the war between king and parliament was concerned, the D'Ewes brothers would always be allies in blood.

History has not been unconditionally kind to our studious and dedicated knight from Stowlangtoft. Those who have taken the time to pay attention to Sir Simonds D'Ewes in the past have often been dismissive of both his character and his contribution to the epic saga that was the English Civil War. Referring to his prolonged stint in parliament and his parliamentary journals, which are drawn on extensively throughout this book, John Bruce wrote derisively in the nineteenth century that D'Ewes 'went on, day by day, constant in his attendance, always ready to talk, often talking the merest nonsense in the world, in a pompous grandiloquent way, altogether ludicrous'. Fellow writer John Forster, on the other hand, painted a more encouraging picture of the man's capabilities and worth, again in the middle of the Victorian period. He described Simonds as a 'learned and careful reporter, zealous for the originality of his notes, sensible of the power derived from exercise of such an art, and resolved to abate no jot of the influence it gave him'. He also noted generously in the same work that D'Ewes's strong puritanical leanings 'and the deference really felt for, and paid to, his knowledge of precedents and constitutional forms, caused him to act steadily with them'.[1]

Simonds's religious outlook requires acknowledgement here. Posterity considers him a typical Puritan of his time, possessing conservative views that encouraged a kind of revulsion for sinful behaviour and godly neglect. J. Sears McGee has observed in recent years that D'Ewes 'was a Puritan in an era during which Puritanism was an enormously powerful force politically, religiously, and culturally. The religious dimension is utterly central to D'Ewes's story'.[2] We have much to thank McGee for; his dedicated reappraisal of Simonds in the mid-2010s, woven into a competent and commanding biography of the man, has exponentially helped bring D'Ewes and his busy life out of the shadows of a bygone era. More than this, McGee's work greatly contributes towards separating Simonds-the-human-being from throwaway comments made by the likes of John Bruce in the nineteenth century. No study on Sir Simonds D'Ewes would be complete without a nod to this eminent researcher.

This book is the author's personal attempt to make further sense of, and shed additional light on, both D'Ewes and the dramatic times in which he lived. It is hoped that, together with offering its own informed opinions, it will provide the opportunity for a wider range of individuals to draw conclusions for themselves. For, at the heart of this undertaking, there is the genuine desire to make the hugely fascinating and curiously relatable Sir Simonds D'Ewes known to a new audience.

PART ONE
PEACE

'Divers days of happy content'

Chapter 1

IN THE BEGINNING

DORSET. ENGLAND. 9 DECEMBER 1602.

On this day, in this place, a servant of the esquire Paul D'Ewes, one Thomas Vinnicumbe, was buried in the village of Chardstock near Axminster. The ceremony was probably quite a simple one in all, its unpretentiousness neatly mirrored in the surrounding undulations of quiet, green countryside that made up much of Dorset at the turn of the seventeenth century. For Chardstock was indeed in Dorset in December 1602, and continued to be so until the county boundary was altered nearly 300 years later, transferring the ancient settlement to the easternmost edges of Devon.

As mentioned, Dorset was something of a rural idyll in the early 1600s, much like it continues to be in the twenty-first century. Dominated by stunning chalk downland and acres of enclosed fields containing – at least in the summer months – golden offerings of wheat, barley and oats, and even possessing smaller areas of surviving forest, the county demanded admiration from anybody who chose to frequent it in the closing years of the reign of Queen Elizabeth I. It was much the same story in neighbouring Devon, where the scenery also tended to take the breath away. Here could be found 'wastes, heaths and moors, uphill and downhill among the rocks and stones', according to the seventeenth-century native of Exeter, John Hooker, who avowed that 'the whole province and country within these bounds is in greatness the second to the greatest in this land'.[1]

Whether they had shared a close relationship, Paul D'Ewes was unlikely to have mourned the loss of his servant for long in December 1602. No sooner had Vinnicumbe's grey corpse disappeared beneath the earth than a baby boy was born, rosy-cheeked and screaming, to take his place within the D'Ewes family, on 18 December. The infant in question was the first son of Paul and his young wife Cecilia, who at the time were staying with Cecilia's wealthy parents at Coxden in Dorset, not far from Chardstock. It is by no means an exaggeration to suggest that both mother and father had desired this male child's arrival for many years; indeed, it had been widely supposed that, during the couple's early years of marriage, Cecilia might even be incapable of carrying a baby.

The long-awaited son and heir of Paul D'Ewes was to be named after his wife's family. On 29 December, Simonds (which was his mother's maiden name) was baptised in the open gallery at Coxden, on account of the bitterly cold weather that had then descended on Dorset. Performing the important rite was Richard White, vicar of Chardstock, who would later act as one of Simonds's schoolmasters. The baptism's venue was by all accounts a respectable dwelling in the Elizabethan era, 'being for the most part fairly built of freestone'. Though in no way a building that outdid all other rural seats in the county, the place nonetheless was thought to have been adequately adorned, possessing a central courtyard overlooked by dormer windows, beyond which lay handsome rooms whose walls were elegantly lined with oak panelling. A contemporary description of the dining room survives, made by Simonds himself in later life. 'My... grandfather did... cause to be depicted over the chimney of his dining-room at Coxden in Dorsetshire, his own coat-armour empaled with Lovelace and Ensham,' D'Ewes noted in the 1630s. Upon Simonds's grandfather first taking the house in the late sixteenth century, paying somewhere in the region of £900 for the privilege, it had reportedly been in a dilapidated state. Years later in the 1800s, when Simonds, his grandparents, his parents, his children, and even his grandchildren were all long dead, local hearsay would hint at ghosts stalking the property. 'When we were repairing it,' a nineteenth-century occupant wrote, 'nothing would induce a couple of workmen to remain in it during the night. We have, however, been troubled neither by "the tall old man" nor by "the yellow dog".'[2]

Perhaps 'the tall old man' spoken of was, in fact, Richard Simonds, maternal grandfather of Simonds D'Ewes, and Coxden's well-known proprietor at the end of 1602. Intermittently a justice of the peace in Dorset, as well as a qualified lawyer at the Middle Temple in London, Richard would go on to be idolised by his grandson in the years after his decease, both for his loyal and charitable nature and for the respected place he occupied within the community local to Coxden. The gentleman was 'a man of personage proper, inclined to tallness', according to D'Ewes, 'in his youth valiant and active, towards his latter age full and corpulent, of a full face and clear complexion'. He was quick to anger but apparently willing to forgive just as easily, his grandson continued in his autobiography, having overcome a somewhat inadequate education in his youth by immersing himself in the intellectual – not to mention profitable – world of the law. Certainly, his intellect can be discerned through a surviving sermon on Matthew, written partially in his hand, that now forms part of the Harley Collection at the British Library. Richard had decided to share his prosperous life with Joan (or Johanna), a daughter of William Stephens of Kent, whom Simonds also remembered fondly long after both grandparents had passed away. 'She was a comely tall gentlewoman, even in her old age, and very hospitable, so as her memory [when she died] remained very much endeared amongst her poor neighbours,' he recalled.[3]

The gentry couple Richard and Joan Simonds had a daughter, Cecilia (often spelled 'Sissilia' in contemporary documents), who, as stated, was Simonds D'Ewes's mother. An heiress of her parents, she was born in the market town of Faversham, Kent, in 1579. As with his loving grandparents, Simonds seems only to have collected good memories of this gentlewoman. He described her retrospectively as possessing a 'clear complexion and sweet countenance, often intermixed with modest smiles; her eyes full and quick, being a clear and bright grey, her nose a little rising in the middle'. While merely 'of low stature', Simonds explained in his autobiography, Cecilia D'Ewes's sense of duty was anything but insignificant. For, along with bringing up each of her children to fear God and prioritise faith, she was also known to be a diligent, frugal and hospitable housewife, who strove every day to uphold the reputation of both her husband and her wider family. Despite such sentiments of piety and frugality, Cecilia's position in society meant that she probably dressed relatively well compared to most other people. Paul D'Ewes, in his will, bequeathed to one of his younger daughters, Elizabeth, 'her own mother's gold and pearl border to be delivered unto her purely for her use'.[4]

Paul D'Ewes himself was a complicated and difficult man; his relationship with his eldest son, even more so. Such multi-layered issues, which require due thought and attention across this book, will reveal themselves in the fullness of time. For now, it should be noted that the English esquire was descended from the houses of Cleve and Horne in Gelderland, with Adrian D'Ewes immigrating to England sometime in the reign of Henry VIII in the early sixteenth century. Adrian died in London in 1551, purportedly of the sweating sickness. It is no secret that Simonds would take a keen interest in his Dutch ancestry from a young age, in the same way that he would become obsessed with the complicated lineages of many of his nearest relations and closest friends.

Paul, who eventually purchased a Six Clerks' office in the Court of Chancery in 1607 for a sum just shy of £5,000, seemingly shared his father-in-law's penchant for drafting religious texts. It has been argued that the marriage sermon preached at the nuptials of D'Ewes and Cecilia on 10 December 1594 – which were performed at Axminster – was written by the groom himself, 'with his own hand'. According to Simonds, theirs was an outwardly content arrangement from the beginning. A window onto the playful nature of the relationship the couple shared comes from an anecdote imparted by their eldest son in his autobiography, dating to the months before Cecilia was due to give birth in 1602. Returning to Coxden from London one day, Paul is said to have embraced his wife and communicated his delight that she was pregnant again. 'Ay, indeed,' Cecilia had allegedly replied, 'I am with child; but this is none of yours!' She had meant to imply that her father, Richard Simonds, was planning to claim the child as his own, because it was to be born in his house. Smiling slightly, Paul had listened as the woman had insisted for a second time, 'It is none of yours.'[5]

There was nothing particularly straightforward about the first weeks and months of Simonds's life in rural Dorset. At his birth on 18 December, for instance, the deformed neck of Cecilia's midwife purportedly frightened the expectant mother, who was then forced to watch in horror as the practitioner 'exceedingly bruised and hurt' her baby's right eye as he was being delivered into the world. Such was the damage done that there were genuine fears that the eye would be lost altogether. Towards the end of April 1603, the difficulties surrounding the prized infant only continued. Preparing to leave the quiet and emptiness of Coxden for the noise and grime of London, Paul asked that his wife accompany him on the journey so that she could travel onwards to Wells Hall in Suffolk, to 'look to his household affairs there'. Thus, Simonds was brought along in the coach with his parents and grandfather as far as Dorchester. No amount of breastmilk or singing maids, however, could stop the infant from screaming terribly as the wheels of the coach clattered again and again over 'craggy and uneven' roads en route to the county town. Not even a selection of soft pillows, 'on which they laid me', could keep the baby calm and still. At Dorchester that night, it was supposed that the ride up from Coxden manor had been so traumatic for little Simonds that he would in all likelihood not last until the morning. In light of this, Paul decided to postpone moving off to London for twenty-four hours 'to advise of some course for my safety'.[6]

The sickly child, to everybody's immense relief and gratitude, survived to see a new day dawn – crisp, spring-like and full of resolution – over Dorchester. Paul's solution to his present quandary came in the shape of a local wet nurse, the wife of one Christopher Way, whom he planned to engage to look after Simonds while he and his wife resumed their passage northwards. In the end, though, D'Ewes left for the capital alone. Doting Cecilia could not bear to be parted from her son until she was satisfied that he was in no further danger of death, even after the protestations of her own father, Richard Simonds, that all would be well. Two weeks on, and it would appear that the baby's condition had stabilised enough for Mrs D'Ewes to willingly make her own way up to London, where she then planned to head north-east to East Anglia, in the direction of Wells Hall.

As Simonds was careful to highlight in his autobiography, the introduction of a wet nurse ultimately failed to protect the vulnerable infant from the myriad hazards of a seventeenth-century childhood. Three incidents of note in Dorchester alone dripped forbiddingly from pen to paper in the future antiquary's study. The first concerned a kind of sore that developed in Simonds's right eye, no doubt brought on by the negligence of the incompetent midwife who had helped to deliver him at Coxden manor. A 'great rupture' that risked the baby's life all over again constituted the second, which may well have killed Simonds, had it not been for the quick thinking and evident competence of one Margaret Waltham of the parish of Melcombe Horsey. Her remedies, she being something of a local wise-woman and healer, meant that, in just ten weeks, Simonds was completely cured of whatever had made him so unwell in the first place. The third incident, meanwhile, 'left behind it a large and deep depression' in Simonds's skull, which he appeared to carry around with him until the day he died in 1650.[7] Paul and Cecilia would maintain that the indentation came as a result of a nasty fall suffered by their son while in the care of Mrs Way; the said wet nurse and her husband, however, would tirelessly argue that another sore, like that observed in Simonds's right eye, had caused the disfigurement.

Before his daughter had vacated Dorset to join her spouse in the capital, Richard Simonds had promised to do all he could to keep the couple's dear child safe and well at home. This he continued to do to the best of his ability throughout Simonds's early childhood, minding the infant to an even greater extent when he was moved back to Coxden from Dorchester to live with his grandparents once more. Until he was about 8 years old, Simonds flitted between here and the house of the vicar of Chardstock, Richard White, at which abode he eventually began to receive a gentlemanly education. With White, the student would learn to read

English, although 'his indulgence and tenderness over me... was so great as I found little amendment of any of my errors by residing with him'. The vicar would also take particular care to periodically 'purge out atheism' from Simonds, and to advise him 'to a reverent and high esteem of the Scriptures'.[8] It is very possible that such interactions with Richard White formed the foundation of D'Ewes's strict Puritan faith in later years.

Yet, even during this period of close mentorship and earnest, godly instruction in and around Coxden, mishaps persisted in Simonds's day-to-day living. A stream that snaked prettily past Richard Simonds's manor house revealed its more dangerous side one wet day, when, attempting to cross a slender bridge over it while blindfolded, his grandson slipped and fell in. Though no harm was done to the fearless boy due to the speedy reflexes of some of Richard's tenants, who happened to be working nearby, an older Simonds appreciated in hindsight that he had narrowly avoided drowning. On another occasion, again at Coxden, but this time within the property's courtyard, young D'Ewes found himself in more trouble upon playing with a ball near some coach horses. The ball rolling away from him and directly beneath one of the animals, 'which stood a little straddling with his hind legs', Simonds scrambled under its belly to retrieve the plaything without sparing a thought for the potential consequences, before re-emerging from between the horse's back limbs – toy in hand.[9] His parents and grandfather, rightfully so, were furious with his behaviour; having seen the little boy disappear from view from their vantage point at the opposite end of the courtyard, they had all felt certain that he would be kicked to death in a matter of seconds.

In the pious keeping of Richard White in Chardstock, furthermore, a particularly bad case of the measles – a common childhood sickness in the seventeenth century – would take hold of Simonds, provoking additional expressions of anxiety from those closest to him. The profuse bleeding that apparently preceded his disease was alarming to say the least, and encouraged Cecilia D'Ewes to care for her son personally as he battled deliriously towards recovery. Richard Simonds would once again shoulder much of the emotional burden for the family when, in 1610, his grandson contracted a second major illness, being a 'very violent and long fever' that lasted between eight and nine weeks. The physician John Marwood of Colyton became concerned enough about the malady at one stage to think it prudent to prepare Richard for the worst. In response to this dire forewarning, the aged grandfather declared openly that '[Simonds] hath now made me weep for him once, but surely, if through God's mercy he may but recover, I will carry him home to avoid any more such scarings'.[10]

Thankfully, Simonds did, for a second time, escape the unforgiving clutches of a seventeenth-century childhood ailment. While the actions of both his grandparents could be partly attributed to such a happy resolution, there is credible reason to believe that they were not entirely faultless when it came to the touch-and-go episode. Because Joan Simonds was old, frail and indulgent, and Richard often away on legal business in London, activities within their Dorset mansion were frequently known to include drinking, swearing and 'corrupt discourses'. Such antics were made considerably worse by the plentiful store of alcohol that Richard kept in constant supply in his cellar, consisting of cider, beer and various wines. 'I drank so liberally of them all,' Simonds recalled, 'as I verily believe it inflamed my blood, and was the cause of a most dangerous fever I afterwards fell into.'[11]

Whatever had caused the young boy to go down with such a serious illness, Richard Simonds seemed to feel, following his grandson's merciful recuperation, that it was high time he travelled up to London to see his metropolitan father. In October 1610, therefore, final preparations were made for the pair's departure northwards. Simonds's naivety prevented him from understanding the tearful countenance of his grandmother in the last hours before the travelling party set off for Blandford Forum in western Dorset, which was to be the first port of call on the road; nor could he properly get to grips with why she chose to say very little to him at their parting. As it turned out, the gentlewoman had somehow sensed a sad truth: that she would never lay eyes on her beloved grandson again.

CHAPTER 2

OUT OF DORSET

THE MARKET TOWN of Blandford Forum, Simonds's first real taste of life beyond the Dorset-Devon border, offered up an exciting incident when the curious boy and his grandfather briefly stayed here in the autumn of 1610. Lodging at the Red Lion inn, young D'Ewes, in his enthusiasm for a new place, decided to chase after a flock of birds picking greedily at a heap of horse excrement in the alehouse's yard. Little did he or his attendant know that a puddle sitting stagnant nearby, covered over with a layer of 'dry litter', was in fact concealing a low and muddy hole, into which Simonds proceeded to sink up to his knees. He was immediately pulled out by his attendant, a clerk, who then slipped clumsily into the filth himself. 'Being come into the house,' Simonds wrote in his autobiography, 'we were assured from all hands, that if I had passed on but one foot further I had been swallowed up into a deep pit, [dug] there on purpose to receive the stable-dung.'[1]

There was to be little tomfoolery on display once London's great, formidable shadow fell across Simonds and the rest of his travelling companions. With Paul D'Ewes arriving on the scene during a convivial dinner that his son and father-in-law were enjoying together one evening, Simonds's excitable mood cooled altogether. Indeed, the boy seemed to realise in this moment that the halcyon days of his early youth had drawn to an informal close, and that life would never quite be the same again. What made such a turning point especially difficult for him to digest was the thought of not spending every day in the company of his kindly grandparents, whom he viewed essentially as a surrogate mother and father. Without question, he felt a closer bond with Richard and Joan Simonds than he did with Paul and Cecilia D'Ewes.

The 7-year-old Simonds became yet more convinced of change ahead following his grandfather's suggestion that he visit his actual mother in Wells Hall, Suffolk, for an extended period. The boy obviously had little say in where he was to be moved to from London. Soon, accompanied by a tenant of Richard Simonds, one William Ceafe, he found himself breaching the capital's northernmost suburbs and traversing uneven East Anglian roads bordered by infinite, rolling countryside, his juddering coach bound for the place where Cecilia and his sisters were in residence. Suffolk, like Dorset, was a pretty enough county in the early seventeenth century. Largely undisturbed by urban development, the region for the most part consisted of large swathes of farmland, grassland and, in the north-west, marshy fenland, the majority of which was occupied by crops and livestock. 'The soyle receveth not in every place [one] certain kind but in some places, as among the enclosures, it is heavy with clay and sometime intermixed with Chalks, in other places, as neare the

Champion, it is lighter and with a variable and sandy earth,' one R. Reyce wrote in 1618.[2]

That Cecilia was pleased to have her son with her at Wells Hall is beyond any doubt. Simonds joined not just his mother here, but also several of his siblings. By late 1610, he had four living sisters to amuse him and keep him company, which, given the high infant mortality rate circulating in Jacobean England, was a relatively healthy number of children. These included Johanne, his older sister (born in 1601); Grace (born in 1604); Mary (born in 1608); and Cecilia (born in 1610). A younger brother, Paul, had died in infancy by the time Simonds embarked on his travels, while an additional brother and sister (Richard and Elizabeth) were yet to be conceived.

The fluid nature of Simonds D'Ewes's stay in Suffolk was confirmed when, in 1611, he was sent to school in the village of Lavenham. This was an area of the county that Paul D'Ewes himself, now in possession of a Six Clerks' office in the capital, would take a financial interest in. Around this time, the esquire acquired the manors of Overhall, Netherhall and Lavenham from Isaac Woder – of Gray's Inn in London – for £2,500, to include the advowson of Lavenham (meaning that Paul would be able to appoint a member of the clergy to a vacant benefice there, or at least recommend someone for the role). Excluded from the conveyance was a piece of land called 'Lavenham Parke', which was seemingly attached to Lavenham Hall, where the widow of Sir Thomas Skinner, Mary, was still residing when D'Ewes made his hefty purchase midway through King James I's reign.[3]

While Dame Mary Skinner continued to enjoy her comfortable life at Lavenham Hall, Joan Simonds, herself not yet a widow, was slowly fading away in the West Country. She died in early 1611, veritably robbed of the chance to see and speak to her grandson one last time, and was buried at Chardstock on 23 February. Her widowered husband, overcome with sadness at the gentlewoman's passing, dreamt some weeks later that his deceased wife 'came to him' from the other side and 'called him to follow her'. A spell of bad weather in the summer, during which there was a 'great and long shower of rain', served to transform this vision into an upsetting reality for the gentleman's family. On 27 June, Richard Simonds also passed away at Coxden, having been 'driven by the wind... with much violence upon the right side of his body' en route to Shaftesbury from Salisbury.[4]

Richard's relatives and friends gathered in Chancery Lane in London to mourn his death. Here we can assume the will was discussed at some length, a full copy of which survives to this day as part of the records of the Prerogative Court of Canterbury, where the document was eventually probated. Its content is useful in shedding even further light on Richard Simonds's personality, the relationships he shared with family members and his household servants, and the sort of life he may have led both at Coxden and in London. 'To each of my loving brothers William and Thomas Symonds I give several pieces of plate... to the several values of £10 apiece,' he willed, 'which I hope they will thankfully accept as an assured pledge of my unfeigned and never dying brotherly love towards them.' For the poor of Chardstock, there was £5 put by in the will; for the needy of Taunton, the same amount again. Richard's servants, additionally, were all to be given 20 shillings each, save for one Thomas Tibbes, who was to be bequeathed the larger sum of £15. The Dorset esquire desired that Paul D'Ewes might 'have care' of this particular servant when he was dead and buried, which showed him to be, if nothing else, a considerate and compassionate master.

Of course, the will directed that there was to be money aplenty for Richard's close family. Johanne, Grace, Mary and 'Sissilia', his granddaughters, could each expect to receive £50 upon either their wedding days or their eighteenth birthdays – whichever event came first. Simonds himself, meanwhile, had been earmarked to one day take over the lucrative manor of Coxden, his grandfather's estate in Dorset. The thinking was that the boy might even take up residence there, for the good of the local community it would appear, as much as for his own comfort and pleasure. 'If it be his will... I beseech him... dwell where I do and there keep a house to the credit and remembrance of me his grandfather and to help relieve the poor,' Richard wrote emphatically.[5]

On 5 July 1611, the time had come for the entire family to leave London and return to the Dorset-Devon border for Richard's burial. For Paul and Simonds D'Ewes, there had been important business to attend to beforehand. Father and son had paid a visit to the Middle Temple, one of the four Inns of Court, on 2 July, to admit Simonds to the prestigious establishment in preparation for his legal training further down the line. Paul D'Ewes had been admitted himself some twenty-six years earlier, on 3 July 1585; Richard Simonds had also been a member until his death that year.

Had he still been living, it may have been a comfort to Richard to know that his grandson and namesake would be following in his footsteps at the Middle Temple, where a profitable and honourable career as a barrister awaited him. All that remained of the man and his thoughts and feelings now, however, was a corpse lying limply in a coffin at Coxden, ready to be interred beneath the floor of the church in Chardstock. On 11 July, such a removal came to pass. In the presence of his loved ones and the vicar Richard White, who had been given a mourning gown to wear as he delivered the funeral sermon, Richard Simonds was laid to rest beside his wife 'without pomp', as per his last wishes. His will had further called for the erection of 'some monument cut in stone of her and my semblance' within the wall near to his usual pew, which Paul D'Ewes seems to have eventually honoured as well. Centuries later, a fragment of this church memorial was rediscovered and described in minute detail by a contemporary, being a shield measuring 4¼ inches wide by 5 inches deep, 'carved on an ornamental block of the same material', which itself was partially gilded. It has been surmised that this small portion of the monument commemorated the marriage of Paul and Cecilia in 1594, and by extension the coming together of their two great families.[6]

The proud D'Ewes dynasty lost the manor of Wells Hall in Suffolk just a short time later. Young Simonds D'Ewes, who was once more residing in his beloved Dorset, could not be expected to feel any meaningful sense of grief over the rather sudden dispossession; that was for his father alone to come to terms with. Instead, the boy focused on furthering his education as 1612 inched steadily closer, under the guidance of Christopher Malaker of Wambrook, a village near Chard. Malaker's tutoring of D'Ewes commenced enthusiastically in September 1611; such was their warm association and mutual understanding, in fact, that Simonds would even spend Christmas in Wambrook at the end of the year. The knight recalled decades later in his autobiography developing a recreational taste, in between lessons with his tutor, for wandering across to the public gallows in Chard and watching the executions that took place there.

Where Simonds's professional future within the criminal justice system was concerned, the state of play was somewhat uncertain by the autumn of 1611. At a 'parliament' held on 25 October at the Middle Temple, Jerome Hawley and Edward James came forward to petition that the 8-year-old's claim to their room be voided immediately (having previously been occupied by his grandfather), because the space consisted 'but of two small parts besides the studies, and can be convenient for two students only'. After due deliberation, the petitioners' request was granted on 7 February 1612, at which time it was ordered that 'Hawley and James only shall be admitted, and Dewse's admittance be void, so that no more than two shall henceforth be admitted to the said chamber'. The disappointing situation was only rectified months later in June, when it was announced that a room was to be made available for Simonds upon his beginning at the Middle Temple after all – provided that one of its two occupants, somehow including Hawley, had vacated it by then. If the room was still fully occupied when D'Ewes entered the Temple to initiate his legal career, the treasurer had agreed to provide another 'convenient chamber for him'.[7]

For now, then, all was well. About 1613, amid plague that is said to have ravaged neighbouring Axminster, Paul and Cecilia D'Ewes left Coxden and the many memories it held for both of them for the last time, in effect bringing to a close the earliest chapter of Simonds's eventful life. The boy himself, who was now turning into an intelligent and eligible young man, finally vacated the county in November 1614. One of Paul's last acts in relation to his and his wife's permanent move away from Dorset was to arrange for a large amount of the couple's household belongings to be sent via sea to the Suffolk coastline, where they were then to be carted inland to Lavenham. It was a decision that would spare the items involved from a devastating fire at the Six Clerks' Office in London some years later.

Chapter 3

STOWLANGTOFT

WHEN A COLD and distinctly autumnal November 1614 arrived in Dorset, the month brought with it the pertinacious calls of Paul D'Ewes to his only living son, ordering him back to London at the earliest opportunity. Simonds received a surprisingly happy welcome at his father's office in Chancery Lane upon his arrival there, finding 'much comfort by the sight of both my parents and my four affectionate sisters'.[1] Yet, the boy's summoning to the capital was not merely for the purposes of a loving reunion with his family, however pleasant this might be for all involved; nor did it constitute an opportunity for Simonds to spend time idly in recreational activities that could only be pursued in the city. There were still academic subjects to be mastered, as well as gentlemanly qualities to cultivate. Soon, the obliging student was again under the instruction of an able tutor, one Henry Reynolds, who kept a house in the medieval parish of St Mary Axe.

While Simonds would not always regard Mr Reynolds fondly, or even courteously, there can be no doubt that he was admiring of some of the man's qualities and capabilities. In his autobiography, he wrote:

> And yet he had a pleasing way of teaching, contrary to all others of that kind; for the rod and ferular stood in his school rather as ensigns of his power than as instruments of his anger, and were rarely made use of for the punishment of delinquents; for he usually rewarded those who deserved well with raisins of the sun or other fruit.[2]

He was also complimentary about Reynolds's daughter, Bathshua, whom he praised at her father's expense. '[She] had an exact knowledge in the Greek, Latin, and French tongues,' Simonds remembered, 'with some insight also into the Hebrew and Syriac; much more learning she had doubtless than her father, who was a mere pretender to it.'[3]

1614 was a monumental twelve-month period for the D'Ewes family. The manor that came to define them, that of Stowlangtoft in Suffolk, was purchased this year, forming a significant part of the reason Simonds was able to put Coxden behind him as easily as he did. The estate was sold to Paul D'Ewes by Sir Robert Ashfield, who had until then been living in the manor house on the site, known locally as Stow Hall (or Stowhall). In 1615, the last of the land was released by Penelope Ashfield to D'Ewes, enabling Paul to press ahead with the innumerable building projects that had been lined up for his new country bolthole. These projects were begun in earnest on 26 March, three months before Simonds himself would set foot in Stowlangtoft for the very first time, as a wide-eyed visitor to his father's most recent acquisition.

When referring to his initial viewing of the manor house at Stowlangtoft in his autobiography, Simonds had surprisingly little to say about its finer details. He described Stow Hall simply as 'a goodly and pleasant seat', which 'my father, after he had bought it, enlarged and beautified very much with brick-walls and buildings'. Happily, documents and odd snippets of information survive that allow us to flesh out this rather characterless account of a building that, at least in its seventeenth-century form, no longer exists. Through an inventory of household goods taken at Stow Hall on 15 June 1613, for example, we know that, when Paul D'Ewes took over the property a year later in 1614, the place would have been made up of numerous rooms that had, until recently, all been comfortably furnished. These comprised a hall and parlour, with the parlour having been home to 'a dozen cushions of Turkye worke' in Sir Robert Ashfield's time; a great chamber, where a long table had formerly been set up for meals; a room called 'the Duke's chamber'; a 'blue chamber' and an 'inner blue chamber', where curtains were known to have hung about the windows; a long gallery that ran between the blue chamber and an additional 'green chamber'; and an 'inner green chamber'.[4] Outside, and probably spread across the grounds, there was a brewhouse, a kitchen, a larder, a pantry, a backhouse and a gatehouse. In the chamber over the gatehouse, when Ashfield had lived at Stow Hall, a bedstead, two blankets, a coverlet and a mat could be found.

How exactly Stow Hall developed over Paul D'Ewes's tenure is difficult to ascertain, but not impossible. Again, we turn to the valuable last will and testament as a mine for relevant information. In his own dating to the late 1620s, Paul offhandedly mentioned a study at his beloved Suffolk mansion, where 'all my old and new golden coins in a little leather purse' were kept. He also referred to 'the Duke's chamber', which had apparently survived intact since the days of Sir Robert Ashfield in the 1610s. During Simonds's own reign as lord of the manor of Stowlangtoft, between March 1631 and his death in April 1650, further records indicate that improvements to the house and grounds continued unabated. An agreement was made in April 1634 between D'Ewes and one Robert Winnif, for instance, for setting up a 'horse-mill' at Stow. Another document, meanwhile, tells us that Simonds arranged for the 'arms and inscriptions' of his family to be 'annealed in glass' and then 'put into the windows of his house of Stow Hall'.[5] In his autobiography, D'Ewes elected to mention that the property was in fact moated in the middle of the century, with brick bridges crossing the water at various points. However, this descriptive morsel was only spoken of incidentally, while the knight relayed the somewhat peculiar tale of how he and his future wife, Lady Anne Clopton, had once fallen from a boat into its depths.

In the days of William the Conqueror, at the latter end of the eleventh century, Stowlangtoft had merely consisted of a mill; stores of wood for about twenty or so hogs; a flock of thirty sheep; 8 acres of green meadow; and a church with 40 acres of free land. Jump forward to the early 1600s, and the manor's basic composition was not likely to have been too dissimilar. It was into such rural obscurity that Richard D'Ewes, the third son of Paul and Cecilia, was born on 14 October 1615. Paul D'Ewes being away from Stow Hall at the time of his coming into the world, Cecilia took the opportunity to name the baby after her late father, because 'he had a full grey eye' that was very like Richard Simonds's had been.[6] This was the first time that Cecilia had given birth in over five years. Therefore, the infant's arrival was a surprise to almost everybody – not least his mother and father.

The timing of Richard's birth at Stow Hall was curiously fortuitous for the D'Ewes family. Having returned to London in the spring of 1616 to resume his academic studies, Simonds caught smallpox over the summer months, becoming at one point so ill with a fever that it was thought Paul might lose his heir to the disease. Fortunately, smallpox did not progress as far in the 13-year-old boy as it did in some sufferers. 'After they [the characteristic spots] once appeared, though I had them very thick, yet through God's goodness I was never in any further danger whilst they continued, nor [in] any way disfigured by them after they were departed,' Simonds wrote gratefully in his autobiography.[7] His recovery, among many other things, allowed him to witness a royal dinner at the Palace of Whitehall on 4 November, which followed on from the inauguration of Prince Charles as the Prince of Wales that morning. Simonds saw Charles dressed in full regalia, his father King James I looking proudly down on him from a viewing gallery, and James's favourite, the future Duke of Buckingham, standing close by to his regal master. He was allowed an even better view of Buckingham when the courtier descended from the gallery to pay Prince Charles a compliment from the king, with the two talking for a good while and exchanging several smiles.

Less satisfying for the revitalised boy was the breaking down of his educational relationship with Henry Reynolds, his tutor in London, at the tail end of 1616. A series of 'divers emergent grudges' between the two encouraged Simonds to call for urgent mediation from his mother in Suffolk, who, ever willing to help her children in any way she could, arranged for her son to be removed from Reynolds's instruction and sent to the King Edward VI Grammar School in Bury St Edmunds instead.[8] Located just a few short miles from the manor of Stowlangtoft, this respectable institution would act as a convenient site of learning for Simonds, enabling him to satisfactorily wrap up his preliminary education before enrolling at the University of Cambridge.

Bury St Edmunds in the early seventeenth century still found itself dominated by the remains of the abbey that had for so long been the supreme authority in the town. John Leland described the settlement's outlook in 1539, shortly before the abbey was dismantled as part of the Dissolution of the Monasteries:

> A city more neatly seated the Sun never saw, so curiously doth it hang upon a gentle descent, with a little river on the east side; nor a monastery more noble, whether one considers the endowments, largeness or unparalleled magnificence. One might think even the

monastery alone a city: so many gates it has... so many towers, and a church, than which nothing can be more magnificent; as appendages to which, there are three more, of admirable beauty and workmanship, in the same churchyard.[9]

When Simonds arrived to take up his place at Bury's grammar school in 1617, it had been almost ten years since a major fire had swept violently through the market town. Some 160 houses had been consumed in April 1608 upon the outbreak of the said blaze within a malt house, causing damage amounting to upwards of £60,000. According to contemporary reports, the situation could have been even worse if not for a miraculous stroke of good fortune. 'In a most strange and sudden manner,' one account described, 'through winds, the fire came to the farthest side of the town, and as it went left some streets and houses safe and untouched.'[10]

Chapter 4

A UNIVERSAL EDUCATION

ON 20 MAY 1618, Simonds set off from Stow Hall with a servant and one of his father's clerks, bound for the ancient town of Cambridge. After years of pursuing a disjointed education with a number of tutors of varying abilities, in a number of different locations, the time had come for the 15-year-old to take the academic step that was expected of any gentleman's son when he reached a certain age in his youth. This would be the day that Simonds was enrolled at university.

St John's College within the University of Cambridge, where D'Ewes was to be admitted as a student, had been established for over a hundred years by 1618. Founded by Lady Margaret Beaufort in 1511, its studentship had thus far included the poet Sir Thomas Wyatt; the eminent statesman and royal adviser to Queen Elizabeth I, William Cecil, 1st Baron Burghley; Henry Wriothesley, 3rd Earl of Southampton; and the ill-fated supporter of Charles I, Thomas Wentworth, 1st Earl of Strafford, who had first passed through the doors of St John's as an undergraduate in 1609. Paul D'Ewes could not count himself among this distinguished list of alumni. Instead, the esquire had attended the equally impressive colleges of Magdalen in Oxford, where he had matriculated in 1581, and Pembroke in Cambridge, at which he had been a student from 1584.

Simonds's journey through East Anglia to Cambridge cannot have been an altogether agreeable one in the spring of 1618, for when he and his attendants arrived at St John's, the first thing that they all did was gratefully strip off their hats, boots and cloaks. This completed, the enrolment proceeded to take place. Simonds's tutor for the duration of his studies at Cambridge was to be one Richard Holdsworth, then a junior fellow of St John's College. Eventually, Holdsworth's championing of modern methods of educating would see him become master of nearby Emmanuel College, cementing his name in the long history of the university. 'I know him to be a most learned man, and I am confident that he would be most ready to further a reformation in the church,' Simonds would say of him much later, when moves were made to secure the academic a bishopric.[1]

It would be several weeks more before D'Ewes officially began as an undergraduate at St John's. The date of his departure, July 1618, could not come quickly enough. The young man found himself both lonely and listless in the intervening period, craving purpose yet finding little in Bury, though he continued to engage intellectually with the schoolmaster of King Edward's, Mr Dickenson. At long last, the time came for him to bid farewell to his friends and family in Suffolk, and to trek back through the East Anglian countryside to Cambridge. Simonds's quarters at St John's were to be in the first or 'old' court, which, apparently, contained less pleasant air than the second or 'new' court.[2] Meanwhile, he was to share his rooms with William Cason (this being the traditional set-up at university), whom D'Ewes was already acquainted with through mutual attendance at a previous school.

The blissful first days of Simonds's undergraduate studies at Cambridge, which consisted of playing tennis, dabbling in the odd game of bowls, and taking walks around the college, were all of a sudden shattered when news of the worst possible kind was brought to him late one evening. At around midnight, the student was awoken by a series of urgent knocks upon his chamber door, the incessant rapping the work of one of his father's dutiful clerks. The man had come to inform Simonds that his mother was gravely ill, and likely to die. Dressing by candlelight, and taking heed of some words of comfort offered by his tutor, Richard Holdsworth, D'Ewes promptly left St John's with the sober messenger who had unleashed such panic in his rooms, galloping with all haste towards Stowlangtoft as the summer sun rose hopefully above the horizon. The sheer urgency of the journey 'spoiled' the horse that Simonds rode that morning, the animal having originally accompanied him out of Dorset.[3]

The pair's arrival at Stow Hall would do nothing to quell the mounting fears of Cecilia D'Ewes's eldest son. A sombre reception indeed greeted the weary travellers within the inner courtyard of the house, with Simonds's father, plus William Latham, a cousin of the family, both fighting back tears as they ushered the newcomers indoors. Simonds, with Paul's blessing, was taken straight to the chamber in which his mother lay dying. 'I saw her so changed and altered with her sickness,' the bereft son recollected, 'as that I scarcely knew her.' Cecilia was able to talk to Simonds with a thin, faltering voice when he entered the room, seeming to recognise in her grown-up child the intense grief that he was experiencing as a result of her illness. 'Ah child, thou hast a sick mother,' she reportedly said from her bed.[4] While Cecilia was undeniably close to death in this intimate moment, in reality the gentlewoman would survive for several more days at Stow Hall, sometimes appearing to recover a little in the eyes of her relatives, yet ultimately growing frailer and frailer as July drew to a close. Eventually, a physician confirmed to the despondent family, who had been hanging off his every word, that there was no chance of her recovery. Cecilia died quietly just an hour later, on 31 July.

The funeral, unlike those of her parents, was held at neighbouring Stowlangtoft church, where the matriarch was also buried. Paul D'Ewes would in time be interred close to his first wife, beneath a marble monument that would feature both of their likenesses, mentioned in the introduction to this book. The ceremony was by all accounts performed 'with very good solemnity' that late summer day, being the hallmark of a seventeenth-century aristocratic funeral in England.[5] Guests included an interesting mix of the privileged and the desperately needy; of local gentry families looking to pay their respects, to say goodbye to one of their own, and casual paupers looking for a burial dole or an edible handout. Simonds was convinced that the sermon, conducted by one Mr Chamberlain, would linger in the minds of the congregation for a long time after the final word on Cecilia's many desirable qualities and characteristics had been spoken.

If the Cambridge student believed that the sudden death of his mother would bring him closer to his temperamental father, in grief if in nothing else, he was sorely mistaken. Before Cecilia's body had even gone cold, heated arguments erupted between Simonds and Paul over the former's university expenses, which the latter considered totally unreasonable and, as a consequence, unacceptable. It was only at the last minute, when Simonds made to depart Stow Hall for Cambridge again, that Paul D'Ewes gave in and agreed to part with the money that his son had asked for. The discerning Simonds was aware that such a financial system was not sustainable in the long term. To ensure a more secure agreement with his father where finances were concerned, therefore, he enlisted the help of his tutor, Richard Holdsworth, who also stood to lose out if Paul's unpredictable attitude towards expenses continued. Both Holdsworth and his pupil presently returned to Stow Hall to put on a united front. The confrontation, needless to say, worked a treat; with his tutor present, Simonds managed to negotiate a £50 stipend from the esquire of Stowlangtoft.

The astute teenager seemed to encounter no difficulties in crafting several close friendships at St John's College in the second half of 1618. One such companion acquired by Simonds was James Wriothesley (the eldest son of Henry Wriothesley, 3rd Earl of Southampton), who would go on to die aged just 19 years old in November 1624. Within the grounds of the college, when the weather was particularly hot, D'Ewes claimed that the two could often be found sitting beneath the canopy of a walnut tree talking familiarly with one another. Otherwise, they might be discovered playing tennis, or, rather unusually for Simonds, engaging in a game of cards after supper.

In many ways, D'Ewes also found a friend in the academic Richard Holdsworth during his first months at St John's. On a dark November morning, for example, both junior fellow and undergraduate looked out of the window in Holdsworth's chamber – in a moment of companionship – to glimpse a brilliant comet blazing across the inky sky, with the two appearing to be equally astonished at what they could see beyond the glass. 'It grew soon after to a length so formidable, in the shape of a fox's tail, as to fill men's minds with dismal conjectures,' D'Ewes wrote later. The Simonds of the 1630s was rather fixed on the celestial notion that the 'portentous star' may have presaged a catastrophic accident that the young student was about to suffer, which was to occur not long after the comet disappeared from the heavens.[6]

The near-fatal accident in question took place on 21 December 1618, just days before Christmas. That morning, Simonds woke to the familiar sound of a bell ringing out across St John's, which encouraged him to get up, dress, and walk across to the place where the instrument was located. His intention, as he wandered through the dark, deserted college towards the melodic din, was to ring the bell himself to get a little recreational exercise from it. The reality of the experience, however, was far from leisurely for all who were unlucky enough to be involved. Sometime after he had taken control of the rope from the previous ringer, Simonds became so physically tired from the activity – having ignored the helpful suggestions of the students who were with him – that 'I could neither well guide the rope I held, nor my own body'. This fatigue caused the undergraduate to accidentally tread on, and get himself caught up in, the said cord attached to the bell, which then led to the jerking upwards of his whole person to an undetermined height above the floor, before he was thrown down again onto his unprotected head. It was anything but a soft landing: skull and a thin layer of tissue collided with a hard, concrete 'half-pace' in the passage.[7]

Not only did nobody think to catch Simonds as he hurtled towards the step, but the incident happened so suddenly, and with such violence, that it seemed to shock every witness into running from the scene as fast as possible. Just one boy felt guilty enough about what had transpired to return to assist the stricken D'Ewes, who 'lay upon the ground as dead'. With some difficulty, he managed to get Simonds to his feet and returned to his chamber, where the patient proceeded to slip into a wholly senseless state while his tutor and a surgeon were hastily sent for. It did not look at all good. Well into the afternoon, blood poured relentlessly from Simonds's pale ears and gradually pooled on his bedclothes; deranged cries of anguish escaped from his lips, echoing awfully around the room; and 'ghastly fits of convulsions' coursed through his entire body.[8] In fact, he was given up for dead several times by the surgeon attending him, one Dr Allott, who presumably had enough experience of dealing with injury to know when a situation was hopeless.

Upon the patient stabilising somewhat in his chamber, plans were made by Allott and another Cambridge surgeon, Mr Lichfield, to remove a section of Simonds's skull that the men believed was pressing dangerously against his brain. It was while they were in the process of tying down the undergraduate's arms (so that he would not be tempted to prevent them from performing the surgery) that D'Ewes came to his senses sufficiently to point out that the dent identified by the surgeons, which appeared by sheer coincidence on the side of his head, was an old wound from years ago, and should not be cut into. This fact being confirmed by another student, one Chambers, who was deemed to have a more reliable mind in that moment, Allott and Lichfield decided that the damage was not as great as had been originally feared.

Miles away in the capital, Paul D'Ewes was informed of the dramatic sequence of events unfolding in Cambridge by special messenger. In an instant, his festive cheer, already heavily subdued by the death of his beloved wife in July, crumbled. The esquire had no idea whether his son was dead or alive as he hurried out of London with his eldest daughter, Johanne, who was ready to support her distraught father if required. Rumours on the road to the university town hinted at both a sorry conclusion and a miraculous outcome where Simonds was concerned; while one scholar told Paul that his son was almost certainly dead, 'slain two days ago by ringing of the college bell', another maintained that the student had, against all the odds, survived his ordeal.[9] Consequently, the father and daughter did not know what to believe as they passed through Cambridge towards St John's College, though, because the scholar had mentioned that he knew young D'Ewes personally, they were inclined to believe the latter report. Happily for them, it was indeed the case that Simonds had made a full recovery.

Having brought sufficient funds with him from London in the event that he would be required to pay for his son's funeral, Paul instead used the money in

Cambridge to celebrate Simonds's swift recuperation. The esquire of Stowlangtoft may have come to regret so willingly parting with this monetary sum early the following year. In a cruel but fairly typical twist of fate, the spring of 1619 would see the eldest D'Ewes child, now 16 years old, yet again in poor health when he was struck down with a 'sharp and long tertian argue'.[10] No obvious remedy or potion would ease Simonds's discomfort at St John's. Soon, the student came to the conclusion that only a change of air would be able to properly cure him of his debilitating ailment, which he found first at Bury St Edmunds and then at neighbouring Stow Hall in Stowlangtoft. Though Simonds relapsed rather seriously on one occasion at Stow, by the concluding days of May he was well enough to travel back to Cambridge.

A very public figure who would not be so fortunate in early 1619 when it came to her own health was Queen Anna of Denmark, the wife of King James I. Simonds mentioned the passing of the consort in his autobiography, noting briefly, 'it pleased God in the beginning of this year to take out of this vale of misery our Royal Queen'. Anna had been ill for a while by the coming of spring, with her brother, King Christian IV of Denmark, failing to materialise as he had promised to lift her dwindling spirits. At Hampton Court Palace, where she was to spend her final weeks, the queen's physicians became inventive in their attempts to drag the sick woman back from the abyss. One doctor firmly believed that instructing Anna to saw wood for hours on end would get her circulation moving again, an interesting prescription that, perhaps unsurprisingly, led to a second haemorrhage. In the early hours of 2 March, all were in agreement that there was nothing more that could be done. With Prince Charles, the Archbishop of Canterbury, the Bishop of London, her doctors and her Danish maid, also called Anna, in attendance, the queen began to slip away. 'Your properties, madam. Can I have those?' Charles frantically asked his mother in her last moments, because she had not made a will. 'Yea,' she replied, in a barely audible voice.[11] Not long afterwards, Queen Anna was dead.

Though it did not go on for the late queen consort of England, who was to be buried on 13 May within Westminster Abbey, life naturally did go on for Simonds D'Ewes and his family. The summer months that year were to be particularly significant for the soon-to-be 17-year-old. It was during this balmy period that Simonds first laid eyes on the girl – bedecked in mourning dress to observe the death of her father – who would eventually become his much cherished first wife. It is no exaggeration to refer to Lady Anne Clopton as a mere girl in 1619; when D'Ewes met her at Clare Priory in Suffolk, the country home of her maternal grandparents, she was not even 7 years old. Accordingly, Simonds had no inkling then that he and Lady Anne would end up sharing a life together; nor could he have begun to appreciate the profound effect that her premature death would have on him several decades later. 'I never imagined, that of all women living, God had ordained her for my wife,' he wrote in his autobiography.[12]

Simonds's being at Clare Priory in the first place was on account of a familiar association he had developed with Sir Nathaniel Barnardiston, a cousin of Anne Clopton's. The two seem to have been introduced by Abraham Gibson, preacher at Kedington in Suffolk, where Nathaniel also lived at Kedington Hall – and where

Simonds had been invited before the friends travelled the short distance to Clare. Though there was a fourteen-year age gap between Barnardiston and D'Ewes (Nathaniel was born in 1588, Simonds in 1602), theirs was to be a companionship that would stand the test of time.

Nathaniel Barnardiston, like Simonds D'Ewes, became a steadfast follower of a sober branch of Christianity known as Puritanism. However, unlike D'Ewes, the moment of his conversion was recorded for posterity, being described thus:

> For the time of his conversion, it was when he was young, the Lord enabled him to remember his Creator in the days of his youth, by casting in the Seed of Regeneration when he was at school, the very time when others of his rank and quality give up themselves to the greatest degrees of licentious wantonness, and immoderate excesses; pretending that the heat of nature, and strength of the buds of youth, produce a sufficient apology and discharge for the same: but at that very time did infinite grace so effectually seize on him, that with the devout young Abel he did offer his first-fruits unto God.[13]

There seemed to be very little in Barnardiston's comparatively long life that was worthy of criticism. Even his physical appearance was lauded by his contemporaries, with one commentator noting admiringly, 'the make of his body, even from head to foot (not to be too particular) was competently gentile and brave'.[14]

An upstanding member of the Suffolk gentry who would sit in several parliaments over his lifetime, Nathaniel was considered a model husband, father and grandfather. When it came to the bringing up of his children in particular, the proprietor of Kedington Hall ensured that they were well educated and coached to value religion above all things. These were qualities that he also inspired in his servants, with Barnardiston giving them 'good example in himself, and [failing] not to instruct them in the most useful things for the benefit of their souls and bodies'. Kedington Hall itself came to be regarded as a 'spiritual church and temple, wherein were daily offered up the spiritual sacrifices of reading the Word; and prayer, morning and evening, of singing of psalms constantly after every meal, before any servant did rise from the table'.[15]

CHAPTER 5

THE ROAD TO THE TEMPLE

THOUGHTS OF SIMONDS'S intellectual and professional life after university began to grow in intensity for both the student and his father as a new decade of the seventeenth century arrived. Having spent Christmas with Nathaniel Barnardiston in Kedington, which turned out to be a subdued affair owing to the recent death of Nathaniel's grandfather, Sir Thomas Barnardiston, Simonds devoted a large portion of his waking hours to study in early 1620. This included regularly attending lectures delivered by Andrew Downes, professor of Greek at Cambridge, as well as D'Ewes turning his hand to Aristotle's physics, ethics and politics. Further reading material consisted of Florus's *Epitome of Roman History*, which Simonds took detailed notes from; Henry Stephens's *Apology for Herodotus*, first published in Latin in the sixteenth century, but read by D'Ewes in English; and Edmund Spenser's *The Faerie Queene*, an epic poem dating from the 1590s. The latter two works were perused by Simonds in the evenings, which was deemed by him a recreational use of his time.[1]

On 13 May 1620, the diligent student at last received a letter from his father stating that he was shortly to be moved to the Middle Temple in London. Simonds no doubt harboured mixed emotions about leaving St John's College. While greatly admiring the learned men who had tutored him since his arrival at the university in 1618, notably Richard Holdsworth and Andrew Downes, D'Ewes's Puritan instincts had gradually served to sour the regard he held for his peers, many of whom were inclined to drink, fight, swear and even – God forbid – flirt. 'The power of godliness, in respect of the practice of it, was in a most atheistical and unchristian manner condemned and scoffed at,' he lamented later. This is not to say that Simonds was entirely innocent of the worldly preoccupations of the young men surrounding him at St John's. Looking one's best mattered as much to the heir of Stowlangtoft as it did to any other esquire's son, as is evidenced in the surviving accounts of the things he chose to spend considerable sums of money on as a student. One such set of accounts mentions the purchase of a doublet of green silk, designed in the fashionable French style, a pair of hose finished with silver lace, and a pair of Spanish leather shoes.[2]

As the summer of 1620 beat down on Jacobean England with clement intent, it was not just Simonds's professional future at the Middle Temple that started to be seriously considered. Visiting Paul D'Ewes at Stow Hall in August, the delicate topic of marriage was discussed at some length by both parties. Now approaching the ripe-for-the-plucking age of 18, Simonds took the seeds of this idea with him to his acquaintance, Abraham Gibson of Kedington, upon his return journey to Cambridge a short while later. Even then, it would appear that Gibson had a few candidates in mind for his unmarried protégé. One of these was a daughter of Sir Henry Hobart, Lord Chief Justice of the Common Pleas, whom Simonds quickly dismissed because of her age (being only 12 years old). He was also reticent about pursuing the match on account of the fact that he had never seen the girl before, and knew next to nothing about her. Nonetheless, going forwards, D'Ewes became somewhat consumed by the notion and associated possibilities of an advantageous union, to the degree that his studies at St John's began to suffer as a result.

Temple politics, blighting Simonds's initial admittance to the institution in 1611, had conjured up additional distractions in June. A new 'controversy' regarding his intended chamber within the Middle Temple had seen the parliament take further steps at the end of the month to ensure that the room would indeed be ready for D'Ewes to move into, when the time came. The chamber, somehow, had fallen into the possession of one James Dier, who, the parliament had ultimately decided, would be allowed to retain his quarters until the day that 'Dewse shall actually come into commons *bona fide*'.[3]

Probably to the regret of Dier, that particular day was drawing ever closer. On 22 September, Simonds left Cambridge for the leafiness of rural Suffolk, and with it his life as a carefree undergraduate. Accompanying him home was Richard Holdsworth, his 'loving and careful' tutor (rewarded with a costly pair of gloves for his efforts in teaching the Cambridge pupil), who sought payment from Paul D'Ewes at Stow Hall for a handful of outstanding bills – as well as to bid his student a fond farewell.[4] The well-meaning, warm sentiment would begin and end with the kindly St John's theologian. Simonds was forced to contend with nothing but his father's infamous fury following Holdsworth's departure, which lasted for four, long days and encouraged the 17-year-old to actively dread how close they would soon be living to each other in London.

However much it might feel like a deliberate or targeted attack, Paul's propensity for cantankerousness was not personal to his son. Records indicate that the esquire could be hostile towards all manner of individuals who made unwelcome appearances in his day-to-day life, including one Edward Shorland, with whom Paul had entered into a dispute in the early 1600s that had resulted in arbitration. The process had not gone well at all; a narrator of the proceedings wrote that 'Mr D'Ewes' had dealt both 'unfairly' and 'indirectly' with his opponent, Shorland, who had formerly held the manor of Wells Hall in Suffolk.[5] Whether Paul D'Ewes genuinely felt as though Edward deserved to be treated in such a poor way is unknown.

The capital city called out to his son, Simonds, now that he had put his days at the University of Cambridge behind him. In October 1620, the adolescent arrived in London with his family to begin a rather different chapter in his life, though he soon received the displeasing news that certain issues with his Middle Temple chamber remained unresolved. Forming one of the four Inns of Court, the others being the Inner Temple, Gray's Inn and Lincoln's Inn, the Middle Temple had existed for hundreds of years by the 1620s, boasting among its illustrious members everybody from the explorer Sir Walter Raleigh, admitted in 1574, to the architect Inigo Jones, admitted in 1613. Yet, even so, it held a general reputation that was not entirely unblemished in this period, intriguing flavours of which have survived in the records compiled from the colourful sittings of each of its regular parliaments. Around the time that Simonds was first admitted, for example, the following was recorded:

> In consequence of the complaint of John Dashfeild and Mary, his wife, of the injuries suffered from gentlemen having chambers in the new buildings near the Temple Churchyard, 'by casting out of chamberpots and other annoyances out of their chamber windows'; it is ordered that gentlemen having casements [part of a window set on a hinge, so it opens] or open lights on the north side of the said buildings shall remove their casements and hang them to open into their chambers, and the lights are to be wired outside with strong wire, and the gutters cleansed at the cost of such offenders.[6]

One hopes that the very curious practice spoken of was at least made less severe by the measures that the parliament proposed to introduce to its members.

Certainly, straight expulsions as a result of inappropriate behaviour were not uncommon at the Temple, if the crime committed was deemed serious enough. Gyles Garton was eventually expelled in 1610 after striking a fellow Middle Templar, Thomas White, across the face with a knife during supper one evening. On 25 May 1614, meanwhile, the parliament decided to permanently remove Mr William Callow 'for having... with two others disordered [himself] in the street'. The young men in question had been dragged back to the Temple gate by the city watch at 2:00 am on the night of the said incident, where they had then proceeded to smash the windows of 'divers Benchers and gentlemen both of this Society and of the Inner House'.[7] Such blatant vandalism could not be forgiven.

Various issues, not necessarily related to the students, were present when Simonds himself lodged at the Middle Temple in the early 1620s. Crumbling staircases and dilapidated private chambers preoccupied the parliament when it met to discuss business in October 1621. A year earlier, it had been back to the familiar problem of sanatory arrangements. 'Every gentleman shall forthwith provide some convenient pot or other vessel to hold all such water and other noisome things, and cause the laundress or other servant to empty and cleanse it daily in places convenient,' the parliament had ordered brusquely. The laundresses in particular had been warned about the consequences of emptying chamber pots 'in places unseemly or unbefitting'.[8] Any servant caught performing this unhygienic activity would now be sacked on the spot, without appeal, and their employer fined 10 shillings.

At least the food at the Middle Temple could be quite good – on special occasions, anyway. The accounts drawn up in the years after Simonds D'Ewes's tenure show that bountiful feasts were not beyond the institution, and might include various wines, cider, venison and doe pasties, tarts, mutton, fish, bacon, beans and fruit. One assumes that this is the level of comfort that Simonds hoped for, or even expected, at the Temple as his legal career finally got off the ground. In the end, it appears that almost anything would be preferable to spending time around his father in those early days of his adulthood, who, we are told, erupted into anger as soon as the D'Ewes family alighted in Chancery Lane in October 1620. As was often the case (though unjustly so), it was Paul's eldest son who was to blame for this latest outburst. Having entered 'the chamber where they kept' and apparently opened a casement too enthusiastically, which was already hanging 'but by one gimmer', Simonds had made the grave error of pulling the whole contraption off its hinges by accident.[9] It was the very opposite of a good start.

Considering Paul D'Ewes owned substantial property in London, including three houses 'standing near Charing Cross', which were leased to Thomas Southwell in the early reign of Charles I, it may have felt cruel to Simonds that he was not granted permission to lodge somewhere other than his father's small office. What the young man could put his mind to as a consolation, however, was getting out and exploring as much of the great metropolis as possible. This the expectant Middle Templar did gladly in his spare time, visiting and climbing St Paul's Cathedral, viewing the stately monuments housed within Westminster Abbey, and taking in the magnificent form of the Banqueting House in Whitehall, where, unbeknown to him, King Charles would meet his maker in January 1649. On top of sightseeing, there was also the Middle Temple itself to prepare for. Within the first few days of being in the capital, Simonds set about organising a whole new wardrobe for himself in anticipation of the fashionable company he would soon be keeping beside the Thames. He was, in truth, ashamed of the 'rustic accoutrements' he had brought with him from Stowlangtoft, being so conscious of his substandard appearance that he chose to hide himself away in back alleys – and even his father's office in Chancery Lane – while 'a gown and a new suit of clothes' were made up for him at the tailor's.[10] When the articles were finally ready to be worn, Simonds considered that he was a changed man, now able to walk about wherever he pleased in London. One of the first places he visited in his finery was the nave of St Paul's Cathedral, known colloquially as Paul's Walk, where gossip was shared and news imparted by the somebodies of society.

Life wasn't all frills, gowns and keeping up appearances as Simonds approached his landmark eighteenth birthday in the city. Religion had begun to occupy a profound spot in the teenager's psyche since his immersion in the heady delights of higher education, and this was no different in London, a place crammed full of medieval churches stretching back to the days of the twelfth-century Anarchy and before. Not long after his arrival, for instance, Simonds eagerly relayed a sermon he had heard at St Ann Blackfriars to his sisters, which had been delivered by the Puritan minister William Gouge. Sadly, the impromptu lecture was cut short by the appearance of his disapproving father, who deliberately drew his daughters' attentions away from Simonds's religious oration by engaging them in an unrelated topic of conversation. When the budding lecturer tried again to pass on the wisdom of Gouge's sermon to his siblings that evening, the act was met with even fiercer resistance from Paul, who 'declared that many suns would not suffice to eradicate his anger'.[11]

It was somewhat ironic that, the following month, the D'Ewes patriarch would come to rely on the Christian teachings of the Bible more than ever. On 17 November, amid a heavy snow that left the ground sodden and treacherous across much of London, Cecilia D'Ewes, one of Simonds's younger sisters, died of a fever aged 10. This premature loss (perhaps occurring rather too soon after the death of her mother and namesake) would have come as a blow to every member of the D'Ewes family, not least the emotional Paul. For, even though child mortality rates were undeniably high at this time in England's history, there was still very little that could prepare a parent for the sheer anguish that came with the passing of one of their offspring – especially when the son or daughter had grown out of infancy and become a miniature adult in their own right. Simonds himself appears to have been profoundly affected by the death of his sister. Before Cecilia's life had even reached its sudden end, he had raced through the wintry capital with several of his siblings to get to the place where she lay dying, through sheets of thick snow and over roads made perilous by the cold weather. Clearly, there had been a desperation in him, and in his sisters, to see the girl alive one last time.

Bad news followed bad news in the concluding days of November. The disagreement over Simonds's earmarked room within the Middle Temple rumbled tiresomely on when the institution's parliament met at the end of the month, with an order being made that James Dier, 'who claims to be admitted into the chamber', should demonstrate why 'the son and heir-apparent of Paul Dewse' was not entitled to the divisive space now that he was 'come into commons'.[12] Luckily, the dispute was close to reaching a resolution by the arrival of the new year. On 9 February 1621, the Masters of the Bench at last decided that the chamber was rightfully Simonds's, though Dier was given some breathing space and not coerced into leaving straight away.

Before this victory – and a victory it certainly was after so many years of fighting for Simonds's right to occupy the chamber – there had been the Christmas period to enjoy at the Middle Temple. 'Enjoy', perhaps, might have been too strong a word for the ever-watchful parliament; more properly, there had been a seasonal interlude to observe with minimal celebrating and modest good cheer. 'Christmas shall be kept solemnly, not grandly. Commons shall be continued until next term. A cartload of coals, 40 shillings for the minstrels, and £3 for the officers' commons shall be allowed,' it was announced in the run-up to the festivities of 1620.[13] The conservative attitude of the parliament towards the festive season is hardly surprising when one peruses the records that have been left behind in a little more detail. It would seem that this time of year could inspire less than palatable behaviour in the young men who forever crowded the chambers, staircases and halls of the Temple, throwing their chamberpots into the open streets and drinking illicitly at ungodly hours. Around the time of Richard D'Ewes's admittance, in November 1632, the following was recorded:

As the order of 25 Nov, 1631, for redressing disorders at Christmas time has produced no good effect, it is ordered that no commons be kept in this House next Christmas. Commons shall break up the Saturday before St Thomas's day, when the Hall doors shall be locked up; and shall begin again upon Saturday after Twelfth day. Certain officers are to attend to guard the House [in the] meantime [...] In the presenting and performance of revels, no gentleman of the House shall make use of the gallery over the screen, or bring down any lady or gentlewoman to see their ordinary revels, or dance with them in the Hall in the absence of the Bench, or use the Reader's chair or any other pre-eminence for their master of the revels, on pain of censure.[14]

Chapter 6

JEMIMA WALDEGRAVE

VERY MUCH AWARE that he was leading a strained existence in London in the keeping of his erratic father, Simonds again found himself considering his marital prospects in late 1620 – though, this time round, as a quick means of breaking free from Paul D'Ewes's ire. A friend in the capital by the name of Boldero, by a happy coincidence, had a new candidate in mind for the young suitor, in the form of a young, aristocratic woman whose ancestry, money and good looks certainly represented an attractive package. She was the daughter of Sir Edward Waldegrave of Lawford Hall in Essex, and her name was Jemima.

When Simonds ultimately summoned up the courage to put the match to his widowered, cantankerous father, it was met with general approval. Yet the subsequent negotiations, which were absolutely essential for the Jacobean aristocracy to enter into before any firm decisions were made regarding a marriage, were slow to start. They were so slow, in fact, that Simonds's head was turned in the interim by another woman. Her name and prospects had been dangled in front of his nose once before, by Mr Gibson of Kedington in Suffolk: it was Mary Hobart, daughter of Sir Henry Hobart, Lord Chief Justice of the Common Pleas. D'Ewes's cautious interest in Mary was reignited when he fell into conversation with one Mr Wade at the Middle Temple, during the subdued Christmas festivities that took place there. Wade was one of Sir Henry's 'gentleman', therefore possessing an intimate knowledge of the family and its array of personalities.[1]

Pretending to be acting on behalf of an acquaintance, Simonds casually managed to arrange 'a sight of the damsel' with Wade as they conversed, which was to occur the very next day at Hobart's house in St Bartholomew's, near Smithfield. The morning of 6 January 1621 saw D'Ewes's plan going exactly as he had intended it. Standing at the front door of the residence claiming to be looking for Mr Wade, Simonds soon caught a glimpse of young Mary Hobart emerging 'to speak to a poor woman, who had brought her mother some oranges and lemons'. There were without question two motives at work in this moment, as D'Ewes himself would freely admit. For, as well as becoming genuinely curious about Mary and wanting to see the aristocratic Hobart daughter for himself, Simonds seems to have been keen to compare her with the eligible Jemima Waldegrave. 'Nature had done sufficiently for both' as far as D'Ewes was concerned, but, when all was said and done that January morning, he appears to have walked away from the townhouse believing that Jemima outdid her love rival because of the money she would be able to bring to their marriage.[2]

Romantic considerations temporarily evaporated from Simonds's mind on 30 January 1621, to be replaced by an all-consuming concern for pomp, circumstance and state business. With the coming together of the third parliament of King James's reign, D'Ewes counted himself among the surging crowds who had assembled to watch the sovereign proceed from the Palace of Whitehall to Westminster. Accompanying the king, himself wearing a crown 'most royally caparisoned', was his son, Prince Charles, riding a horse and sporting 'a rich coronet' between serjeants-at-arms wielding maces and pensioners clutching poleaxes. The procession was considered unique by Simonds in that James apparently looked upon his people favourably for once, choosing to bless the throngs as he passed them, instead of hissing that a plague or pox should befall anybody who came too close to the place where he rode. The chivalrous mask slipped only once. It is said that, as the king drew level with a window packed with 'gentlewomen and ladies' dressed in yellow bands, he shouted up to them, 'a pox take ye, are ye there?'.[3]

Fanciful musings of wedlock could not fail to re-emerge within Simonds a week or so later on 7 February, the day that his older sister, Johanne, was married to William Elliot of Busbridge in Surrey. In fact, following the ceremony at St Faith under St Paul's, it was noted by several of the wedding guests that the bride's younger brother looked thoroughly miserable. The lack of progress in his own matrimonial affairs seemed to be the cause of D'Ewes's melancholy amid the merriment, dancing and feasting on display in the Strand. Thankfully, the Middle Templar would soon enter another period of reassuring movement, beginning with the introduction of a Mr Littlebury to the negotiations with the Waldegraves, who was a neighbour of the family's in Essex. Added to Littlebury's input was Paul D'Ewes's own decision to extend the hand of friendship to Sir Edward Waldegrave, Jemima's father, via a cordial letter, to get the ball properly rolling between the two parties. In no time, Simonds was so confident about the outcome of the business at hand that he arranged to have his portrait painted by a limner in Chancery Lane, which he intended to have sent down to Lawson House for the Waldegrave family's consideration.

The world, a previously dark expanse with little hope of light in it, was made even brighter for Simonds when, in March, he travelled with his father to the home of his newly married sister, Johanne, at Busbridge in Surrey. Here had lived the gentle Elliot family for many decades, occupying 'a handsome timber house, placed in a bottom between hills, and excellently accommodated with large and well-stored fish ponds'.[4] It was here as well that Simonds, given an entire chamber for his own use by William Elliot, could now throw himself wholeheartedly into the study of the law – and even learn to enjoy it.

While young D'Ewes's accrual of legal knowledge appeared destined to take care of itself, the matter of his proposed marriage to Jemima Waldegrave represented a more complicated undertaking. Negotiations would require the proactivity and consent of numerous individuals to reach a favourable resolution, even with the promising inroads that had already been made. In May 1621, Paul D'Ewes and Sir Edward Waldegrave, the chief negotiators, finally met in person to discuss the match, only for discussions to resolutely break down upon D'Ewes learning that Waldegrave was 'not prepared to give his daughter any portion in hand'. Such was the bumpy course of any marriage treaty in seventeenth-century England. Shortly, the participants of the match were drawn back once more to the bartering table, with Simonds paying his prospective father-in-law a visit with Boldero (the man who had first suggested Jemima as a worthy catch) after supper one evening. 'The good old man' was just going to bed when the pair arrived, though he 'sat a pretty while discoursing with them in his nightcap'.[5]

Given money to buy a new set of fashionable clothes, and carrying the blessings of his father with him out of London, Simonds wasted no time in travelling to Lawford Hall in Essex to plead his case to the wider Waldegrave family in person. The journey was far from a smooth one, considering the relatively short distance between the capital and Colchester. Boldero, for one thing, contracted smallpox en route and was forced to pull out of the matrimonial expedition altogether. D'Ewes himself, meanwhile, made it as far as Maldon, near Chelmsford, before realising that he had accidentally left his money behind at a previous pitstop. Yet, somehow, Simonds arrived in Colchester in one piece – and more or less unperturbed – in time to meet his acquaintance, Mr Littlebury, at the King's Head inn. From here, almost straight away, the men were lucky enough to trace Jemima herself to the nearby house of a refugee, who originally hailed from the Low Countries.

D'Ewes set out for Lawford Hall the next day, accompanied both by Mr Littlebury and by a certain confidence that all would turn out well. The house and grounds alone impressed him; so did their custodians, who appeared one after the other in their finery to welcome Simonds and Littlebury to the Waldegrave country seat. Sir Edward Waldegrave was the first to greet the guests, steering the men into light conversation within the dim interior of the hall, before his second wife, Sara, and his two daughters – including Jemima – joined the party from an upper storey. It was when everybody moved outdoors to inspect the gardens that Simonds identified an opportunity to take Jemima to one side. For an hour, they walked privately together, with the young lady initially 'unwilling, for the general, to try the married life', but seeming to soften a fraction towards the end of their discourse. The pair were able to speak again in Jemima's chamber following dinner, after which Simonds found himself in an uncomfortable conference with the steely, disapproving Lady Sara Waldegrave (formerly Bingham). Lady Waldegrave appeared to have already decided, perhaps upon first sight of the youth, that D'Ewes was not the correct suitor for her valuable daughter after all. Somewhat unexpectedly, this unappetising revelation only encouraged Simonds to pursue the alliance with Jemima more vigorously, and with renewed enthusiasm. At the earliest opportunity, the Middle Templar guided the Waldegrave daughter back out into the grounds to talk with her some more. 'I received as many tokens and signs of her gracious willingness,' D'Ewes wrote of the encounter, 'as none had ever before received the like.'[6]

Back in London a short while later, Paul D'Ewes continued to blow hot and cold in his opinions on his son's love match. The middle-aged esquire was also, nearly three years on from the death of Cecilia D'Ewes, toying with the idea of a new marriage of his own. Dropping the bombshell when Simonds was least expecting it, the younger D'Ewes's reaction was to feel nothing but sheer horror at the prospect of his father remarrying, especially to one whom he believed it appropriate to describe as 'a young light woman' herself. Relations between the two deteriorated further upon Simonds returning to Lawford Hall with letters from Paul addressed to the Waldegrave negotiators. This simple act, outwardly designed to move discussions along and nothing more, turned out to be as damaging to Simonds's cause as throwing a flaming torch on the entire D'Ewes-Waldegrave marriage treaty. Already highly unsure about the suitability of the Middle Templar, Lady Sara was spooked by the peculiarly authoritative tone of Paul D'Ewes's written words, deciding from them that her daughter, Jemima, was at real risk of 'coming under [Paul's] power'.[7] A third visit to Lawford did nothing to remedy the situation, with Jemima kept upstairs for the duration of her suitor's stay (the girl having been categorically forbidden from showing her face). It quickly became obvious to all – even to the Waldegraves' chambermaid, whom Simonds had befriended – that Lady Sara would die before allowing her child to go through with the match.

For Simonds D'Ewes and Jemima Waldegrave, then, there was to be no storybook conclusion to look back on fondly. While Simonds would now have to let go of any futile thoughts of continuing with this particular matrimonial mission, he had at least become newly free to pursue other avenues. Even so, D'Ewes did not exhibit an overwhelming keenness to replace Jemima Waldegrave with another object of desire as 1621 moved into its autumnal stages. Other more agreeable developments seemed to keep the Templar occupied throughout this season, including the breaking off of his father's dubious marriage treaty in October, which came as particularly cheering news to Simonds when he received it. Up to then, Paul's furious disagreements with his son over money and matters of inheritance had purportedly become unbearable. The esquire's marital miscalculation was followed at the end of the month by more heartening tidings from the Middle Temple, where it was declared unequivocally by the parliament that 'Mr Symondes Dewes has absolute right' to the chamber that had been in dispute for so many years.[8] On 22 November, Simonds could finally call the room his own, having agreed in advance to pay the expenses incurred by Mr James Dier in wainscotting and amending the space to suit his various tastes.

Significant wins on the part of Simonds erupted into terrible tragedy for the entire D'Ewes family on 20 December. With mere days to go until Christmas Day, a fire broke out at the Six Clerks' Office in Chancery Lane, gutting every inch of Paul D'Ewes's lodgings there. Blame for this accident was later laid on one Mr Tothil, also of the Six Clerks' Office, who was thought to have been careless with his hearth and allowed flames to jump destructively down into 'the woodwork under the chimney'. When Simonds arrived on the scene in the early morning to inspect the damage (his father had already left London for the holidays), he was confronted with little more than a gaping, smouldering ruin. So much of value – both on a monetary and a sentimental level – had been lost to the fire that the stunned Middle Templar could barely stand to contemplate it. Among the possessions burned to a cinder were copious amounts of legal paperwork, including inheritances and leases relating to London and the West Country; £3,000 in gold; and, most distressingly for D'Ewes, 'an ancient testimonial, in Latin, written on parchment, and sealed and signed by the Duke of Cleves's principal herald'. A few noteworthy survivals among the smoking debris helped prevent the incident from being an insurmountable catastrophe for the D'Eweses. Picking through the rubble, Simonds was able to retrieve roughly £500 in 'scorched gold', as well as, quite remarkably, his mother's wedding ring.[9]

The road to recovery was clearly going to be a long and complex one where the gutted Six Clerks' Office was concerned. Records indicate that, even five years down the line, articles of agreement were being drawn up between Paul and various tradesmen to reconstruct parts of the destroyed building. The act of painstakingly sifting through the wreckage in December 1621 was also to leave a lasting mark on Simonds himself. 'For my own part,' he recollected in his autobiography, 'I had contracted so much illness for my care, cold-taking, watchings, and the ill smells of the ruins the fire had left... as I was necessitated for the future to spare myself.'[10]

For the D'Ewes clan, such circumstances probably rendered December and January noticeably devoid of the warming celebrations that one might have expected with the coming of the festive season. The Waldegraves of Lawford Hall, too, were in for a rough start to 1622. On 12 February, Sir Edward Waldegrave, who had but a matter of months earlier entertained Simonds at his home in London in his nightcap, died. His passing, curiously enough, would go on to throw up a succession of unforeseen opportunities for both families, mainly in the shape of marital propositions that had formerly been considered impossible. Paul D'Ewes not only reconsidered the status of the abandoned match between his son and Jemima Waldegrave in the wake of Sir Edward's passing, but also his own eligibility with regard to the ancient Essex dynasty. Briefly, the Suffolk esquire actively entertained the idea of attempting to take the widowed Lady Sara Waldegrave as his second spouse. Both schemes would, ultimately, come to nothing.

Chapter 7

CITY LIVING

THROUGHOUT 1622, SIMONDS made good progress with his legal studies at the Middle Temple. While he had become rather tired of applying himself to the law by the arrival of autumn, describing it as 'difficult and unpleasant', the student continued to soak up as much relevant information as possible in London, making it his business to attend the Court of Star Chamber every Wednesday and Friday to take notes on the cases presented there. He also made it his business to keep abreast of domestic and foreign affairs, something that would forever keep him occupied into later life. 'I heard some newes as that things went ill in the Palatinate,' D'Ewes noted in June; in July, he observed, 'Of newes I understood much that, domesticke, I thinke not worth the remembrance; for forraine, it was that the King of Bohemia had removed all his gold plate from the Castle of Heidelberg.'

Alongside his vocational commitments, Simonds also kept up an active and interesting personal life. It would seem that there was rarely a dull moment for the Middle Templar in the vertiginous metropolis. On 25 February, a poor boy whom D'Ewes had taken in and clothed out of his own pocket 'ran away from me to a dancer's, [and] I being at first troubled was at length glad so to be rid of him[,] being but a rogue'. The next day, Simonds decided that the absconder should not be allowed to get off so lightly after all, and therefore set about contemplating how best to punish him for his behaviour. On 13 June, meanwhile, D'Ewes visited Sir George Stoughton's house and played bowls 'and other sport' with the knight's mother, seemingly until they could bear it no longer. A few weeks later, in July 1622, he even went at night with 'some other gentlemen... to wash myself in the Thames'.[1]

Through rain, sunshine and heavy snowfall, Simonds's considerable social calendar spilled liberally and plentifully into 1623, with regular trips to church in the capital and further afield taking up much of January. In March, an ecclesiastical visit of especial significance occurred when his father, having entered negotiations for a relatively short period, married for a second and final time. Paul D'Ewes's new wife was Lady Elizabeth Denton, the widow of Sir Anthony Denton of Tunbridge Wells, and originally an Isham of Lamport Hall in Northamptonshire. Because Simonds had ended up playing an integral role in cementing the marriage treaty, the 20-year-old likely felt a sense of personal satisfaction as he witnessed the couple exchange vows in St Faith under St Paul's on 5 March. He was certainly sufficiently at ease with the development to wish Paul and Elizabeth a safe journey to Elizabeth's 'jointure-house' in Tunbridge Wells three days later, although a cold suffered by him at the time made the amicable encounter rather a chore.[2]

There is no question that Paul D'Ewes came to regard his second spouse with great affection. When he eventually wrote his will, the esquire referred to Elizabeth as 'my well-beloved wife the Lady Denton, an honourable lady whom I have found to have been to me... most loving, careful and obedient... so towards all my children a very mother'. There is also no question that the two endeavoured to create a meaningful life together in the years that Paul had remaining – which, unfortunately, were few in number by the early 1620s. Thus, we have records in 1623 of the esquire attempting to make good some of his properties in Suffolk, including those found in Lavenham, the manor of which he had purchased around a decade before. Even Lady Denton, however, try as she might to avoid them, could not escape entirely the fiery outbursts that so heavily characterised her husband's treatment of those with whom he came into contact. Simonds recorded in one of his Latin diaries a particularly troubling episode involving his father and stepmother in February 1624, which is worth briefly mentioning here. Visiting Lady Denton one day on a whim, D'Ewes found the gentlewoman extremely upset and in need of consoling, presently establishing that she had fallen out with Paul over a new gown that she had recently purchased. 'Such was her goodness that she much grieved at his anger,' Simonds wrote. 'I therefore did comfort her what I might, [and] told her I did not doubt by her patience [and] mildness it would soon be blown over – as indeed it was.' Paul D'Ewes's will shows that the man was not always averse to his second wife indulging in her appearance – though, obviously, it was a trait that did not generally become a God-fearing woman. 'I do give... and bequeath unto my said loving and faithful wife,' Paul wrote at one point in the document, 'that... diamond ring and that diamond hatband which she hath used to wear since our marriage.'[3]

In terms of Simonds's own activities, there are plenty to speak of across the rest of 1623 and into 1624. The young man lost a valuable watch that had been lent to him on 16 April, and found it again on 18 April. On 1 May, he accompanied Lady Denton to see a training exercise 'in the field', before joining his whole family, including his younger brother, Richard, for a walk in the gardens at the London Charterhouse. Two months later, Simonds's grafting at the Middle Temple finally paid off when, to the utter delight of his father, he was 'called to the bar' and made a barrister at the age of 20.[4] The Middle Templar had been exceptionally nervous beforehand that he had not done enough to pass, even supping in the company of his stepmother to try to take his mind off the outcome. Paul D'Ewes's genuine elation at the news that his eldest son had qualified as a barrister manifested itself in the esquire immediately adding £40 to Simonds's annual allowance, which, naturally, was excellent news for Simonds himself.

September 1623 constituted perhaps even more of a milestone for the brand-new legal practitioner, however. In this month, as he was at pains to note in his autobiography, Simonds began working through the great collection of records held at the Tower of London, which sparked within him – probably more than any other activity thus far had done – a life-long passion for antiquarianism. 'I at first read records only to find out the matter of law contained in them; but afterwards,' D'Ewes wrote emphatically, 'perceiving other excellences might be observed from them, both historical and national, I always continued the study of them after I had left the Middle Temple and given over the study of the common law itself.'[5]

A different kind of passion erupted mere weeks after Simonds's first perusal of the Tower documents. Walking in the footsteps of a great many zealous gentlemen in this period, the youthful barrister found himself on the verge of a bloody duel in November 1623, following a heated exchange that had taken place between D'Ewes and one James Scudamore of the Middle Temple. Simonds appears to have been more than prepared, sword in hand, to defend his honour against the backstabbing Scudamore if necessary, though he very much hoped that 'I might [go] to field without killing or being killed.'[6] The whole would amount to very little upon push coming to shove, with Scudamore apparently losing his appetite for the challenge and deliberately scheduling the duel to coincide with Simonds's absence from London. Nevertheless, it was a close thing.

Through 1624 and the final year of the reign of James I, religion in various forms reigned supreme in Simonds's everyday life, colouring much of his later experiences in London as a young man. In March, he heard at Whitehall – seemingly with considerable suspicion – an impassioned sermon preached by none other than Dr William Laud, champion of Arminianism and pre-Reformation doctrine, who would eventually turn the religious landscape of England upside down through his reforms in the 1630s. Simonds noted disdainfully of the event that the preacher 'was suspected to be somewhat popish'. Over the rest of the year, there would be many more such sermons delivered across the city that could count the fresh-faced Puritan as an attentive audience member. Generally speaking in the early 1620s, Simonds listened to every religious expounder in the city from Dr John Everard, renowned theologian and alchemist, to Richard Holdsworth, D'Ewes's own tutor at Cambridge.[7] Each would make a small but significant impression on the barrister, and would moreover work towards sculpting the particular branch of Christianity to which Simonds subscribed as an adult.

Faith additionally presented itself through the dealings of a forward-thinking Paul D'Ewes in June 1624, of which Simonds himself must surely have been a part. On 25 June, articles of agreement were drawn up between the esquire and one Jan Janson, a stonecutter based in St Martin-in-the-Fields, for the erection of a monument dedicated to Paul and his wider family within Stowlangtoft church. It was to cost its main subject a sizeable £35 to set up (about £4,600 in today's money), and was intended to last forever inside the hallowed edifice of St George's.[8] Seventeenth-century men like Paul D'Ewes, often proud and influential lords of the manor, loathed the idea of being forgotten in a place where they had previously held sway; the installing of a church memorial after their deaths, complete with lifelike effigies and identifying epitaphs, helped ensure that this would never happen. By all accounts, anybody who met the lord of the manor of Stowlangtoft while he was alive would need no such visual prompting to recollect a gentleman who was known to have an outlandishly bad temper.

His father's mortality thus looming over him like the shadow of the great marble monument itself, Simonds busied himself with antiquarian pursuits when not bogged down in the business of the law or fulfilling his religious obligations. On 1 July 1624, at Paul's picturesque seat in Suffolk, the barrister carried out the following:

> I perused over divers of the old evidences of the manor of Stowlangtoft with much delight, having now by my study of records gotten reasonable skill and ability in the reading of those old hands and

characters, in which the elder deeds had been written for about 500 years past. By them I easily discovered that the ancient appellation of the town had been singly Stow, and that it having been possessed by the family of Langetot, from about William I's time, till the latter end of King John or the beginning of Henry III...[9]

This work was interspersed with familial visits and preoccupations. In August, Simonds returned to Busbridge in Surrey, the home of his beloved older sister and her husband, to meet his new nephew for the first time, who had been born to Johanne and William Elliot on the nineteenth of that month. While Baby Elliot had been delivered relatively safely considering the innumerable risks associated with early modern childbirth, Johanne had unfortunately gone into labour three weeks early, brought on by a hallucination of 'a villain stood close at her bedside with a knife in his hand'.[10]

Furthermore, there were social calls to pay and close friends to catch up with in between Simonds's commitments, which might not always leave the man feeling rested and refreshed afterwards – particularly during the winter months. In January 1625, D'Ewes visited Sir Martin Stuteville at Dalham Hall in Suffolk, near Newmarket, and came away from the place feeling utterly wretched and full of cold, having suffered from the ill effects of the thin bedclothes with which he had been provided by his hosts. Simonds, in fact, grew so ill following his sojourn with the Stutevilles that Paul D'Ewes, not for the first time, had reason to believe that his son's life may be in danger. The complaint did not turn out to be as bad as all that. With Simonds looking likely to make a full recovery yet again, Paul had soon returned to his own material concerns, which included negotiating with a bricklayer to have building work completed at Stow Hall.

⟵⟶

The years-old English constitution began to quake slightly on 27 March 1625, upon the death of King James I at the age of 58. Simonds dedicated a portion of his autobiography to the monarch's final days at Theobalds Palace in Hertfordshire, noting that 'His Highness's sickness was at first but an ordinary ague, though at last it turned to a burning fever.' The king's death knell, according to D'Ewes, was ultimately sounded by George Villiers, 1st Duke of Buckingham, the courtier having reportedly administered a potion and 'plasters' to his ailing master that had made him fatally unwell. Up to then, there had been hopes of a full recovery among James's physicians. When the late sovereign's body was opened up to commence the tricky embalming process a short while later, it was found to be in a very bad way indeed. Save for the liver, which was 'as fresh as if he had been a young man', every one of the dead ruler's organs was either blackened, swollen or shrunken.[11]

Such was, and continues to be, the nature of the British monarchy that there was no kingly void left in the wake of James's passing. No sooner had the Stuart monarch died than his son, Prince Charles, took up the orb, sceptre and crown – in a figurative sense – to become King Charles I, aged 24. He was proclaimed sovereign at Theobalds Palace, former home of the Cecil family, where his father had breathed his last. One of Charles's first duties in his new role was to act as chief mourner at King James's state funeral, which took place on 7 May in London, amid huge crowds that lined the streets from Somerset House to Westminster Abbey. Simonds D'Ewes was there that day. The barrister found himself a 'most convenient place in the Strand, near Somerset House, on the other side of the way', where he was able to watch the procession pass in all its solemnity and ostentation.[12] A good record of the pageantry surrounding James's death, funeral and burial comes from the Tuscan diplomat Alessandro Antelminelli (also known as Amerigo Salvetti), who wrote the following regarding the deceased king's lying-in-state at Somerset House:

> The rooms of the palace were hung from floor to ceiling with black cloth, and the bed chamber with black velvet. The body, which was embalmed and placed in a leaden coffin, was deposited under the bier, and a figure, an excellent likeness of the late king, lay on it dressed in the royal costume and robes, with the Imperial crown upon its head, the sceptre in the right hand, and the globe in the left... On each side of the bed there were three candlesticks of silver, of the value of 1,500 crowns each, which the present king had ordered to be made in Spain. At night only were the wax torches lighted. Two days before the funeral the body was removed by a private stair and placed in another bier in the presence chamber, whilst the other, with its canopy, was moved into the guardroom.[13]

King Charles was present, 'attended by the court and heralds', when his father's body was moved in preparation for the state occasion.[14]

As for the funeral itself, Antelminelli described it as a day of unimaginable soberness in the capital, complemented by lashings of unmatched pomp and ceremony. Leading the funeral procession alone were some 400 poor men dressed in black garments, their cloaks trailing against the ground as they walked, followed by servants, ministers, gentlemen, members of the nobility, and the Archbishop of Canterbury, George Abbot. After the French ambassadors and a selection of gentlemen from the royal household, who were holding aloft the dead monarch's helmet, sword, gauntlets and golden spurs, came the ornate effigy of King James through the thoroughfares of London, an undoubted highlight for spectators such as D'Ewes. Antelminelli commented:

> ...[the effigy was] richly dressed and crowned and laid on the bier, which was supported on a funeral car open on all sides and covered with black velvet; the car being drawn by six horses, caparisoned in black velvet, with black feathers on their heads, and guided by two coachmen and twenty-four grooms who assisted at the car, all being dressed in black velvet; whilst on the car were two gentlemen of the royal chamber dressed in black cloth, one placed at the head and the other at the feet of the effigy which they appeared to support.[15]

Charles I walked in the shadow of the elaborate funeral car, garbed in a cloak and hood and looking appropriately downcast, his person covered by a black-cloth canopy. Inside Westminster Abbey, the new sovereign was shown to a table and seat that had been specially prepared for him, from which he inspected 'the twelve standards and all the other emblems or things belonging to the late king', before depositing pieces of gold and silver 'in a large silver basin'.[16]

Flavours of what was to come in England under King Charles found their way into Alessandro Antelminelli's correspondences in the succeeding weeks, with the ambassador noting on 20 May 1625 that the monarch had decided to delay the opening of his first parliament until his young bride, Henrietta Maria of France, had arrived in the country. On 17 June, Antelminelli confirmed in another letter that the French queen was now at last on English soil, having landed at Dover on the twelfth.[17] Simonds similarly recorded the events of Henrietta Maria's arrival and subsequent meeting with Charles in his autobiography, describing how the royal couple initially dined with each other in Dover, travelled to Canterbury together, and then consummated their marriage at St Augustine's Abbey. The pair had been married by proxy before Notre-Dame de Paris on 1 May.

D'Ewes went on to see Queen Henrietta Maria with his own eyes in Whitehall on 30 June, believing her to be an attractive consort with many appealing qualities. 'Her deportment amongst her women was so sweet and humble,' he remembered, 'and her speech and looks to her other servants so mild and gracious, as I could not abstain from divers deep-fetched sighs to consider that she wanted the knowledge of the true religion.' This last was an overt reference to Henrietta Maria's Catholic faith, which was completely at odds with the Protestant doctrine that Simonds placed on such a high pedestal in his own life. Luckily, only the latter religion would be present in Suffolk on 22 September, when Simonds's younger sister, Grace D'Ewes, married Wiseman Bokenham of Thornham Hall at Stowlangtoft church. The ceremony was made yet more pleasurable for the visiting barrister by the erudite abilities of its preacher, Mr Richard Danford (or Damport, some write), who, while not always a friend to the D'Ewes family, on this occasion 'made one of the neatest and well-penned sermons that I ever heard preached'.[18]

Into 1626, Simonds would have had little clue that his own wedding day was now approaching, the associated marital negotiations suspended just beyond the horizon, out of sight. In the meantime, there was a coronation to be excited for in early February, which D'Ewes would make sure that he was a part of when the day arrived. Antelminelli observed of the event in a letter:

> The coronation of King Charles took place yesterday in Westminster Abbey but without the customary royal cavalcade, and comparatively without the magnificence characteristic of the ceremonial; it being resolved, from motives of economy, to save 300,000 crowns which it would have cost and to use the money for other important and needful purposes. It was at the same time desirable to avoid bringing together a numerous assemblage of the people whilst the plague still infests the city in various places.[19]

The Tuscan ambassador was clearly underwhelmed by Charles's crowning on 2 February, even though he possessed a good understanding of why the various ceremonies had been curtailed. Simonds, on the other hand, appears to have been entranced by proceedings – perhaps because he had seen nothing else like it in his lifetime.

Early on 2 February, D'Ewes remembered hurrying across London to the house of fellow antiquary Sir Robert Cotton, whose property (backing on to the Thames) had been chosen to receive Charles and his entourage on their way to Westminster Abbey. It was no secret that Cotton's gardens were to be employed for this purpose; many other gentlemen and ladies of quality filled the windows of the antiquary's townhouse that morning, all wanting to catch a glimpse of the bedecked king before he was coronated. Frustratingly for everybody concerned, the barge carrying the royal party sailed straight past Sir Robert's gardens, which had even been carpeted in anticipation of King Charles's landing, and instead docked at the stairs leading directly to the Palace of Westminster. 'The landing was dirty and inconvenient of itself,' D'Ewes relayed bitterly, 'and that incommodity increased by the royal barge's dashing into the ground and sticking fast a little before it touched the causeway.' This setback was not to deter him, however. Wandering through Westminster and beside the abbey a little later, Simonds came across a door that was less heavily guarded than the rest and slipped inside unopposed, then finding the stage on which Charles was to be crowned and settling down there. Shortly, the king himself appeared 'bareheaded to the people', ready to partake in the mystical rituals of the day.[20]

Sir Robert Cotton had become one of Simonds's closest friends in the capital, meaning that there would have been little love lost between the two over the former's embarrassing blunder. The men's shared passion for antiquarianism held them together in a kind of intellectual union, like glue. Years later, D'Ewes would choose to hang a portrait of Cotton in his library at Stow Hall, the painting of which, in the first place, had been organised by him in July 1626. There were several other meaningful friendships of this ilk enjoyed by Simonds in London in the 1620s. One such companionship D'Ewes struck up was with the learned Sir Albertus Joachimi, who had become the United Provinces' ambassador to England following the death of Sir Noel de Caron in 1624. They seem to have first met in March 1626, not long after the coronation. Riding in the ambassador's coach after a mutual visit to the de Veres' London townhouse (Simonds had taken an interest in Robert de Vere's claim to the earldom of Oxford), D'Ewes became attracted to the obvious intellect of Joachimi, a man who could himself write fluently in Latin. The rest, as they say, was history.

D'Ewes's accelerating enthusiasm for antiquarianism led him to pursue fanciful notions when drafting a copy of his last will and testament on 26 March. William Camden, antiquary and famed author of *Britannia*, had been buried at Westminster Abbey in November 1623, with a white-marble monument erected in his memory soon afterwards in the south transept of the cathedral. Simonds, in considering his own posthumous fate, felt that he also deserved this honour if he were to die in London. 'I desire that a monument be set up in Westminster church,' he wrote, 'just by Mr Camden's tomb, on the right-hand, in everything according to the form and pattern of that as near as may be possible.'[21]

CHAPTER 8

ANNE CLOPTON

THE RESPECTIVE ARENAS of the law and antiquarianism continued to coexist in Simonds's day-to-day life throughout the spring and early summer of 1626. When not attending to business at the Court of Common Pleas in Westminster Hall, where he could be found most mornings at one stage, the intellectual occupied himself with antiquarian research and the transcribing of texts instead, including *Fleta*, a treatise on the common law of England.

Soon, however, there was a more important matter in need of consideration by D'Ewes, coming in the encouraging form of a fresh matrimonial opportunity for the young suitor. Lady Anne Clopton's name seems to have first sprung onto Simonds's radar as a potential candidate for marriage sometime at the beginning of 1626. She was the daughter of the wealthy Sir William Clopton of Kentwell Hall in Suffolk, a 'civill and quiet' gentleman of distinguished descent, who had died in March 1619 in his late twenties, leaving his attractive Long Melford property in the care of his second wife, Elizabeth Pellicini.[1] Anne's mother was Clopton's first spouse, Anne Barnardiston, herself the daughter of Sir Thomas and Dame Ann Barnardiston (née Bygrave), who had also passed away in 1616. Hence, she was a relation of Sir Nathaniel Barnardiston, whose father had been her mother's half-brother.

As mentioned, Simonds and Anne had first met – without any agenda particularly – in the summer of 1619 at Clare Priory, when Anne had only been a very young child, and indeed an orphan. Aged 13 in April 1626, she was still rather juvenile upon Simonds entering into discussions with his friend Nathaniel Barnardiston about the possibilities of a match with her. By May, Anne's grandmother, Dame Ann Barnardiston, had given her blessing to the D'Ewes-Clopton union and entrusted the inevitable negotiations to two of her step-grandchildren: Nathaniel himself, respected lord of the manor, and his younger brother, Arthur. Paul D'Ewes, as ever, did not intend to make the ensuing months easy for either party; as early as June, the esquire of Stowlangtoft's stubbornness led to the hard-won treaty coming undone before his anxious son's very eyes. Naturally, Simonds began to wonder at this point if he would ever be able to secure himself a wife.

Lady Barnardiston rubbed salt into the wound the following month, being responsible for her own bit of derailing by choosing to pursue an alternative match for her granddaughter with 'an Essex gentleman'. When it seemed unlikely that this scheme would come to anything, the savvy gentlewoman then set her sights on a grandchild of William Fiennes, 1st Viscount Saye and Sele, who was called James. Distressing as these countermoves were for D'Ewes and his reputation,

Simonds had plenty of other worries with which to contend in July 1626. Writing to his close associate Sir Martin Stuteville one day, the barrister complained that 'my head hath been so full of moots [his legal responsibilities] as I scarce have had time in the better part of a week to visit my father or my lady'. Therein lay another of his distractions. Simonds's father and stepmother were ill with an undisclosed sickness in July, requiring near-constant medical attention from professionals. It is with some surprise that we learn from his letter to Stuteville that Paul had allowed himself to be 'a patient man under the physician's hand'.[2]

All traces of uncertainty, disquietude and general affliction would be washed away in cleanly fashion come August, much like the contents of the chamberpots at the Middle Temple. Not only was the marriage treaty between D'Ewes and Clopton reopened this month, but the terms of the union had more or less been agreed on by the time Simonds travelled up to Kedington Hall, the Suffolk home of Nathaniel Barnardiston, on the twenty-fifth. Here were also in residence Lady Barnardiston and Anne Clopton herself, 'whose person gave me absolute and full content as soon as I had seriously viewed it'.[3] So beguiled was Simonds by his future bride that he wasted no time, a week later, in sending a servant to Clare Priory to present Anne with a diamond carcanet, together with a few romantic lines, which ran thus:

> Fairest,
> Blest is the heart and hand that sincerely sends these meaner lines, if another heart and eye graciously deign to pity the wound of the first, and the numbness of the latter; and thus may this other poor enclosed carcanet, if not adorn the purer neck, yet lie hidden in the private cabinet of her whose humble sweetness and sweet humility deserves the justest honour – the greatest thankfulness. Nature made stones, but opinion jewels; this, without your milder acceptance and opinion, will prove neither stone nor jewel. Do but enhappy him that sent it in the ordinary use of it, who, though unworthy in himself, resolves to continue your humblest servant, Simonds D'Ewes.[4]

The servant, returning to his master that night, reported that these gestures had been well received by the young lady. Successful relations between the pair continued on 4 September, when Simonds visited Clare Priory himself to get to know Anne Clopton even better. It would appear that the more he learnt about her, the more he liked her.

There were a few uncomfortable issues to iron out before Lady Barnardiston would give the absolute go-ahead for her granddaughter to marry Mr D'Ewes. One such sticking point concerned Anne's limited years on the planet. Even seventeenth-century contemporaries were aware that 13 was a young age at which to be entering into a marriage, and an even younger age at which to be having sex. It was this last truth that troubled the girl's grandmother particularly as negotiations between the two families were formally wrapped up. Simonds did his best to persuade Lady Barnardiston that he merely desired 'to have the marriage consummated, and would forbear to reap the fruits of it till all danger in that kind should be passed'.[5] Because his words were sincere enough, and because she had no reason to doubt D'Ewes's honest intentions based on what she had seen of the man so far, eventually the matriarch yielded.

Thus, on 6 October 1626, members of both the D'Ewes and Barnardiston dynasties rode together in a coach towards London. While Anne Clopton, Lady Barnardiston and one of her daughters were all to stay in Blackfriars in the lead-up to the wedding, at the house of a relation, Simonds's plan was to temporarily take himself back to his chamber at the Middle Temple for a few weeks. The parish register of St Ann Blackfriars records that 'Simon D'ews & An Clopton' were married at the church on 24 October, around a fortnight later. Nobody was more pleased about the significant milestone in D'Ewes's life than his ageing father, who, though at times a resentful and oddly pessimistic fellow, 'received much comfort at the instant, seeing my happiness in the choice I had made'. Indeed, there was a palpable air of light-hearted celebration long after the ceremony itself had concluded, particularly at 'my cousin Bygrave's house' in Blackfriars, where the newly married couple had chosen to stay immediately following their nuptials. 'We enjoyed there divers days of happy content and rejoicing together in each other,' Simonds recalled.[6] Like a balloon popping and turning to nothing but ripped shreds, such euphoria finally came to an end on 1 November, when it was time for Lady Barnardiston to leave her granddaughter to the mature delights (not to mention challenges) of early modern marriage. Anne D'Ewes could not hide her tears, which ran thick down her cheeks, as the old woman who had educated her ever since she could remember rattled away from Blackfriars in her handsome coach, headed once more for East Anglia.

Opportunities for renewed festivities in the family would be numerous at the closing of another busy year. On 4 December 1626, one more of Simonds's sisters, Mary D'Ewes, was married to Sir Thomas Bowes of Much Bromley in Essex, the wedding taking place at St Faith's church in London. This was followed just two days later by a personal triumph for Simonds himself, who thus far remained without a title. Paying somewhere in the region of £364 for the privilege (making it, therefore, perhaps both a personal and a costly win), D'Ewes was knighted by the king on 6 December. Possibly he had felt ever so slightly coerced into the expensive enterprise by Lady Barnardiston, his new wife's grandmother; she had written to Paul D'Ewes in September, voicing her ardent desire that her grandson-in-law 'might undergo that ordinary step of honour... that so [Anne] might avoid the contempt of some ill wishers to these proceedings and he gain further respect amongst her kindred by these little additions'.[7] Whatever his motives had been, it was all for the greater good that the barrister and antiquary could now call himself, and be so named in return, Sir Simonds D'Ewes.

Chapter 9

WOLVES

SIR SIMONDS WAS in an enviable position in January 1627. The knight was newly titled; more than fulfilled when it came to his recreational activities; in a reasonably good place with his father, which certainly had not always been the case; and, most importantly, married to a young woman whom he found both physically attractive and sufficiently eligible. 'As my greatest worldly comfort consists in the enjoying of your sweet affection and most desired company... I shall ever account myself most happy to see and know you, to grow every day more and more sincere and conscionable in the fear and service of God; that so you may get knowledge and faith sufficient to discern whether you be in the estate of salvation or no,' he wrote to Anne on the thirty-first, his own assurance of salvation being notably strong. Anne D'Ewes's pleasing material assets were something that was particularly on her older husband's mind at the beginning of the year. Struggling along muddy, rutted roads, a telltale sign that winter had settled on the English countryside, Simonds embarked on a tour of the East Anglian lands that she had inherited soon after the Christmas holidays, including the manor of Newenham (near Ashdon in Essex). He was accompanied to the latter estate by two of its feoffees: Sir Nathaniel Barnardiston of Kedington, Suffolk, and Sir Giles Alington of Horseheath, Cambridgeshire. The aim of the exercise was simple: to begin the taxing process of collecting the manor's outstanding rents.

Hopefully experiencing better weather now that springtime had arrived, D'Ewes was back at Newenham Hall in April, where he continued to see to his wife's business and 'gave order for the receipt of divers quit or chief rents which were in arrear[s]'. In June, meanwhile, his various projects brought him into contact with Sir Richard St George of London's College of Arms, whom Simonds had instructed to amend his father's crest so that it included a wolf's head 'with a collar bezantée about the neck'.[1] This striking – and somewhat disconcerting – imagery had supposedly been found on the coat of arms of his ancestors in Gelderland. Whether true or otherwise, the wolf's head was accordingly granted to the D'Ewes family that summer, ears pricked, wild-eyed and collared, with flaming fur and a tongue that leapt from its mouth like a dagger.

The height of the hot season saw Simonds ushering his young, vivacious wife through golden fields and verdant pastures to Stow Hall in Suffolk for the first time. Paul D'Ewes threw open his doors gladly to his son and daughter-in-law upon their arrival at Stowlangtoft, the esquire being especially pleased to see that Anne D'Ewes had grown into herself a bit more since their last meeting. Indeed, the gentlewoman was now 14 years old, and, strictly speaking, no longer a child. While there were some who might have felt that such an age was still a little too tender to be engaging in the sorts of activities that defined a seventeenth-century marriage, there were few who would have denied the couple the enjoyment of taking a boat out on the scenic moat at Stow Hall on 1 August. Perhaps someone should have warned them of the unexpected dangers. Through a catastrophic miscalculation, both Simonds and Anne ended up falling backwards into the water during the innocent jaunt, with the knight struggling to reach the surface of the moat due to shock, and his wife, 'terrified with fear and astonishment', hardly able to recover from the incident afterwards.[2]

From Stowlangtoft, the D'Eweses travelled across to Cambridge at the end of August, where Simonds had been a student at St John's College nearly a decade earlier. The ex-undergraduate – who, incidentally, had never finished his degree – was eager to show Anne every corner of the town that he had once called home. The couple even climbed King's College Chapel beside the River Cam during their short stay, at the top of which Anne had her foot 'set… and her arms cut out within the compass of the foot, in a small escutcheon'.[3]

By the autumn of 1627, Simonds had left a great many things that were once inextricably linked to his life behind him. Along with his university days at Cambridge, D'Ewes's time as a barrister at the Middle Temple was also no more; for, now that he had married into money, the comfortable gentleman could afford to abandon the profession and concentrate on his personal interests instead. Irrespectively, there remained a curious air of reminiscence and reflection into the chilly month of November, which exhibited itself most obviously in a surprising reunion Simonds shared one afternoon. 'I went to visit Mistress Jemima Crew,' he wrote in his autobiography, 'lodging in Holborn at this time, my wife's kinswoman, now the wife of John Crew.' This was, of course, the knight's former flame from Lawford Hall near Colchester, Jemima Waldegrave. As Simonds noted, the Essex gentlewoman was married herself now, to the gentleman John Crew, distinguished Puritan, MP and future 1st Baron Crew of Stene. Tactlessly expressing how content he was with his own marriage, Simonds then listened to his companion that reflective afternoon as she remarked that Anne was likely to make him a much better wife and partner than she could ever have done. D'Ewes replied optimistically that 'God decreed matches in heaven; and when they are once accomplished, every man and woman ought to compose and frame their hearts to a persuasion that the husband or the wife they enjoy is best for them.' Jemima's answer to this was short and wistful. 'Ay,' she said, 'if one could do so.'[4]

Simonds seemed to be learning quickly as a young, compassionate man that happiness was not a God-given right in the seventeenth century, and that there were many people who were, in fact, deeply unhappy. He had felt the heavy emotion himself on several occasions in the past, though never with any profound or lasting seriousness. It was a condition that would – albeit fleetingly – again affect his spouse in early 1628, when the time came for the couple to leave Albury Lodge in Hertfordshire, where they had been staying since Blackfriars, for the capital. Albury was the home of Anne D'Ewes's aunt, Hannah Brograve, the youngest daughter of Dame Ann Barnardiston. While many new tears were shed upon Simonds and Anne's departure from this pleasant house on 6 February, these were soon replaced by warm and gleeful expressions once more in London. Paul D'Ewes and his second wife, Lady Elizabeth Denton, far from finding the development an imposition, were nothing short of thrilled to welcome the two youngsters to the former's office on Chancery Lane for the foreseeable future.

Simonds's Puritan anxieties got the better of him in May 1628. Witnessing what he believed to be abhorrent scenes at court upon the occasion of a diplomatic audience hosted by King Charles I, he relayed to Sir Martin Stuteville:

> The horrible profanation of Sunday was se'nnight you have heard, where the afternoon being spent at Court in giving the Russian ambassadors audience from dinner till three. About an hour after, the Garter Knights, attended with their followers, went in their greatest pains towards my Lord Mayor's. Thousands, in getting seats and places, exchanged both service and sermon; and the streets were no less filled with the meaner sort, nor windows stuffed with the better sort, than on a Lord Mayor's day. Having come thither, healths, and quaffing, and plays, spent the residue of the time till almost the next morning.[5]

Regrettably, this 'profanation of Sunday' was nothing compared to the wider misfortunes that were about to follow in England. Though he probably hoped very much that he was wrong, Sir Robert Cotton, D'Ewes's friend and fellow antiquary, hit the nail on the head in July 1628 when he warned that English politics was on a knife-edge, and that there was 'no certain happiness in this life to be expected'.[6]

For Simonds personally, the next few months were a mixture of both welcome occurrences and disturbing episodes, thrown side by side against a gradually deteriorating national backdrop. October 1628 was a particularly fruitful period for the blossoming antiquary. D'Ewes purchased the library of the late Ralph Starkey, another antiquary, this month, whom he unapologetically branded 'an ignorant, mercenary, indigent man' in his autobiography. It is possible that Simonds, in fact, had been slowly acquiring Starkey's collection (which included an impressive twenty volumes of transcripts) since as early as 1623.[7]

In November 1628, meanwhile, hissing, spitting flames signalled tragedy. The unlucky structure to be devoured on 19 November was the 'new brick house' of Sir Edward Cecil, 1st Viscount Wimbledon, which had been hired out by Sir Albertus Joachimi for the Dutch ambassador and his family to live in. Hence, it was a conflagration that Simonds himself naturally became involved in, given his intimate association with Sir Albertus at this point in his life. It would appear that the fire caused untold damage to the Joachimis' possessions and valuables, as had been the case in December 1621, when Paul D'Ewes's lodgings were consumed in Chancery Lane. The scenes in November 1628 were arguably even more desperate than those of seven years earlier. Whereas Paul had at least been elsewhere at the time of the incident at the Six Clerks' Office, Joachimi's wife and two of his children were in Cecil's house when it caught fire in the middle of the night, leading to the terrified trio escaping the property in nothing but their nightclothes. Simonds, who later consoled the shellshocked family as best he could, was of the impression in the 1630s that Lady Joachimi had never fully recovered from the ordeal.

On 28 February 1629, with the festivities of Christmas well and truly over for another twelve months, D'Ewes rode to Bury St Edmunds to dine with the high sheriff of Suffolk, Brampton Gurdon. Once the men had finished their meal, the two set off to meet Justice Hervey, a judge of the Court of Common Pleas, who was approaching the town as part of his circuit. Though their initial greeting in the countryside was breezy enough, the topic of conversation as the small party rode back towards Bury was decidedly heavy. Hervey had brought with him ill tidings from other parts of the country, especially London, where he feared that the sitting parliament was about to come unstuck. 'We heartily condoled the near approaching breach,' Simonds recollected, 'and the infinite miseries that were likely to ensue upon it.'[8]

Just forty-eight hours later, a breach is exactly what took place. On 2 March, a day described by D'Ewes as 'the most gloomy, sad, and dismal... for England that happened in five hundred years last past', Charles I drafted a royal proclamation conveying his intention to dissolve parliament, following a serious collapse in relations between the king and Westminster. Various issues had presented themselves in recent weeks that the two factions had simply been unable to agree on, no matter how lengthily, or indeed how tirelessly, they had been debated in the House of Commons and House of Lords. Among them were Charles's continued collecting of tonnage and poundage: customs duties that were traditionally granted by parliament to a monarch for life, but that had been denied the present king over fears that the historical privilege might be exploited. Religion, obviously, was another bone of contention that could not be settled tidily, particularly the differences in Christian doctrine that existed between the sovereign's inner circle at court and members of the Westminster elite.[9]

Perhaps underhandedly on that fateful date of 2 March, Charles chose to inform the Speaker of the House of Commons, Sir John Finch, that he merely wished to adjourn parliament until 10 March. Yet even this redacted message from the king, which Finch duly read out for the benefit of those men gathered, was enough to cause certain members of the assembly to smell a rat. Accordingly, when Mr Speaker made to rise from his chair once more, the communication having been delivered to his satisfaction, several MPs leapt into action in a furious attempt to prevent a political catastrophe from occurring. Like predators, Denzil Holles and Benjamin Valentine caught hold of Sir John Finch's arms and roughly directed him back to his seat, where he was forcibly held down while Sir John Eliot, an outspoken and defiant parliamentary representative, loudly denounced tonnage and poundage and Charles's proposed religious reforms. The move was deemed shocking by many, but there is no doubt that it was vigorously welcomed by others.

The sheer pandemonium sparked by the intervention was relayed to Paul D'Ewes at Stow Hall by Justinian Isham, who wrote to him on 5 March from London:

> ...as [the Speaker] was about to go out of the House, they plucked him back by force, and held him in his chair. So locking the door to themselves, they laid the key upon the table; which done, after divers speeches by sundry men spoken, with a general voice they proclaimed that none should have tonnage and poundage; and also, that they were traitors to the king and state, who either favoured Arminianism or popery, as Bishop Laud, said one, as my lord treasurer, said another; every one particularising whom he thought fit.[10]

Isham reported to his kinsman that concerned messengers sent by King Charles himself, one after the other, had been continually denied entry to the chamber as the stunning mutiny had played out. When tensions had threatened to bubble over and the doors had finally been unlocked, the serjeant-at-arms, poised to cross the threshold, had apparently instead been carried away in the crowd. 'It is said,' Isham remarked, 'that a Welch page hearing a great noise in the House cried out, "I pray you let hur in, let hur in, to give hur master his sword, for they are all fighting!".'[11]

This was not a fight that any parliamentary representative could win, however. On 4 March, the proclamation drafted by Charles two days before was published, officially dissolving parliament. The act marked the start of a highly controversial period of personal rule in England, which would continue, without interruption, for the next eleven years.

PART TWO
UNEASE

'All things hasten apace to confusion and calamity'

Chapter 10

NEW LIVES AND OLD

SOMETHING WAS TROUBLING Sir Simonds D'Ewes in 1629.

It was not, as might be expected, the dissolving of parliament by the king on 4 March, which had led many a hardened gentleman to fret about the future of the English constitution. Nor did it concern his antiquary activities, which were coming along just fine by the end of March. Simonds, at this point, had begun transcribing records from the Tower of London that would eventually make up his most celebrated work, entitled *The Journals of All the Parliaments During the Reign of Queen Elizabeth*.

It did not relate to certain difficulties faced by D'Ewes with regard to the manor of Coxden in Dorset, either, although these probably weighed heavy on his mind as well. In need of funds to take up a townhouse in Islington this year, Simonds would be forced to lease out 'a great part of my west country estate' for a century, in the process 'taking great fines, and reserving small rents, in which I lost some considerable sums'. He would also find himself in a dispute with the vicar of Axminster in 1629, 'who had abused his trust in cutting down trees within the manor of Coxden in Dorsetshire'.[1] The knight would go on to take a petition detailing the finer points of the outrage directly to Sir Thomas Coventry, Lord Keeper of the Great Seal of England.

No, it was none of the above. The 'something' that bothered D'Ewes was much more intimate than matters of antiquarianism, or an altercation with a neighbour. It had to do, in actuality, with his wife's fertility. Simonds and Anne had been married for close to three years by the summer of 1629, yet no child, male or female, had thus far been born to them. Even Simonds's visiting his young wife's inheritance of Kentwell Hall in Long Melford on 7 August, which he described as 'a goodly, fair, brick house', could not entirely take his mind off this predicament. It came down to the gentleman's pride fundamentally, as well as D'Ewes's concern for the continuation of his family name and line through a son – a preoccupation that consumed the thoughts of almost all men of his social standing in the early modern period. Simonds's case was especially troubling because his father was now unlikely to produce any further male children in his advancing years, while his 'dear and only' brother, Richard D'Ewes, 'was yet a child'.[2] A third brother, Paul, had died during infancy long ago, his loss constituting a painful episode that would later be preserved on his namesake's monument within Stowlangtoft church.

But there was hope. The coming of the 1630s in England may have heralded a decade of governmental anxiety and kingly egotism for the country as a whole, but for Simonds himself, it offered fresh optimism regarding the way ahead for his family. On 30 April 1630, in the early hours of the morning, Anne D'Ewes gave birth to the couple's first child. The miraculous baby was a girl, whom her parents decided to also call Anne, after her 17-year-old mother. Of course, it was not lost on Simonds that little Anne was not the son who would be able to secure the good D'Ewes name for generations to come. However, that the infant had been born at all was encouragement enough for her happy mother and father that male heirs would soon be arriving to join her in Islington, where the household was then resident. It is recorded within the parish records of St Mary Islington that 'Ann, the Daughter of Sir Simon and Ann Dewes' was baptised at the church on 13 May.[3]

Simonds had been a father-in-waiting for a sufficient time by 1630 to know how he might go about raising his children. He would write in a commonplace book that parents 'are especially bound to instruct the children, pray for them and train them up in fear of God because they drew original corruption from their loins'. Certainly, his Puritan ideology may have led him to question the methods of whoever had been responsible for raising – or dragging up – Dudley North, 3rd Baron North, and his wife, who, one day in August, showed themselves up unforgivably by talking of nothing but a deceased canine for hours. '[They] did so fill up all the dinner time with the needless and vain discourse of a dog they had which died a little before,' Simonds wrote distractedly, 'as it showed them to be ill-catechised in the principles of religion.'[4]

The puritanical edge to D'Ewes's everyday life and values was evident again at Christmastime, when the knight refused to participate in the sinful games of dice and cards, choosing instead to spend the holiday interlude studying, paying 'harmless visits' and entering into 'useful discourses'. Such strict religiosity and respectable behaviour had obviously rubbed off on Simonds's younger brother by early 1631. Fifteen years old in February, Richard wrote to his father in Latin to convey his eternal gratitude for Paul D'Ewes's kindness in providing him with so well-rounded an education, as well as for every other 'benefit' he had 'placed in me'. The teenager 'beseeched God that he may serve thee under his protection', and additionally made it known that he wished to follow Paul's example 'in all things'.[5]

Colourful, passionate, independent and headstrong, and very rarely boring to a modern audience, the esquire of Stowlangtoft was reaching the end of the road upon receiving his youngest son's affectionate letter. About 22 February, Paul D'Ewes contracted an illness from which he would not recover. Simonds described the complaint as a 'fever, joined with a pleurisy, of which disease he lingered three weeks before he deceased, during which time I had many sad and heavy journeys to him'.[6] Blood was much thicker than water in these final days of Paul's life; whatever differences had come between father and son previously were now quite forgotten, to be replaced by mutual feelings of great love and respect only. This renewed relationship was to prove a blessed comfort to both within the four walls of the Six Clerks' Office, particularly when considering that the severity of the ailment, while destined to be a fatal one, would ebb and flow as physicians continued to re-evaluate the situation.

Dr Giffard and Dr Baskerville among them, the medical practitioners attending Paul's sickbed would try all manner of remedies to get their patient better.

One treatment that was attempted time and again into March was the practice of bloodletting, a procedure that, on the failure of its fourth application, was abandoned altogether. Simonds appears to have witnessed more than once the (supposedly) tainted blood come pouring out of his blanched father in red, oily streams, commenting that it was the most 'infected' he had ever laid eyes on. Paul's physicians became worried relatively early on in treatment that they were expelling too much of the bodily substance from the invalid. The esquire himself was less concerned; a doctor having anxiously informed him on one occasion that he had ceased letting blood because he was frightened that he would lose more than was good for him, Paul replied that 'thou needest not, for what thou leavest will shortly be in the grave'.[7]

27 February was a sobering day for everybody. Taking Holy Communion together in Paul's chamber on Chancery Lane, Simonds then left the visiting minister alone with his father to discuss the prospect of dying, and how he might prepare his soul for the inevitable end. 'I conceive he felt more inward comfort and resolution to die,' D'Ewes concluded afterwards, having considered the overall outcome of the spiritual consultation. Given how unwell Paul was now becoming, this stoic attitude can only have been a merciful development for his immediate family. 'Mr D'Ewes, saith my author, is not like to live many days,' the Reverend Joseph Mede reported gravely to Sir Martin Stuteville on 6 March, just a week or so before the man's death.[8] Paul allegedly revived a little on 12 March, to the point where – for a brief period, anyway – Simonds seems to have been genuinely convinced that his father would make an inexplicable recovery. Just two days later, however, on 14 March, the fantasy volatilised almost as fast as it had emerged.

Word was sent to the knight in the morning that Paul D'Ewes was unexpectedly entering his final hours, and that if he wished to see his father alive, he should come at once to Chancery Lane. Simonds ran most of the way to the Six Clerks' Office. Anne D'Ewes followed her husband in her coach, being heavily pregnant at the time with the couple's second child, yet earnestly desiring to continue playing the dutiful daughter-in-law while she was still able. When it came to the melancholic deathbed scene, though, the young gentlewoman was forced to draw the line. The 'doleful and deep-fetched' groans that escaped Paul's lips as he lay dying simply proved too much for Anne in her condition; indeed, they would have been difficult sounds for anybody to hear, including Simonds himself.[9] His wife safely out of the chamber and recovering from her unpleasant experience in another room, the eldest son and heir continued by his father's side until the awful groaning subsided, leaving in its place a rather sad silence. Without a single person noticing, Paul D'Ewes of Stowlangtoft died sometime after 5:00 pm. To check that he was in fact dead, and not just unconscious, a mirror had been held in front of his face to see if any trace of breath had appeared upon the glass. There had been nothing.

Paul's widow, Lady Elizabeth Denton, was obviously distraught at losing another spouse and life partner. Nevertheless, even before the esquire had died, the woman had gathered herself sufficiently to begin seeing to his personal affairs. Legal administration in the wake of an aristocratic death could be a complicated, contentious and uncomfortable business in the mid-seventeenth century; ideally, the bulk of the paperwork needed to be dealt with as quickly as possible, and in a way that was both methodical and seamless. Lady Denton knew this as well as anybody of her rank, and, therefore, had passed a box containing her husband's last will and testament to Simonds before the end arriving for his father in his Six Clerks' Office chamber.

Once opened, Paul D'Ewes's will would unleash a multitude of headaches for the new lord of the manor of Stowlangtoft. Court proceedings would be threatened and acted on, including by members of Simonds's close family; certain inheritances would be vigorously disputed; and even Stow Hall itself, that quiet and inviting mansion in Suffolk, would find itself at the centre of a controlled row over which rooms Lady Denton could continue to use as part of her jointure. Beyond the assets-based content of the document, there would be further squabbles over the directions Paul had given for his burial within Stowlangtoft church. He had asked that Mr Chamberlain ('a religious neighbour' of some respectability) deliver his funeral sermon, which did not go down at all well with St George's incumbent rector, Richard Danford, who saw the role as his own and nobody else's. '[Danford] absolutely refused to permit him to preach,' Simonds despaired in his autobiography.[10]

The exact provisions made, and directions given, in D'Ewes's will are worth exploring briefly here, for they paint a picture of the man that is not necessarily apparent in most contemporary accounts. In the first place, his numerous instructions reveal an indisputable concern for fairness after his death, as well as familial harmony. On the future of Stow Hall, for example, he willed the following:

> During [Lady Denton's] widowhood she should live and dwell at Stow Hall with my son, being fittest for them both, which son of mine I do charge and command upon my blessing to observe and respect her with all love and duty and to let her choose for her own dwelling in Stow Hall, my principal house, the most convenient rooms and lodgings for herself and her family and her friends, with stable room for her coach and coach horses, all which I do now give and bequeath unto her.[11]

Furthermore, the legacies he left to society's less fortunate members show Paul to be a compassionate and caring leader of the local community – even though it was quite normal for the impoverished to be provided for in wills. For the poor and needy of Lavenham alone, there was to be £20 put by; for those of Stowlangtoft, £10; and for those of Godalming in Surrey, where his daughter lived with her husband, another £5. One Amy Albert, 'an old deaf woman', was to personally receive 40 shillings.

Paul D'Ewes's respect and deep concern for his household particularly is also apparent in the document. His plans for Elizabeth, his youngest daughter, were as follows:

> And because my daughter Elizabeth is yet young and not able to 'marriage her portion' I have often in my lifetime and now... I do [?]

my well-beloved wife the Lady Denton to take her (she being of her own name) unto her own government, ordering and breeding and to give unto her a godly, religious and worthy education as heretofore during our marriage she hath with good commendation performed to my good liking.[12]

For his servants, meanwhile, there were to be further monetary bequests distributed to see to each individual's immediate financial needs. Susan Goddart, 'my late servant', was to get the respectable sum of 20 shillings; Magdalen Dufford, described identically, 40 shillings, plus 20 shillings each for her two daughters; John Lawson and his wife, £5 apiece; George Wright, £10 in plate; Anne Denton, his widow's 'woman', £3 in plate; and John Scot, 'my ancient servant', another £10 in plate.[13]

Paul's story, which had begun decades before in 1567, was reaching its very last pages on 17 March 1631. His corpse having been wrapped in a cerecloth and put into a strong coffin, this day it was carefully loaded into a coach and taken from the Six Clerks' Office in Chancery Lane as far as Brooke Walden in Essex, where it would rest for the night. Simonds followed the body out of London and kept his father's lifeless remains company that evening. The next day, the coach carried on to Stow Hall in Suffolk, bringing Paul back to the place that he had loved more than any other. Uncertainties surrounding the late esquire's burial in Stowlangtoft remained until the morning of the scheduled funeral solemnities, on 25 April. Even then, Simonds was rather unsure whether Richard Danford, still incensed that he had been utterly excluded from proceedings, would allow a rector that was not him to deliver his father's funeral sermon. He appears to have backed down only at the last minute, agreeing to admit the parson of Lavenham, Dr Ambrose Copinger – not Mr Chamberlain, as Paul had wished – to St George's church to preach.

Despite the problems that had arisen, Simonds found the day as a whole to have been conducted both 'orderly and fairly' in hindsight.[14] Paul's coffin left Stow accompanied by every one of his children, apart from Johanne, and arrived at the church doors nearby with 'due solemnity'. Inside, there were then tears aplenty from everybody present as his body was interred close to where Cecilia D'Ewes's remains had been deposited thirteen years earlier.

CHAPTER 11

THE LAVENHAM BRASS

FINAL PARTINGS CONTINUED to stalk Simonds in the weeks and months after Paul D'Ewes's funeral. Following his father to the grave in May 1631 was Sir Robert Cotton, one of the knight's great friends in the antiquarian world, who died with his library still determinedly closed up on the orders of King Charles I. It was believed at court that the library's contents had the potential to be damaging to monarchical opinion in the aftermath of parliament's dissolution. 'He was so outworn within a few months with anguish and grief, as his face, which had been formerly ruddy and well-coloured, and such as the picture I have of him shews, was wholly changed into a grim blackish paleness, near to the resemblance and hue of a dead visage,' D'Ewes lamented.[1]

During the summer, there was one more death to come to terms with, though this latest loss was perhaps the worst yet for Simonds. The sorrowful tale began a fortnight earlier, on 24 June, when a son was finally born to the D'Eweses in Lavenham, one of the family's manors in Suffolk. All was positively joyful for the growing brood until 7 July. On this day, as was the case with so many newborns in the seventeenth century, Clopton (named after his mother's family) began to sicken. By 9 July, what was suspected to have been nothing more than a minor complaint had turned into a life-threatening illness, characterised by a 'violent and little intermitting lask [looseness] or scouring'. There was little to be done. Around 4:00 pm, the infant 'had some intermission' and seemed to settle somewhat, but by 6:00 pm Clopton had breathed his last. Simonds and Anne were naturally devasted; being in Lavenham still, they arranged to have the newborn interred in the chancel of the church there on the afternoon of 10 July, 'about the middle of it'.[2]

To memorialise the son that he had desired above almost all things, but that he had tragically lost, Simonds afterwards installed a monumental brass in St Peter and St Paul's church, Lavenham, of a baby swaddled in a chrism robe, together with a brass inscription. The inscription, written in Latin, spoke of Clopton being cruelly taken out of the world just four days after his baptism. Beautifully preserved in the chancel of Lavenham church, this 'baby brass' and its accompanying inscription can still be viewed in the twenty-first century, fixed innocuously to a stone slab and surrounded by a sea of coloured tiles. Nowadays, it has been respectfully cordoned off so that the intriguing installation might survive for centuries to come.

As much as he may have wished that it was not so, the bereft esquire of Stowlangtoft did not have the hours in the day to mourn Clopton D'Ewes for an extended period. All too soon, Simonds's exertions had been redirected towards his younger brother, Richard, who had reached university age by April 1632, and was therefore ready – at 16 years old – to continue his education at Cambridge. The pair set off for the town separately on 7 April, where, unlike his older sibling, Richard D'Ewes was admitted to St Catharine's College as a student. Simonds returned to his family in Islington only the following day, relieved to find that his sole child, Anne, had fully recovered from an illness. Further relief came through D'Ewes's subsequent perusal of certain deeds relating to 'the families of Knyvet and Chasteleyn', being a continuation of his antiquarian undertakings. By 1633, records indicate that Simonds had multiple servants working for him to transcribe these old documents, and that it was not a solitary pursuit in the literal sense of the word.[3]

A short while later, on 19 April, D'Ewes again found himself making good Richard's future by taking his brother to the Middle Temple in London, where the teenager was to be admitted. Richard was then sent back to Cambridge to begin his studies at St Catharine's. 'It was my chief care,' Simonds noted in his autobiography, 'to have him religiously and virtuously educated, and therefore, before his departure to Cambridge, I gave him especial cautions and instructions to beware of evil company, the very pests and poisoners of the younger sort that are sent thither.' Alas, the knight's careful words of advice for his sibling fell on deaf ears. Stories were quickly fed back to Simonds that Richard had been getting up to all sorts of mischief with his university friends at St Catharine's, including plying young D'Ewes's coachman with strong drink until the servant could barely stand. This led to Simonds restating to his impressionable brother just how important it was to rise above such behaviour, and that it was better for his companions to view him as uptight or 'proud' than to have them 'trample upon the innocence of your youth and enrich themselves with the spoils of your good beginnings'.[4] Whether Richard took any notice of the only father figure left in his life is not altogether clear.

Together with taming young Richard, who had once written such a devoted, godly letter to Paul D'Ewes before his death in March 1631, Simonds was made to reconsider his living arrangements towards the end of 1632. The knight spoke in his autobiography of a 'terrible censure... passed in the Star Chamber against one Mr Palmer' on 7 November, purportedly 'for staying in London the last long vacation, contrary to the king's proclamation', which had spooked him into concluding that it was about time his family left Islington and returned to Suffolk. This they had already done by December, though the spacious Stow Hall in Stowlangtoft had not been an option for them as a place to move their young family to; as per Paul's last will and testament, the best rooms of the country house continued to be used by his widow, Lady Elizabeth Denton. The nearby town of Bury St Edmunds, where Simonds had attended school for a time as a child, in any case turned out to be a more than agreeable alternative in which to set up home. 'Most happy we were, during our continuance here,' D'Ewes recalled warmly, noting that he and his wife were frequently engaged in religious activities of one kind or another in the parish of St Mary's.[5]

Anne D'Ewes possibly felt that she had never been more in need of sound spiritual guidance early the following year. The young gentlewoman, barely 20 years old even after half a decade of marriage, found herself heavily pregnant again in March – this time with twins. 'I heartily wish your good lady a happy and safe deliverance, which we shall be as glad to hear of as any poor friends you have, unto whom I desire you to present my best service,' William Elliot, Simonds's brother-in-law, wrote to him on 1 March, having also raised the delicate subject of a legacy that his younger son was due from Paul D'Ewes's generous estate.[6] The man knew, as did Simonds himself, that there was much riding on the upcoming Suffolk birth. Something that Elliot did not know, however, were the problems that Anne had already been facing in Bury in recent weeks. Life appeared to have no intention of making things easy for the D'Eweses now that they had a second chance at bringing a son into the world. For a start, the couple's daughter had come down with the measles at the end of February, causing her mother to fear that she would catch the disease as well. There had also been a particularly bumpy coach journey for Lady D'Ewes to endure through the streets of the market town one day, with the vehicle's wheels bouncing over cobbles and all manner of other obstacles.

Both incidents were considered to have had a negative impact on Anne's precarious pregnancy, at least according to a despairing Simonds. Accordingly, neither baby would last long once it had been delivered prematurely on 10 March 1633. What made the episode decidedly painful for each parent was the bittersweet discovery during Anne's difficult labour that both twins were boys. The first to be born was called Adrian, after Simonds's paternal great-grandfather; the second, and more sickly of the two, Geerardt, in honour of Paul D'Ewes's father. Geerardt faded fast following his delivery. His father had him baptised near enough straight away 'in my wife's chamber', before the newborn died early in the afternoon.[7] His little body was then taken in Simonds's coach to Lavenham, where he was buried in Clopton D'Ewes's grave on 12 March.

Though Adrian would cling to life for a little longer in Bury St Edmunds, Simonds believed it prudent to also have the baby baptised on 11 March, a day after the birth. In attendance at the understated ceremony, again conducted in Anne's chamber, were his sister Elizabeth and good friend Sir Nathaniel Barnardiston. The older twin ultimately joined his brothers in eternity on 13 March, while Simonds was away on business in London. 'I came safe thither... well hoping of the continuance of the life of my little Adrian; but God... had otherwise decreed,' he wrote melancholically in his autobiography.[8] Once more, a coach was taken out to Lavenham on 14 March, where Adrian's tiny corpse was deposited in the chancel of St Peter and St Paul's alongside those of Clopton and Geerardt.

Chapter 12

LAUD

RICHARD D'EWES TURNED 18 in October 1633. With this birthday, Simonds's responsibilities as an administrator of his father's will finally came to an end, for his younger brother was now at an age where he could become executor of Paul D'Ewes's estate under law. Thus, on 3 October, the knight departed Stow Hall in a hired coach and travelled south to London, where he planned to pay the student the sum owing to him.

D'Ewes took a coach from Stow Hall of all places because, as of June, he and his family had taken up residence there. What's more, in November, Lady Elizabeth Denton would permanently move out of the property to live at neighbouring Ixworth Abbey, allowing the D'Eweses the run of the place at last. This development had its drawbacks, as well as its plus points. The main advantages were, of course, that the house was large and attractive, the gardens rambling, the surrounding countryside charming, and the memories of happy family occasions many. As for the few disadvantages, they all seemed to lead back to one particular individual. Richard Danford, rector of Stowlangtoft, had been relentlessly on the warpath ever since his infamous snub following the death of Paul D'Ewes in 1631. The preacher was not about to rein in his confrontational behaviour now that the repugnant family who had snubbed him were back living in his parish.

'Mr Danford... had wasted much money with me in several suits... [and] practised daily new and malicious devices to vex us, so as we feared we should at last be driven, for very peace and quiet's sake, to forsake our mansion house,' Simonds recalled in his autobiography. Even news of Anne's being pregnant again, early in 1634, could not thaw the intermittently icy atmosphere that had settled on a part of the world that the knight had worshipped since his teenage years. Simonds became so offended by Danford's religious ideology specifically that, one Sunday in April, he decided to take detailed notes during a church service ('unworthy the name of a sermon') that the man animatedly led at St George's.[1] When he could tolerate Richard's relentless profanations no longer, D'Ewes went to the Bishop of Norwich, Richard Corbet, for advice on what was to be done. While initially insisting that he would look into the misdeeds of Mr Danford, it seems that, somewhere down the line, the bishop was paid off by the rogue parson to keep quiet.

Simonds's ecclesiastical anxieties at this time went far beyond the actions of one insufferable minister, however. 'At home,' he lamented later in his autobiography, 'many wicked, anabaptistical or popishly affected divines and scholars in both universities and elsewhere, maintained in the schools and pulpits justification by works, free will, Christ's bodily presence in the sacrament of the Lord's Supper, and a world of other corrupt and noisome tenets.' D'Ewes was here referring to the string of religious reforms that had been introduced to England since King Charles's accession in 1625, namely by the theologian William Laud, who had risen to the post of Archbishop of Canterbury in 1633. To many, and particularly to Puritans like Simonds, such extensive Protestant revisions smacked of a national return to the tenets of Catholicism. It is not difficult to understand why Laud's reforms were so frequently viewed in this way by contemporaries. Changes more or less enforced by the archbishop, himself a follower of Arminianism, included a requirement to stand during certain parts of a religious service or ceremony; the railing in of altars, with parishioners up and down the country now expected to kneel when receiving communion; the restraining of lectures delivered by Puritan clergymen; the permitting of recreational activities on the Sabbath; and a ban on wearing hats in church.[2]

Though ministers who defied their superiors in these matters were at serious risk of being punished for it, this did not stop a good many of them from exhibiting bold displays of resistance. The Court of High Commission heard the case of one Anthony Lapthorne, rector of Tretire in Herefordshire, on 9 October 1634, who was charged with multiple counts of religious malpractice within his respective ministry, including refusing to administer the sacraments correctly and branding his ecclesiastical colleagues 'Great Rabbis', 'Great Clergy-monsters', 'Idol Shepherds', 'Dumb-dogs' and 'Soul-murtherers'.[3] Lapthorne was further accused of the following:

> In expounding he inveighed at some of his parishioners with whom he was offended. He never observed any holy days or fasting days except at Christmas, Easter, and Whitsuntide. At baptism he refused to take the child into his arms, or to sign it with the cross. In the Holy Communion, after having said the words of benediction to one or two, to the rest he said, 'Take and eat', or 'Take and drink'. He reviled some of his parishioners who bowed at the name of Jesus. Held a fast on the Friday before Trinity Sunday... and invited many foreigners of other parishes to be present, in whose presence he stated that certain of his hearers who had not profited by his teaching were possessed of devils, and called upon the foreigners to assist in praying them out. He forbade his parishioners to say after him in versicles, or anything but Amen, and singing of Psalms.[4]

The court found the man to be 'incorrigible' and wholly unfit for office. Consequently, those sitting in judgement on him moved to suspend Lapthorne from his livelihood.

A year later, the Court of High Commission found itself dealing with two more outspoken opponents of William Laud's religious programme. Charles Chauncey, vicar of Ware, and Humphry Packer, a local yeoman – who were the defendants in question on 26 November 1635 – seem to have been particularly insulted by the railing off of a communion table within Ware church. 'In the presence of divers of the parishioners,' the surviving court document reads, 'Chauncey used reproachful speeches against the setting up of the rail and bench and the lawfulness thereof, and affirmed that it was an innovation, a snare to men's consciences, superstitious, a breach of the Second Commandment, [and] an addition to God's worship.' These were grave accusations indeed. Packer, meanwhile, was supposed to have 'derided the rail and kneeling bench, and scoffed at the setting up thereof, saying it would serve for better purpose in his garden'. Both men were found guilty of 'raising a schism and distraction' in Ware, with Chauncey, again, being suspended from 'the execution of his ministerial functions'.[5]

No doubt frightened by the consequences of refusing to toe the line, countless other church officeholders chose to react to the steady rise of Laudianism with quiet acceptance. Some even embraced the changes that were filtering down from the king and archbishop. Dr Roger Mainwaring, Dean of Worcester, wrote to Archbishop Laud on 24 September 1635 to enthusiastically apprise him of the remedial action that had been taken in Worcester Cathedral since his assumption of the role the previous year. A rail had been added to 'fence the holy table' in; a new marble altar, draped in a pall, had been installed and 'set upon four columns'; the wall directly behind this altar had been decorated with 'azure-coloured stuff', with 'a white silk lace down each seam'; and the forty or so King's Scholars of the cathedral, who might ordinarily be expected to come into the choir in a rather raucous manner, had now been made to 'do reverence towards the altars' each time they entered the hallowed space.[6]

There is no question that the English population at large harboured deep reservations about the place of Laudianism inside their whitewashed, staunchly Protestant churches. Yet, at the same time, certain aspects of the reforms might be accommodated by at least some congregants. It seemingly took very little persuading to get considerable swathes of England to engage in sports and other recreational pursuits on the Sabbath day, for example, being one of the policies of Laud's regime that was openly endorsed by King Charles himself. Equally, the Laudian proclivity for festivals and other frivolities, including parish ales and morris dancing, found a supportive following in the West Country with relative ease.[7]

As mentioned, what the hostility towards Laud's reforms really boiled down to was a ubiquitous aversion in the country to anything that resembled a resurgence of Catholic worship or influence. It must be remembered that England had been, by the mid-1630s, a devoutly Protestant nation for a century; nobody living could now remember a time when the religious landscape had been any other way. That Charles I surrounded himself with Catholics at court, including his own wife, Queen Henrietta Maria, only reinforced the fear felt by many about the long-term implications of Laudianism. The couple's very marriage treaty contained a clause permitting the French queen to practise her Roman Catholicism at liberty, with an ornate chapel created for her at Somerset House by Inigo Jones, which was consecrated in 1635. Indeed, Simonds himself would write to Elizabeth Stuart, Queen of Bohemia, to convey his own concerns that there were many in the king's circle who 'under the couler of Lutheranisme would sett upp such a masse of superstition and Idolatrie in the Church of God as therbie his Roiall Majestie's best and most loiall subjects of England shall bee utterlie ruined'. Popular contempt for the old faith in this period can be readily observed in an example taken from August 1635, involving the French ambassador Monsieur de Poygne. The devout Catholic riding in his coach near Somerset House one day, seemingly minding his own business, he was suddenly joined in the vehicle by a dead cat 'covered with filth', which had been thrown by somebody standing in the street. 'Such audacity,' the Venetian ambassador Anzolo Correr reported to the Doge and Senate of Venice, 'is intolerable but incorrigible all the same'.[8]

To return to Simonds D'Ewes, the knight arrived in the capital in May 1634 to news that 'much ensadded my heart'. The disturbing tidings concerned the polemicist and devout Puritan William Prynne, who had been censured by the Court of Star Chamber earlier in the year for authoring a provocative book entitled *Histrio-Mastix: The players scourge, or, Actors Tragaedie*, which took aim at the theatrical industry. Having had one ear partially cut already for his seditious words, the man was now about to have the other clipped. These violent acts, unfortunately, did not represent the full punishment inflicted on Prynne as a result of his writing *Histrio-Mastix*. Because the work is said to have offended the queen herself, it had encouraged the Star Chamber to deal with the offence in an especially merciless way. On top of having his ears mutilated, it had been ordered that copies of Prynne's book be 'burnt in the basest manner by the hand of the hangman'; that the Puritan be 'put... from the profession of the law' and expelled from Lincoln's Inn, where he had trained as a barrister; that he be 'degraded in the University [of Oxford]'; that he be fined £5,000; and that, finally, he be 'imprisoned perpetual, or at the king's pleasure'.[9]

The entire affair was, in fact, bound up in a wider programme of printing censorship and control pursued by both William Laud and Charles I between 1625 and 1640. Despised perhaps as much as Laudianism, this movement saw the licensing of publications become stiflingly restricted in England in the 1630s especially, with around '70 acts of [post-publication] censorship' taking place from the king's accession to the year of the convening of the Long Parliament.[10] The penalties for getting on the wrong side of the scheme, as we have seen in the case of William Prynne in 1634, could be severe.

Prynne's experiences at the hands of Laud and the Star Chamber were not to deter him in his quest to disseminate printed information about the things he believed to be irregular or injurious about society. In 1637, as an imprisoned man, he managed again to author and publish a controversial pamphlet that sought to criticise bishops, entitled *Newes from Ipswich*. Once more, thus, Prynne was marched to the pillory in Westminster to be made an example of, along with the vicar Henry Burton and Essex physician John Bastwick, both of whom had also written works attacking the church. The day was one of gentle gestures and bloody deeds. Initially on 30 June, Burton and Bastwick walked to the site of their punishment with their loyal wives in tow, through streets that were piled high with scented herbs and flowers, tossed lovingly by the sympathetic crowds who had come to wish the perpetrators well. However, there was only brutality on display in Palace Yard itself.

Here, further chunks of Prynne's already disfigured ears were removed, before a red-hot iron was stamped against his cheek three times to brand him a repeat offender. As for Burton and Bastwick, they had been sentenced to lose their currently intact ears. Evidence presented in parliament later would point to the viciousness with which this punishment was carried out on one of the two men, Henry Burton, with Simonds himself in attendance as a surgeon's recollections of the day were read out to an appalled audience. 'Then followed the execution,' the report went, 'which... was executed with great cruelty, and... [Burton] bled long and spent much arterial blood before [the surgeon] could come to him; he then attending at Mr Prynne's scaffold.'[11]

Among the mounting controversies of King Charles's personal rule, Simonds's personal life continued to take various twists and turns of its own in 1634. On 3 June, a conveyance was signed at Stow Hall to settle the estate of his late father-in-law, Sir William Clopton, now that his wife, Anne, was 'full of age', being a mature 21 years old that summer.[12] Then on 18 July, at nearby Ixworth Abbey, the couple's fourth son was born.

Named Clopton D'Ewes, again after his mother's paternal family, the infant was delivered at Ixworth, the new home of the widowed Lady Elizabeth Denton, as a consequence of the ongoing conflict between the D'Eweses and Richard Danford, parson of Stowlangtoft. Anne's labour came on before she had even arrived at the property of her stepmother-in-law. Upon entering the house, the expectant mother 'grew so extremely unwell' that it was feared by those present that the midwife (travelling from Bury St Edmunds) would not be able to get there in time for the birth. Thankfully, all would turn out well for the family, with Anne going on to experience a relatively incident-free delivery. Over the next fortnight, however, two wet nurses would come and go, leaving Simonds to 'pitch upon a poor woman who had been much misused and almost starved by a wicked husband'.[13]

Though there was no accident of any particular note to be spoken of during Anne D'Ewes's labour in July, this was not the case the following month, when the gentlewoman, her husband, and two of his younger siblings were journeying back from Melford Hall in Suffolk, having been the dinner guests of Thomas Savage, 1st Viscount Savage. Somewhere between here and Lavenham, the coach carrying Simonds, Anne and Elizabeth D'Ewes overturned. While nothing could prevent Simonds from being thrown dramatically out of the vehicle and onto the ground, Richard D'Ewes, who was riding up ahead, possessed the foresight to bring the startled horses to a halt before any more harm was done.

So much excitement coloured the day-to-day activities of the D'Eweses in 1634 that there were grumbles from close friends that the family had dropped off the radar. Sir Nathaniel Barnardiston of Kedington Hall insinuated as much to Lady D'Ewes in a letter, though on this occasion the landowner specifically referred to the inordinate amount of hours that Simonds seemed to be spending on his antiquarian researches. 'I should be heartily glad if your knight would spare so much time from his studies as that we might enjoy both your sweet companies here,' he wrote frustratedly. 'It is very much that we living so near together in the same [county] should not have leisure once in two or three years to visit one another.' Along with his genealogical work, which Simonds so loved, there was also a young brother to keep a fatherly eye on. On 3 October, for example, Richard would be engulfed in administration and, therefore, in need of support when he was granted a brand-new suite of rooms at the Middle Temple, within 'the new buildings in Elme Court'. This accommodation, which Richard had contributed towards financially, consisted of 'half an outer chamber on the third floor westward on the right of the stairs leading to the chambers westward, with study, woodhouse, bedroom, and servant's bedroom on the east side of the said outer chamber'.[14]

Perhaps Sir Nathaniel would be more understanding regarding his friend's busy life from early 1635 onwards. For it was in these months that young Clopton D'Ewes began to tread the path of his three older brothers, Clopton, Adrian and Geerardt, the toddler becoming intermittently ill. On 3 April, the following occurred:

> ...in the morning, my dearest son, Clopton D'Ewes, being my only male now living, and of a most venust [beautiful] and cheerful, sweet countenance, had a convulsion fit; which dreadful disease at times assaulted him afterwards... yet we little imagined at this time that the issue of it would be so fatal.[15]

Simonds chose not to tell his wife about this preliminary episode, though he could not conceal the second fit from her. Looking back, the knight's impression was that the physicians eventually hired to care for his sick son provided no help whatsoever in the desperate struggle to keep his son alive. One, Simonds asserted, being an Italian doctor from Bury St Edmunds, would even be directly responsible for Clopton's development of rickets.

On 9 June, Simonds's older sister, Johanne Elliot, wrote to him to offer her own opinion on the impending loss of his latest heir, and why she thought the situation might have deteriorated so rapidly. Her expert conclusion was that, in matters of childhood sickness in males, everything came back to the wet nurse – or, more accurately, the lack of one. 'I think it was very ill for your child to suck again, after so long being kept from it,' she counselled. 'I desire to hear whether it had fits, before you tried to wean him, I know not what cause you had but methinks it was somewhat soon to wean a boy.' Beyond suggesting that blood be let from the infant, which Johanne had proposed in a previous letter, the only pieces of advice that the woman could give to her younger brother related to any future offspring that the couple might have. 'The best way I found was to change the complexion of the nurse. When you have another, a brown ruddy complexioned woman I found best for my children,' she noted.[16]

Johanne's counsel would be applicable to Simonds and Anne relatively soon, with the arrival of a sixth child on the evening of 25 November 1635. It was another little girl, whom D'Ewes named Cecilia (or Sissilia), after his loving, late mother. The labour at Stow Hall had been particularly hazardous this time round, though, to everybody's obvious relief, not fatally so for either mother or baby. At any rate, Simonds had felt relaxed enough about the situation the afternoon before his wife had given birth to take notes on a register of ancient wills held at the register's office in Bury St Edmunds.

CHAPTER 13

SHIP MONEY, THE ELECTOR PALATINE AND THE NEW WORLD

At home the liberty of the subjects of England received the most deadly and fatal blow it had been sensible of in 500 years last past; for writs were issued the summer foregoing to all sheriffs of England, to levy great sums of money in all the counties of the same kingdom and Wales, under pretext and colour to provide ships for the defence of the kingdom.[1]

So wrote Simonds D'Ewes on the revival of ship money in England in the mid-1630s, a distinctly unpopular tax levied on the English people by Charles I to raise naval funds independently of parliament.

Ship money found its roots in the medieval period. Traditionally imposed when the country was considered under threat from seafaring, foreign opponents, the idea was that the capital raised from the tax would help protect England's coastlines through the commissioning and building of warships. Thus, it was a levy that historically fell to coastal communities to pay. What made ship money so controversial when it was reintroduced in October 1634 was that, as far as most Englishmen residing by the sea saw it, the threat posed from external invaders was non-existent. The odd 'privateer' from Dunkirk, or corsair skulking in the waters around Cornwall, was not nearly a compelling enough argument to convince them that the tax should be paid indefinitely. To make matters worse, in the summer of 1635, Charles and his advisers, spurred on by the apparent success of the scheme so far, moved to extend the levy inland, targeting counties and communities that had never before had to concern themselves with the defence of the coast and ports. Writs issued by the privy council in August quickly enshrined this arrangement in law, provoking outrage from taxpayers across the length and breadth of the kingdom.[2]

The unenviable task of collecting ship money in the 1630s was officially given to each county's high sheriff, with these ceremonial officeholders tending to delegate the actual handing over of funds to local constables. Records indicate that such constables, together with those who had been charged with assessing how much each man owed the king, could be met with fierce resistance from taxpayers as they toured their jurisdictions looking for financial contributions.

Sometime around the beginning of 1637, for instance, the Bishop of Lincoln, John Williams, became so incensed by the considerable sum that he was expected to pay to fulfil the tax that he demanded that his assessors come to his manor house in person to be held to account. '[He] reviled them,' a contemporary document reveals, 'saying they were base fellows, rascals, and liars, and not fitting to assess him, and that the worst boy in his house was a better man than [the] petitioner or his brother.'[3]

Even the constables themselves might feel strongly enough about the evils of ship money to resist the programme from time to time. In 1635, the constable John Napper of Somerset squared up to the individual who brought him a warrant demanding that he collect certain 'amounts assessed' without delay. 'Napper… at first refused it,' another contemporary document relays, 'but afterwards received it, saying he did not care a fart for it, nor would do anything thereupon, for he reckoned no more of the sheriff or his warrant than for a straw in the ground which with his foot he spurned at, and said he would maintain what he had done if it cost him £500.' It was uncomfortable encounters such as these that had D'Ewes melodramatically lamenting the tax in his autobiography. 'In all my life,' he groaned, 'I never saw so many sad faces in England as this new taxation, called Ship-money, occasioned.'[4]

Into 1636, however, Simonds had reason to smile again. On 2 February, the knight battled wind and rain to reach Newmarket in Suffolk, where both the divisive king and his nephew, Charles Louis, Elector Palatine, were staying. Eighteen-year-old Charles was the son and heir of the now-deceased Frederick V, Elector Palatine of the Rhine, who had married Charles I's older sister, Elizabeth Stuart, in 1613. Years before Frederick died in November 1632, aged just 36, the ruler had lost everything to Ferdinand II, Holy Roman Emperor, in an immense and devastating battle fought on the continent, including his electoral title and the high office of King of Bohemia. He had also been forced into exile. Consequently, Charles Louis, though clinging to his father's usurped title at least, was little more than a nomadic member of the European ruling elite in 1636, with next to no land to his name and even less political power.[5]

D'Ewes had come to Newmarket with the sole aim of seeing the Elector Palatine. Almost missing his chance because the young exile was under the weather, his wife's uncle, Walter Clopton, saw to it that Simonds not only had sight of Charles Louis but also spoke to him in his bedchamber. 'I was brought to him,' he recalled in his autobiography, 'kissed his hand, and received an expression from him, that he took himself to be obliged to me that had come so far to see him.'[6] The next day, Simonds ferried the whole family across from Stow Hall to Newmarket to pay the Elector Palatine a second visit, including his wife, his brother, and his younger sister, Elizabeth. Being treated to a dinner first, the D'Eweses were then taken to the Elector Palatine's guarded bedchamber as his esteemed guests, where the esquire of Stowlangtoft proceeded to delight his generous host with a gift of some Roman coins. Charles felt comfortable enough in Simonds's measured company to gradually draw him away from the main party and engage him in private conversation by a window. Hardly believing his luck, D'Ewes decided to take this very rare opportunity to advise the prince, who scarcely knew what to do next regarding his current predicament, on how best to reclaim his dynasty's lost lands in Europe.

Simonds was of the opinion that his familiarity with Charles Louis in the early months of 1636, unexpected as it was, put him on the map in the eyes of the English court – particularly after he was given the great honour of standing behind the Elector Palatine's dining chair one evening at the University of Cambridge. Whether this would be of benefit to D'Ewes in the long term remained to be seen. For now, it was easy to view the elevation in a mostly positive light; to regard it as part of a broader upswing in the fortunes of his own growing dynasty. That dynasty would be tested yet again in the near future, but not before it witnessed further favourable additions through its union with another distinguished family on 15 March. At Stowlangtoft church that morning, Elizabeth D'Ewes, the youngest child of Paul and Cecilia, married Sir William Poley of Boxted Hall in Suffolk, sometime gentleman extraordinary of the privy chamber. Theirs was to be an affectionate union that seemed capable of weathering any storm, with Sir William insisting in his will, dated 1664, that his wife should continue to enjoy the use of a property called 'Evergreen' in Horton-on-the-Hill, Essex. The house boasted a pretty orchard and gardens, the former of which apparently bore plenty of fruit.[7]

There was one storm in May 1636 that would prove impossible for Simonds to weather successfully. On the ninth of the month, 1-year-old Clopton D'Ewes died at Stow Hall. It would appear that there was just no saving the sickly infant in the end, no matter how hard D'Ewes fought to keep his male heir away from the clutches of certain oblivion. Indeed, the limited effectiveness of medical intervention in the seventeenth century, and the questionable abilities of medical professionals themselves, had been all too apparent throughout Clopton's illness. 'I have before shewed... that by our pitching upon a proud, fretting, ill-conditioned woman for a nurse, it was doubtless the chief cause of his falling into fits of convulsions,' Simonds wrote, 'for the remedying of which an issue had been opened in his neck, and divers other means had been used; but those means having been too violently and unskilfully applied by Dr Despotine, an Italian physician in Bury, so wasted the young and weak body of the sweet child, as it drove him into another disease.'[8]

Unlike his three brothers, Clopton D'Ewes was buried in Stowlangtoft church the following day, near to the spot where his late grandfather slept eternally. Interred with him, needless to say, were any current hopes Simonds had of leaving his name and worldly estate to a living son. It was hard for D'Ewes not to take his chronic misfortune when it came to the fathering of males personally by the time he had laid to rest his fourth boy. The knight began to think despondently that God was bent on making him suffer, or that perhaps He had other, preordained plans for him that did not involve Stow Hall at all – let alone producing an heir to the place. In his autobiography, he reflected that a 'higher providence' might even have been preparing 'a way for my passage into America'.[9]

Simonds boasted several contacts in the New World in the 1630s, who kept him informed of the goings-on within America's principal colonies as each strove to create a functioning and sustainable society, often with very little resources to hand. On 26 September 1633, a former tenant of D'Ewes, William Hammond, wrote to his ex-landlord from New England, telling him that it had not been possible to acquire the 'couple of bullocks' that Simonds had been keen to invest in.[10] The letter went on:

> ...they are wonderful dear here, there is none to be gotten but at a great price. A cow is worth here £25, a calf of this year is worth here £10 and none to be gotten. A mare is worth here £30; there came over this year many people & brought no cattle with them.[11]

That D'Ewes was moving money into America, albeit in small amounts, surely shows that the man possessed, at least at one stage, genuine thoughts of relocating there. A second letter that probably reached Simonds during the winter of 1633–4 allows the modern interpreter to arrive at much the same conclusion. John Eliot, Puritan missionary, composed the following from Roxburgh:

> ...now if you should please, to employ but one might, of that great wealth which God hath given, to erect a school of learning, a college among us; you should do a most glorious work, acceptable to God and Man; and the commemoration of the first founder of the means of learning, would be a perpetuating of your name and honour among us.[12]

It is not known why this 'school of learning' failed to come to pass, though some have suggested that D'Ewes may have felt conflicted about the religious credibility of the enterprise.

Predominantly, Simonds would find himself too preoccupied at home to give up his life in England for a new one in America. On 14 May 1636, the esquire of Stowlangtoft's main concern was harnessing the unbearable grief on display in Much Bromley in Essex. This was the day that Anne D'Ewes, in the dark about her son's welfare up to then, discovered Clopton's sad fate. Approaching the house of her sister- and brother-in-law, Sir Thomas Bowes and Mary D'Ewes, in a notably cheerful manner, the mother did not know that her husband was watching her from a window, dreading the melancholic scene that was about to unfold. When she entered the dining room and saw him ashen-faced with sorrow, however, it did not take long for Anne to realise what had happened. 'Is the boy dead?' she asked promptly, interrupting Simonds as he attempted, through sobs, to update her.[13] D'Ewes had no choice but to confirm that she was correct in her assessment of the situation.

And so it was that life for the D'Eweses continued, the evidence of the high rate of infant mortality all around them. Richard D'Ewes, while not trekking as far afield as America, ploughed ahead with his own agenda by touring the continent in the later 1630s, which only served to unsettle his older brother further. In February 1637, he was even forced to write to Simonds from Paris to allay the knight's fears that he had been lost at sea. Richard explained calmly that the rumour 'had a probable origin; for the same day I came to Rey a bark set out of the haven, the wind being then contrary, for France; the passengers were so negligent, that they omitted to carry provision with them to sea. They all suffered extremely by hunger…'. On 12 May 1638, Simonds penned a letter of his own to his country-hopping brother that restated his general anxieties, the antiquary urging him anew to look after himself and to return 'safe in both soul and body'.[14] The good name of D'Ewes was ever on his mind; if Richard perished, then in all likelihood – as things stood – so would their surname.

Chapter 14

CONFLICT AT HOME, CONFLICT AFAR

IN SOME WAYS, 1638 was not an easy year for Simonds D'Ewes, just as it was not an easy year for England as a nation. While the esquire of Stowlangtoft felt it necessary to reduce the intensity of some of his private devotions across these twelve months, which included decreasing the frequency of his periods of fasting, the wider country found itself drifting dangerously close to conflict with its Scottish neighbours.

The brewing hostilities witnessed between England and Scotland in 1638 could be traced back to one principal subject: religion. As early as the reign of James I, attempts had been made by officials south of the border to alter the Presbyterian Scottish kirk so that it better resembled the Church of England. This was considered especially important now that the two kingdoms were united under a single monarch. Before his death, King James's inner circle had come as far as introducing bishops to Scotland's ecclesiastical hierarchy, though not much further. James's son Charles, on the other hand, had proven to be far more proactive when he had inherited the crown in 1625, setting his sights on the very core of Scottish Presbyterianism. Having always encouraged Scottish clergymen to use the English Book of Common Prayer wherever possible, in July 1637, the king – still ruling without a parliament, and assisted by Archbishop Laud – had given Scotland its very own Prayer Book to employ for worship. This had naturally been one step too far for the Presbyterians. Immediately, riots had broken out in Scotland over the introduction of the book, which in any case had not been approved by any church official residing in the country beyond the bishops.[1]

In early 1638, the protesting was still ongoing. It had gotten so bad by this stage that Charles organised for a proclamation to be read out on 20 February, condemning the abominable actions of those who had dared to reject the Scottish Book of Common Prayer. Infuriatingly, such a move only persuaded the Presbyterian diehards of Scotland to press on with their organised campaign of resistance. On 28 February, at Greyfriars Kirk in Edinburgh, a National Covenant promoting the country's true religion was signed; from here, it was rapidly circulated around the northern dominion for wider endorsement. The Covenant would face serious opposition in Aberdeen in March, where loyalty to the king was unusually strong. Otherwise, it would encounter next to no popular defiance, with the Covenant movement being renewed at Inverness on 25 April without incident.

Amid these rising tensions between the two nations over matters of religion, D'Ewes heard from his brother again in March, this time from Orléans in France. Richard seems to have been tasked with acquiring for the antiquary a picture of the late Jacques Auguste de Thou, French historian and book collector, which he had now achieved. He wrote:

> I have bin since the date of my last at Monsieur de Thou's son's house, but 'twas not my fortune to find him at his lodging. I was at that time presented with Thuanus his picture by his nephews, which they would give me, made by another workman, both, as I conceive, exceeding like; which I had sent you, but that my merchant before dispatched them for England sooner than I thought, and my sudden departure from Paris would not permit me to send it after. I have left it in my trunk at Paris till my coming to town next; and when it shall please God I come for England, you may there make choice of which you best fancy.[2]

There was yet more uplifting news for Simonds over the summer months of 1638. A daughter, Geva, was born. These tidings were followed at the end of July by written confirmation from William Burton, fellow antiquary, that D'Ewes would be allowed absolute creative licence when it came to the authoring of an epistle for his well-regarded book on Leicestershire. 'You may pen for length as you see cause, if the printer will give way, and not gainsay; neither will I alter a letter therein, though present. Your judgement I know is such, that a curious critic may well pass by,' the man remarked. Another letter of antiquarian note, meanwhile, came from William Dugdale in August, politely declining an invitation that D'Ewes had extended to him to sojourn at his house. 'I hope the next summer (God willing),' he continued, 'I shall have leisure to wait upon you.'[3]

In September, Simonds received one more enlightening letter from the far side of the Atlantic, penned by Cambridge graduate Edmund Browne, who had set sail for Massachusetts in 1637. Browne spoke of many exotic things that would have meant little to most seventeenth-century English gentlemen: of wolves that fled humans, as well as mosquitos ('the English gnat') that bit them; of the Native American population and their habits; and, most astonishingly of all, of the security of the environment in which he was living, where an individual could leave their door unlocked for three months and think nothing of it. Even though his real, working knowledge of the land was limited, reading such morsels of information must have regardless been a transportive experience for D'Ewes.[4]

Visions of far-off places and strange customs may have acted as a welcome distraction from the ecclesiastical tempest gathering at home. On 28 November, a General Assembly of the Church of Scotland met in Glasgow to gain back even more control of the compromised Scottish kirk, in the process further defying the will of King Charles in England. With the dissolving of the Assembly in December 1638, January 1639 saw Covenant supporters instructing shires throughout Scotland to raise troops in readiness for an inevitable battle against their English foes. In response, the king officially announced his own plans to muster an army south of the border. These were the initial actions of what came to be known as the First Bishops' War, which broke out properly when the lord general of the covenanter forces in Scotland, Alexander Leslie, took control of Edinburgh Castle by blowing up the gate with a petard. 'They who do not shudder at the very name of intestine war between friends and neighbours... have divested themselves of all love of both religion and peace,' Simonds later wrote to the Scotsman Patrick Young, Keeper of His Majesty's Libraries.

Through the spring months, measured displays of aggression continued to build within each aggrieved country. Then, on 9 May, the situation suddenly deteriorated at Towie Barclay Castle in Aberdeenshire, when, in the middle of an attempt by Sir George Ogilvy to take back arms claimed by the Covenanters, a servant called David Prat was fatally shot. He is thought to have been the very first man to lose his life in the extended period of conflict that had settled on Britain on the eve of the 1640s.

By this time, King Charles was already as far north as Newcastle, the monarch intending to make his way up to Berwick-upon-Tweed on the Anglo-Scottish border to encourage the common soldiers who would be fighting for him. 'There was great debate about the king's going forward or staying there till the army was in readiness,' Edward Norgate wrote to Sir Francis Windebank towards the end of May. 'My Lord of Bristol was very earnest for his stay there, producing a Scot who offered to be hanged if he did not see ten or 15,000 Scots upon their march hitherward, and how unsafe it was to venture the king's person among an untaught and inexperienced army, unentrenched, and perhaps as ill fed as taught, was easy to imagine.'[5]

The English army at Goswick, just south of Berwick, made for a poor show in the courtier Edward Norgate's opinion. Conditions, granted, were against the men; the foot companies had thus far been forced to wade through water that came up to their ankles, leaving them damp and frustrated, while provisions and military lodgings by the coast left a lot to be desired. When Norgate entered the camp, where the king was then situated, he 'marvelled to find [it] so naked and indefensible, without trench or rampart'.[6]

It is probably accurate to conclude that, among the very lowest rungs of both the Scottish and English armies, there was little appetite for fighting during the First Bishops' War. The exact grievances nursed by each side were caught up in a complex theological – as well as political – debate that was much higher than most common combatants. Moreover, many of those in the English camp who possessed a keener understanding of the causes of the conflict were inclined to sympathise with their Scottish counterparts, having been subjected to unwanted Laudian reforms themselves. Sir Henry Slingsby referred to the fleeting nature of combative hostilities in his memoirs, remarking:

> I had but a very short time of being a soldier, which had not lasted above 6 weeks, and I like it as a commendable way of breeding for a gentleman if he consort himself with such as are civil, and the quarrel lawful.[7]

The war itself was over by mid-June, with any kind of confrontation between the two armies being kept to a bare minimum near Kelso in Scotland. The Pacification of Berwick, which effectively stipulated that everybody should pack up and go home, was signed on the nineteenth of the month.

Thirty-six-year-old Simonds discovered that miracles could happen at the end of August 1639. Easing into a country still very much at odds – on a broad, national level – with Scotland on 29 August was Adrian D'Ewes, the knight's fifth and only living son. Evidently he had paid attention to his sister's advice on enlisting the services of a wet nurse who would provide the boy with the best chance of thriving, for, months earlier in May, Anne D'Ewes had received a letter from one Mary Page, informing her that Simonds had prematurely written to request that she breastfeed the expected baby. 'I thank God I have my health and am well and have good store of milk,' Page had commented gratefully.[8]

Simonds refused to leave anything to chance now that he was again in possession of a male heir. On 19 September, he rewrote his will to include Adrian in the bequeathing of his estate. '[I give to] my young son, yet crying in the cradle,' part of the document read, '...my precious library, in which I have stored up for divers years past, with great care, cost, and industry, divers originals or autographs; ancient coins of gold, silver, and brass, manuscripts or written books, and such as are imprinted; and it is my inviolable injunction or behest, that he keep it entire.'[9]

There were bigger fish to fry by late autumn. On 4 November, along with an array of other Puritan esquires, D'Ewes was made high sheriff of Suffolk for a year – a role that he had been considered for on several occasions in the recent past. It was a decision that certainly did not sit well with everybody in local and national government, least of all the royalist champion and dedicated statesman Edward Nicholas, who openly believed many of the sheriffs for 1639–40 to be 'ill chosen'. What ought to have been an honour for Simonds himself, in fact, instead appeared to be viewed by the knight as an additional and unwanted burden – particularly given the climate of the times. 'It hath pleased God to send an unwelcome preferment upon me this year of the shrievalty of Suffolk,' he relayed to his brother in a letter, who was still abroad. 'We are like to have sad and dismal assizes because all things in Scotland hasten on apace to distraction and tumult.' There had been attempts to excuse the new sheriff from taking office, with one friend being 'in some hope to gett him of, and to havee another in his place', but to no avail.[10]

It was true that there were countless pressures ahead for D'Ewes in his new role, including, perhaps above all other things, living up to the standards of his predecessors. His friend Sir Nathaniel Barnardiston had been high sheriff of Suffolk for 1623–4, for example, and appeared to do very well while in office. A contemporary assessment concludes:

> ...he was to God, his King, and the Country for which he served, one of the most exact that ever bore that office. One passage here

I must not let slip; as serving of God was one principal business in every place he was employed in through his life; so here, though he neglected no business that belonged to his present office, yet he had a special care to have God faithfully served, and that even in the weekday, taking with him his Sheriff's men to a weekly lecture at some distance from his house; thereby dignifying that office at an [*sic*] higher rate than usually, if not at any time, is performed.[11]

Balancing the myriad responsibilities of the shrievalty with the commitments that came with his own Puritan faith was something else that Simonds would need to get right over the next year, constituting one more challenge.

The approaching headache that had immediately sprung to mind for D'Ewes in his correspondence with his brother – namely, the Scottish problem – had experienced some worrying developments by the end of 1639. Another General Assembly, authorised to meet by the king following the Pacification of Berwick, had steamed rebelliously onwards with its non-negotiable agenda for the Church of Scotland in August, it having been agreed between the representatives present that bishops should be ousted from the kirk's hierarchy once and for all. This move, in turn, had driven Charles I to conclude in December that another military confrontation with Scotland was the only way to prevent the complete rejection of his religious policies in the country. Thus, the Second Bishops' War now beckoned.

It was not the prospect, or practicalities, of a renewed conflict in the north that had Simonds preoccupied in the first days of 1640. On 25 January, having by now organised the shrieval banner on which his arms were to be painted, the high sheriff of Suffolk received a letter from the Council of the Admiralty bluntly reminding him of his ship-money obligations. 'You were, by writ of November 1639, required to set forth and furnish a ship of 640 tons, manned with 256 men, and double equipage for six months' service,' the correspondence advised, 'to be ready at the rendezvous by the 1st April next, the cost of which you were advertised by this Board would be £8,000.'[12] It was imperative that Simonds step up and follow through with the levying of the tax, or else risk facing punishment at the hands of members of the king's government.

D'Ewes's shrieval duties continued on 6 April 1640, upon the knight entering into an indenture with William Cage and John Gurdon, who were to be returned to parliament as elected members for Ipswich. Unlike ship money, this action did relate to the Anglo-Scottish situation: Charles I, in desperate need of ready cash to fund another war against the Covenanters in Scotland, had decided to summon his Westminster associates again after an eleven-year hiatus of personal rule. The aptly named Short Parliament met for the first time on 13 April, with its parliamentary members having hardly forgotten the outrageous and chaotic way the Commons had been dissolved in March 1629. Neither were they willing to overlook the controversial policies that had been fast-tracked into law in their absence from government. Very soon into the parliament's sitting, on 17 April, MP John Pym took it upon himself to launch a scathing attack on all of tonnage and poundage, Laud's religious reforms, and ship money within Westminster, declaring that no funds for the Scottish campaign could possibly be granted until these atrocities had first been addressed.

It was back to the delicate matter of ship money for Simonds himself just days later, on 21 April 1640. In the wake of another coach accident involving his wife and a flooded stretch of country road, the high sheriff issued a warrant to the constables of the hundred of 'Cofford', requiring them to collect £257 in tax.[13] D'Ewes presently wrote to Sir William Russell, Treasurer of the Navy, to update him on his efforts with the levy thus far:

> I thought good to give you an account of this day's service being the day appointed to almost all the high constables to bring in the whole £8,000 ship money imposed on this county. This day I might have expected to have received £1,000 but fear I shall not get in £200. I beseech you to acquaint the Council with the enclosed certificate and to procure for me some further direction how I shall proceed.[14]

It would seem that Simonds was already in a state of subdued panic about the vast undertaking that lay ahead.

The high sheriff had every right to feel this way. Even close friends would prove unwilling to pay the ship-money levy when D'Ewes sent constables to their front doors for that purpose, including the Barnardistons of Kedington Hall. One of Simonds's men was met with a decidedly frosty reception upon approaching the mansion house with a warrant on 9 May, with Sir Nathaniel Barnardiston's wife, Dame Jane, pleading ignorance regarding her husband's whereabouts and turning him away. Sir Nathaniel certainly had form when it came to the rejection of ship money. 'Witness his suffering under the imposition of ship money, coat and conduct money, and the loan; for refusing whereof he was a long time imprisoned in the Gatehouse [prison], and afterward confined for a longer time in Lincolnshire,' a contemporary account wrote of the esquire's trials in 1627. Furthermore, records indicate over 1639–40 that Kedington was one of Suffolk's recalcitrant parishes that chose not to '[assess] their rates according to their warrant'. As a small consolation, there was at least a degree of compliance on display from Simonds's close kin, namely Sir William Poley of Boxted Hall, who is recorded to have returned £1 and 6 shillings in April 1640.[15]

The ship-money scandal in particular was still dominating proceedings within the House of Commons on 23 April. In a remarkably damning report that surfaced over the day's business, and that would do King Charles no favours whatsoever, it was judged that the levy was 'taken, received, and complained of as a grievance by all the counties, cities, and boroughs of England and Wales'. Therefore, the Short Parliament's official line going forwards continued to be that it would refuse to entertain Charles's plea for capital to go to war with Scotland so long as the tax was not adequately dealt with. The king simply could not understand parliament's behaviour. On 2 May, a message sent from the royal household to the Commons stated exasperatedly that 'His Majesty hath divers times, and by sundry ways, acquainted this House with the urgent necessity of supply [for the war], and with the great danger inevitably to fall upon the whole state, upon his own honour, and the honour of this nation, if more time shall be lost therein'. It went on: 'Nevertheless, His Majesty hitherto hath received no answer at all; and therefore considering, that as heretofore His Majesty hath told this House, that a delay of his supply is as destructive as a denial, His Majesty doth again desire them to give him a present answer concerning his supply; His Majesty being still resolved, on his part, to make good whatsoever he hath promised by himself.'[16]

The Commons was willing to give Charles's communication some consideration, but it would take time for the members to reach a definitive verdict on its content. On 4 May, MP William Lenthall reported from the relevant committee that it had 'spent the whole day in the debate of preparing an answer to His Majesty's message, but could not effect it; therefore [the participants] do desire it may have an adjournment till tomorrow morning at eight o'clock'.[17] However, the king, itching to bring the Covenanters in Scotland into line, felt he had waited long enough for an answer. The following day, he occasioned the repeating of history by impatiently dissolving parliament once more.

On a personal level, things were little better for Simonds by early June. On the first of the month, young Adrian D'Ewes had done what all male infants belonging to the high sheriff seemed to do: he had died. Consoling him in his grief, James Ussher, Archbishop of Armagh, wrote to the esquire of Stowlangtoft to remind him that 'although your proper wisdom is to bear these and similar things, to which we are all subject, you have been abundantly instructed to bear them bravely'. Professionally speaking, there was scarcely anything to smile about either. On 5 June, D'Ewes found himself petitioning the king 'with extreme grief and astonishment' after he had received a letter accusing him of negligently failing to raise the £8,000 of ship money required. Three days later, he felt compelled to petition the Council of the Admiralty as well, arguing that he did not qualify for any kind of punishment because circumstances beyond his control had prevented him from collecting the full tax sum. Simonds cited 'deadness of trading, low prices of all commodities raised from the plough and pail, scarcity of money, [and] great military charges of the past summer' as the reasons behind the shortfall, as well as 'the innumerable groans and sighs' that he had encountered in place of payment.[18]

Predictably, the high sheriff's petitions were jointly read as a distasteful compendium of both grovelling apologies and convenient excuses. Handed to the attorney-general, Sir Edward Herbert, for further scrutiny, they subsequently formed the basis for legal proceedings against Simonds in the Court of Star Chamber in July. 'Now... I myself am a participator in the public evils, I do not know where I shall turn, or what I shall do further,' he subsequently despaired to Albertus Joachimi in a letter. Thank goodness for political developments: these ensured that D'Ewes would never be prosecuted by this accursed body, beginning with the outbreak of the Second Bishops' War that summer.

Simonds, unlike the First Bishops' War, ended up being personally connected to the new campaign: his younger brother, Richard, would be one of those fighting on behalf of King Charles. On 18 August, the 24-year-old soldier was the subject of a warrant issued by Sir Francis Windebank, which required that he be 'furnished, for his money, with four post-horses, to Berwick; whither he is to repair in haste, for His Majesty's service'.[19] There was unease about Richard's going away to war among the whole family. Those praying for his safe return included his sister-in-law, Anne D'Ewes, who wrote to him shortly before his departure north to convey her affection for the young man whom she had now known for well over a decade. The gentlewoman was even planning to travel down to London from Stow Hall to wave her brother-in-law off in person, though she assured Richard that if he had to go sooner, she would understand.

A muster roll taken after the king's army had eventually retreated from Newcastle into Yorkshire suggests that Richard D'Ewes was probably a captain or lieutenant in George Goring's regiment, under the command of Algernon Percy, 10th Earl of Northumberland.[20] The Battle of Newburn, fought between the English and the Scots on the outskirts of Newcastle on 28 August 1640, proved to be the culmination of the Second Bishops' War, and indeed was the only major engagement to take place over its short lifespan. Sir Henry Slingsby observed the following in the build-up to the fight:

> It is strange to see how the ways are pestered with carriages of all manner of preparation for war: thirty pieces of ordinance I met coming from Hull, and abundance of waggons with all things belonging, of powder, shot, and match, tents, pikes, spades, and shovels.[21]

As for the battle itself, Captain Thomas Dymoke of the English forces wrote to Sir Francis Windebank on 10 September to relate the woeful events that had occurred in the field. The covenanter army of Scotsmen, having appeared on the hills above the river crossing at Newburn, had possessed an immediate advantage over King Charles's regiments of foot, who, like sitting ducks, had positioned themselves in the unprotected depths of the valley below. In no time, huge swathes of English infantrymen had been picked off by a great storm of ammunition that had rained down on their 'works' with deadly precision. The attack had caused such terror and confusion within the ranks of the king's foot soldiers that soon there had been no cohesive military presence to speak of among them, allowing the Scottish cavalry to easily overrun the men who had not fled in terror into a nearby wood. While a valiant charge on horseback had occurred on both sides, encompassing a 'most brave but bloody encounter', in the grand scheme of things it had done the English no good at all. By 30 August, the Covenanters had been able to claim both a decisive victory on the field of battle and the taking of Newcastle a short distance away.[22]

An interesting account has survived of what being part of the winning army was like that August. Within the narrative, Scottish soldier John Livingston confirms that a superior force in the mid-seventeenth century did not necessarily mean superior camp conditions. On the Covenanters' march south, he endured the following:

> Our army lay a while at Chusely-wood, a mile or two from Dunce, till the rest of the army came up. I had there a little trench tent, and a bed hung between two 'Leager-Chists', and having lain several nights with my clothes on, I being wearied with want of sleep, did lie one night with my clothes off; that night was very cold, and while I slept all the clothes went off me; so that in the morning I was not able to stir any part of my body, and I had much ado, with the help of my man and my baggage man to get on my clothes. I caused them to put me on my horse, and went to Dunce, and lay down in a bed, and caused them to give me into the bed, a big 'Tin-stoup' full of water, whereby a sweet [sweat?] was procured; so that before night I was able to rise and put on my clothes.[23]

Coupled with this ordeal was the problem of a general lack of provisions, including powder and bread, which 'produced some fears that the expedition might be delayed for that year'.[24] There was a greater sense of optimism around the time of the Battle of Newburn itself. Anybody approaching the Scottish camp at the end of August would have been gradually enveloped in the heartening sound of psalms being sung in the soldiers' huts, as well as the energetic reading and discussing of scripture.

Simonds was acquainted with some vague details about the covenanter occupation of Newcastle through linguist Abraham Wheelocke, who urged his intellectual friend to 'forget the Scots as much as you may'. That said, Wheelocke himself was contemplating leaving the country altogether if the situation there got any worse. 'Newcastle is much abused by them,' he wrote, 'and we here already quake for want of coals.'[25] The linguist's main concern, though, was where on earth he would hide the Anglo-Saxon material he had accrued should the Scottish army decide to advance south.

Chapter 15

THE LONG PARLIAMENT MEETS

ANNE D'EWES SEEMED to take an especial interest in her husband's shrieval affairs when she wrote to him on 31 August 1640. 'I have received your letters from London bearing the date the 27th day of this instant August. I am glad to hear by them that there is some likelihood of your return home, and heartily pray you may see some good issue of the ship money,' she noted.[1] At the same time, the gentlewoman was determined to remind Simonds of his obligations as a spouse and father, mentioning that their eldest child, 10-year-old Anne, was in good health at Boxted Hall in Suffolk, and that Cecilia (or Sissilia) and Isolda remained reassuringly well in Stowlangtoft. Isolda, another daughter, was the latest addition to the D'Ewes family; Geva, who had been born in 1638, had died around the same time as little Adrian D'Ewes, in June of that year.

Sir Simonds's preoccupations the next month lay partly in what the king planned to do now that he had lost his religious war against Scotland. On 1 October, the high sheriff wrote to the Earl of Worcester, Henry Somerset, to offer his informed view on the precarious matter at hand. Unsurprisingly, Charles's policies on ship money going forwards was something that had D'Ewes particularly absorbed:

> Certainly if His Majesty did by proclamation abolish this new oath the Prelates have set forth, and therein also freely remit all arrears of ship money now due, and discharge the present and past Sheriffs from all further collection (which will no way prejudice any right His Majesty supposeth he hath to it) it would not only bring much honour and glory to his sacred person, but also infinitely gain upon the hearts of his loyal subjects...[2]

It is safe to say that Simonds had had quite enough of the despised levy and its awkwardness by this point in the shrieval calendar. In another letter written to Sir Edward Littleton on 10 October, he accordingly spoke with regret about the 'doubts and struggles [sic] which have emergently risen in the execution of my troublesome shreivaltie this fatall yeare'.[3]

One of the last duties D'Ewes undertook in his bothersome role as high sheriff of Suffolk involved overseeing a contentious election, which in fact was directly related to King Charles's next move in London. For, humiliated in the face of an English defeat and in possession of very little money, the monarch had been forced to agree to the summoning of another parliament in Westminster. There were two seats up for grabs at the Ipswich election held on 19 October, the eventual

Right: Paul D'Ewes's monument inside Stowlangtoft church, Suffolk.

Below: Exterior of St George's church, Stowlangtoft. Simonds lived nearby and was buried here in 1650.

Above: Exterior of St Peter and St Paul's church, Lavenham, Suffolk. As lord of the manor, Simonds possessed the right to recommend the church's resident pastor whenever the benefice became vacant.

Left: Portrait of Jemima Crew (née Waldegrave), at one time pursued by Simonds as a potential wife.

The tomb of Sir Thomas Barnardiston, Anne Clopton's grandfather, inside Kedington church, Suffolk.

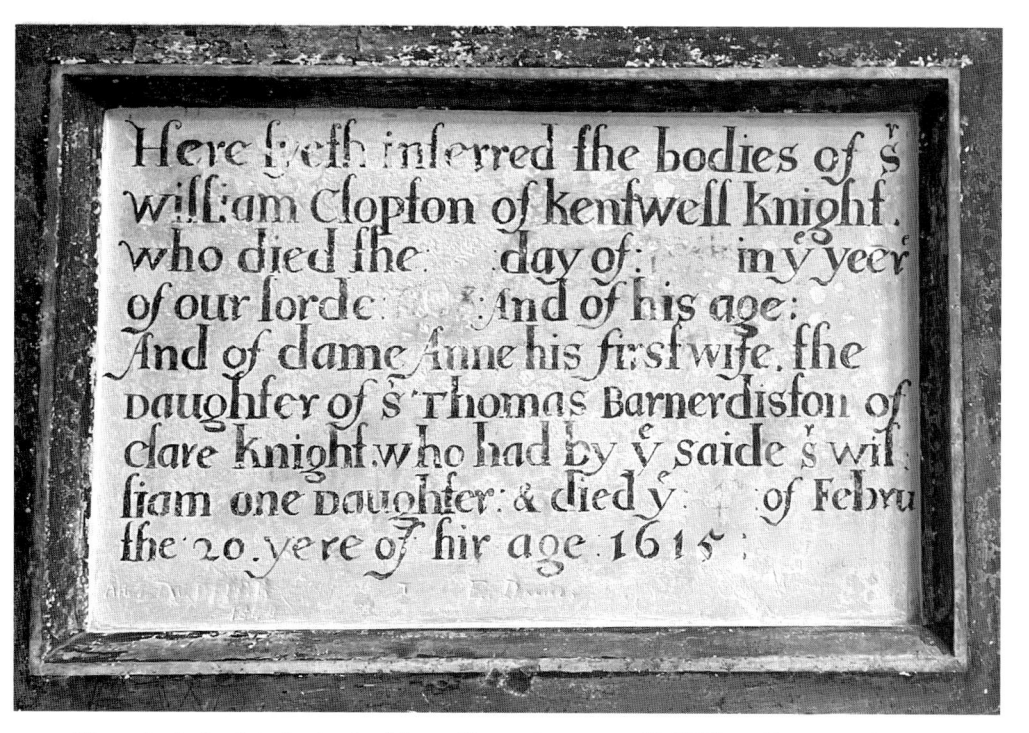

Here lyeth interred the bodies of S[r]
will:am Clopton of kentwell knight.
who died the   day of   in y[e] yeer
of our lorde   And of his age:
And of dame Anne his first wife, the
Daughter of S[r] Thomas Barnerdiston of
clare knight who had by y[e] saide s[r] wil
liam one Daughter: & died y[e]   of Febru
the 20. yere of hir age .1615.

The epitaph fixed to the tomb of Anne Clopton's parents, Sir William Clopton and Dame Anne Barnardiston, inside Long Melford church, Suffolk.

D'Ewes impaling Clopton, depicted in a north-facing window inside Long Melford church.

The 'baby brass' inside Lavenham church. Three of Simonds's sons, all of whom died young, are buried beneath it.

Above: The grave slab of Cecilia Darcy, daughter of Sir Simonds D'Ewes and his first wife, Anne, inside Long Melford church. Her parents' names are prominently engraved upon the stone.

Right: Sir Martin Stuteville's wall memorial inside Dalham church, Suffolk. Stuteville, together with his son John, were close acquaintances of Simonds.

Left: Portrait of Archbishop William Laud, a man reviled for his religious reforms in the 1630s. Eventually found guilty of high treason, he was executed in January 1645.

Below: Engraving of King Charles I and his French queen, Henrietta Maria.

HISTRIO-MASTIX.
THE
PLAYERS SCOVRGE,
OR,
ACTORS TRAGÆDIE,

Divided into Two Parts.

Wherein it is largely evidenced, by divers *Arguments*, by the concurring Authorities and Resolutions of *sundry texts of Scripture*; of the whole *Primitive Church*, both under the *Law and Gospell*; of 55 *Synodes and Councels*; of 71 *Fathers and Christian Writers*, before the yeare of our Lord 1200; of above 150 *foraigne and domestique Protestant and Popish Authors*, since; of 40 *Heathen Philosophers, Historians, Poets*; of many *Heathen*, many *Christian Nations, Republiques, Emperors, Princes, Magistrates*; of sundry *Apostolicall, Canonicall, Imperiall Constitutions*; and of our owne *English Statutes, Magistrates, Vniuersities, Writers, Preachers.*

That popular Stage-playes (the very Pompes of the Divell which we renounce in Baptisme, if we beleeve the Fathers) *are sinfull, heathenish, lewde, ungodly Spectacles, and most pernicious Corruptions*; condemned in all ages, as intolerable Mischiefes to Churches, to Republickes, to the manners, mindes and soules of men. And that the *Profession of Play-poets, of Stage-players; together with the penning, acting, and frequenting of Stage-playes, are unlawfull, infamous and misbeseeming Christians.* All pretences to the contrary are here likewise fully answered; and the unlawfulnes of acting of beholding Academicall Enterludes, briefly discussed; besides sundry other particulars concerning *Dancing, Dicing, Health-drinking, &c.* of which the table will informe you.

By WILLIAM PRYNNE, *an Vtter-Barrester of* Lincolnes Inne.

Cyprian. De Spectaculis lib. p. 244.
Fugienda sunt ista Christianis fidelibus, ut tam frequenter diximus, tam vana, tam perniciosa, tam sacrilega Spectacula: qua, etsi non haberent crimen, habent in se et maximam, et patram congruentem fidelibus vanitatem.

Lactantius de Vero Cultu cap. 20.
Vitanda ergo Spectacula omnia, non solum ne quid vitiorum pectoribus insideat, &c. sed ne cuius nos voluptatis consuetudo delinat, atque à Deo et à bonis operibus avertat.

Chrysost. Hom. 38. in Matth. Tom. 2 Col. 299 B. & Hom. 8 De Pœnitent. a, Tom. 5 Col. 750.
Immo vere, bi Theatrelibus lædi evertis, non leges, sed iniquitatem evertitis, ac omnem civitatis pestem extinguitis. Etenim Theatrum, peccata officina, publicum incontinentiæ gymnasium; cathedra pestilentiæ; fessimus locus; pluribus unaque morborum plena Babylonica fornax, &c.

August nus De Civit. Dei, l. 4 c. 1.
Si tantummodo boni et boni Hi homines in civitate essent, nec in rebus humanis Ludi scenici esse debuissent.

LONDON,
Printed by E. A. and W. I. for *Michael Sparke*, and are to be sold at the Blue Bible, in Greene Arbour, in little Old Bayly. 1633.

The title page of William Prynne's *Histrio-Mastix: The players scourge, or, Actors Tragaedie*. Containing many scandalous opinions on the royal court, its publication in the early 1630s would lead to Prynne losing chunks of both his ears.

Portrait of Charles Louis, Elector Palatine, the exiled nephew of Charles I. In February 1636, while the prince was staying in Newmarket, Simonds would meet him and even advise him on the difficulties he currently faced.

An engraving depicting riots following the introduction of the Scottish Prayer Book to Scotland in 1637.

A depiction of the Scottish and English armies embracing in the mid-seventeenth century, though they fought on opposite sides during the Bishops' Wars.

A portrait featuring the Earl of Strafford, who sits on the left in the picture. The earl's underhand tactics and close friendship with the king would earn him powerful enemies in parliament, many of whom were determined to see him undone.

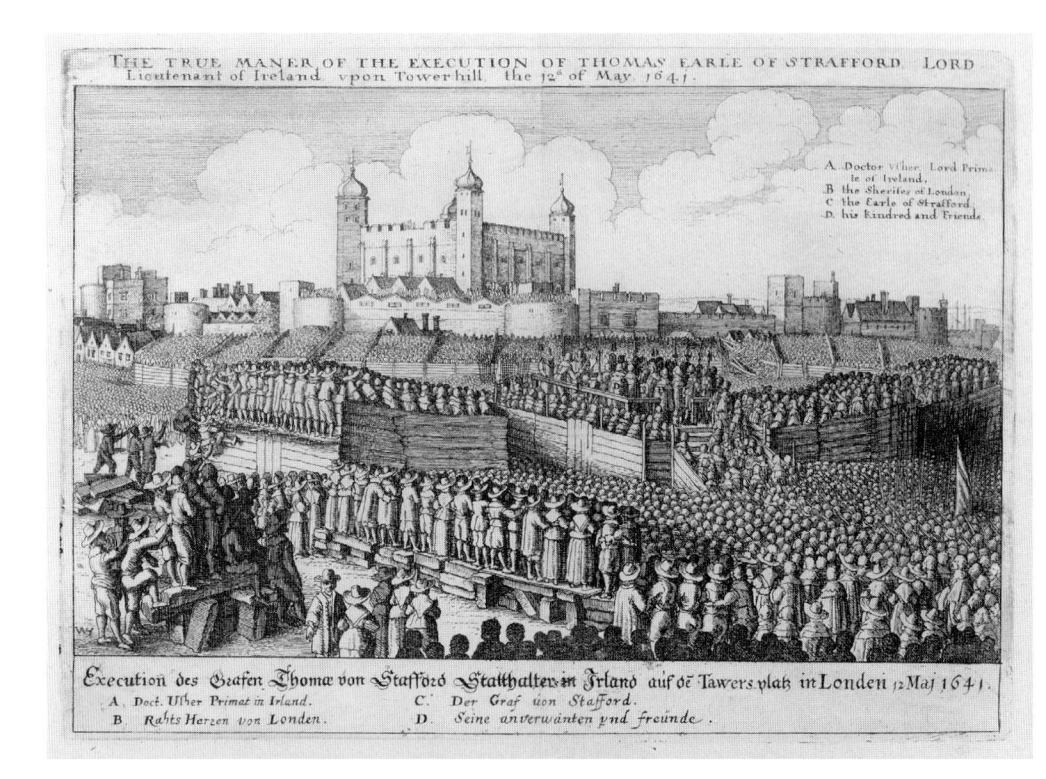

Above: An engraving showing Strafford's execution at the Tower of London in May 1641.

Left: A portrait of John Pym, MP for Tavistock, whom Charles I tried to have arrested in January 1642 for conspiring against the crown.

An engraving of Oliver Cromwell, MP for Cambridge and eventual parliamentary figurehead in the House of Commons.

An engraving of the Earl of Essex, who commanded parliament's forces during the first years of the civil war.

A true and exact Relation of the manner of his Maiesties setting up of His Standard at *Nottingham*, on Munday the 22. of August 1642.

First, The forme of the Standard, as it is here figured, and who were present at the advancing of it

Secondly, The danger of setting up of former Standards, and the damage which ensued thereon.

Thirdly, A relation of all the Standards that ever were set up by any King.

Fourthly, the names of those Knights who are appointed to be the Kings Standard-bearers. With the forces that are appoynted to guard it.

Fifthly, The manner of the Kings comming first to *Coventry*.

Sixtly, The *Cavalieres* resolution and dangerous threats which they have uttered, if the King concludes a peace without them, or hearkens unto his great Councell the Parliament : Moreover how they have shared and divided *London* amongst themselves already.

London, printed for F. Coles. 1642.

A parliamentary pamphlet commenting on the raising of the royal standard in Nottingham in August 1642.

Right: A seventeenth-century playing card depicting the taking of the Solemn League and Covenant in 1643.

Below: A contemporary woodcut showing Boye, Prince Rupert of the Rhine's dog, being killed at the Battle of Marston Moor in 1644.

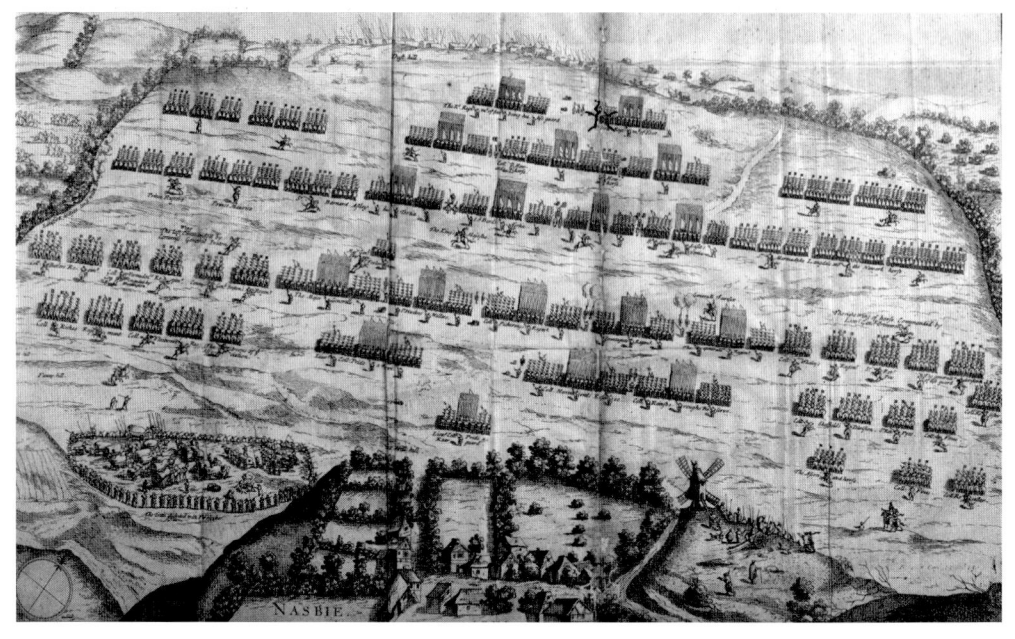

A sketch of the battlefield at Naseby in June 1645.

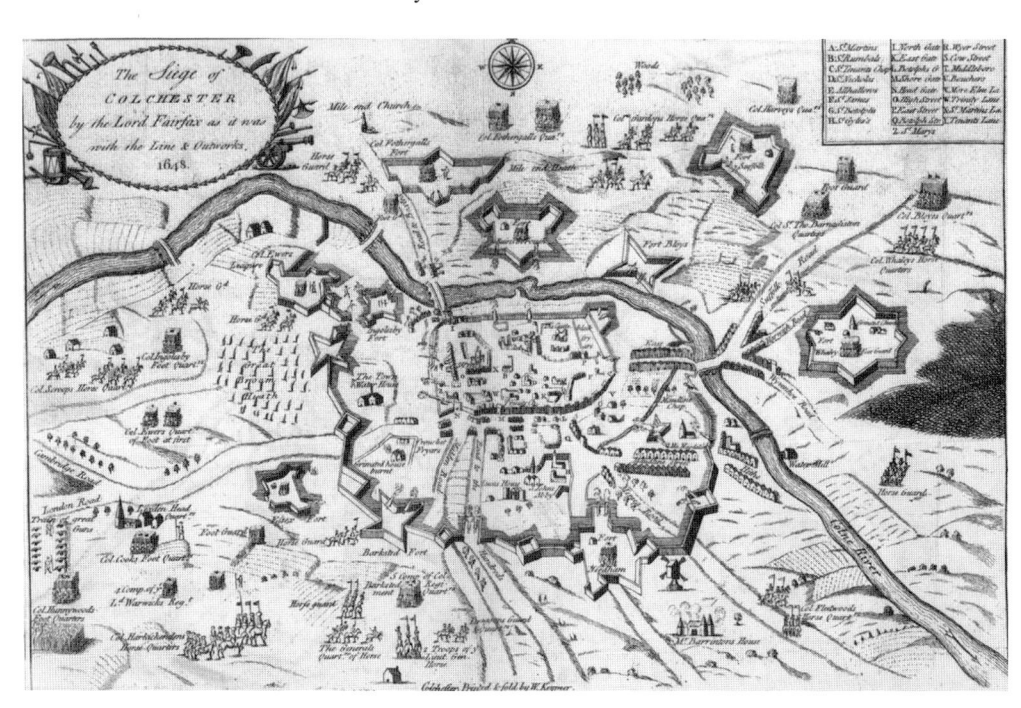

A plan of the siege of Colchester in 1648.

Above: A nineteenth-century portrait of the siege of Colchester, by Abraham Cooper.

Right: An engraving of Charles I at his execution in January 1649.

An engraving of antiquary William Dugdale.

holders of which would represent the constituency of Suffolk (and thereafter be known as 'shire knights'). Sir Nathaniel Barnardiston and Sir Philip Parker, both zealous proponents of the Puritan movement, had previously been elected to the vacant posts before the sitting of the Short Parliament in April; now, Barnardiston, Parker and Henry North, a royalist sympathiser, vied for the opportunity to be the Suffolk constituency members of what would become known to history as the Long Parliament.

The poll was taken in a field, on a cold and windy Monday. Mr North made an early appearance at the grassy site atop a chair carried triumphantly by his supporters, soon to be joined by other members of his raucous party, who made such a commotion upon their arrival that those tasked with setting up the furniture for the event – which included planks and boards – were unable to finish their assignment. After the group had caused the planks to collapse onto Simonds D'Ewes himself several times over, an executive decision was made to relocate the polling to three tables under a tree. Nathaniel Barnardiston, who had turned up some time after North, suggested at midday that the afternoon's polling be held in Ipswich itself, because the weather had now become even more inclement.

Why the election was a contentious one (and many parliamentary elections were in the seventeenth century, it should be noted) came down to the accusations of Sir Roger North, whose son, Henry, went on to lose to Barnardiston and Parker. The father believed simply that Simonds had rigged the voting in favour of his Puritan friends. This a wounded D'Ewes vehemently denied from the off, the departing high sheriff being most affronted that anybody could accuse him of such a dastardly act. 'Yet the said Sir Roger,' a report maintained, 'not satisfied herewith, did, a little after, with [a] company of young gentlemen, and others that followed him, armed... or the greater part of them, go about the Corne Hill in Ipswich, where the Crosse stands, and cried, "A North! a North!", calling the [Puritan] sailors "Water dogges", and otherwise provoking them.'[4]

A week later on 26 October, an unrelated indenture was drawn up confirming that Simonds himself was to be given a place within the Commons division of the Long Parliament. He had been successfully elected as a burgess (or MP) for Sudbury. 'I was elected and by myself returned,' the new parliament man would remark dryly in his famous parliamentary journals, referring to the fact that he was still in his high-sheriff post at the time of polling.[5] Ever the researcher, and a true stickler for the rules, D'Ewes had done his homework beforehand to make certain that his potentially questionable appointment would pass unchallenged.

And so it did. Weeks after the outcome of the poll, in December 1640, a committee sitting on behalf of the Long Parliament would confirm that Simonds had been 'elected without controversy' in October, though, granted, it was not quite so sure about the circumstances surrounding the election of the second Sudbury burgess, Sir Robert Crane. Credible talk suggested that Crane had enjoyed secret dealings with the mayor of the town in the lead-up to polling day (which was conveniently moved from a Saturday to a Monday), and that he had even threatened men to secure himself a seat in Westminster. 'Much hot dispute might have ensued,'

D'Ewes noted of the commotion it caused in the House of Commons in December, 'but Sir Robert Harlow and Sir Walter Earle stood up and spake to the orders of the House, that Sir Robert Crane's election being voted to be good, there ought to be no further dispute of it.'[6]

Whether Crane had been honest, deceitful or something else altogether, Sir Simonds D'Ewes was ready to take his seat in the Long Parliament on 19 November 1640. The parliament itself had convened amid a simmering atmosphere on 3 November, with the Second Bishops' War having formally concluded on 28 October through the Treaty of Ripon. Even before Simonds joined his peers in Westminster, resolute action had been taken to begin to bring the king to book for his behaviour during a disastrous decade of personal rule. While committees had been formed to consider a variety of contentious subjects, including religion and unlawful taxes, MPs had simultaneously begun the long process of presenting petitions from across the nation that concerned governmental grievances. D'Ewes entered the chamber on 19 November to a House of Commons that, as a consequence, was already very much in the throes of agitated debate.

His shrieval responsibilities at last confined to the pages of history, Simonds could now wholly concentrate on the odyssey that lay ahead, which first and foremost involved becoming an effective member of parliament for his constituents. On the esquire of Stowlangtoft's very first morning in the House of Commons, he took the oath required of all MPs, before allowing himself to be introduced to Mr Speaker by Sir Nathaniel Barnardiston, his close friend; acknowledged a few more parliamentary members whom he knew from Suffolk; found his seat on the front bench, opposite one end of the clerk's table; and, just before the business of the day began, revealed the instruments – including ink and paper – that would enable him to commence taking the parliamentary notes that continue to prove so valuable to historians in the twenty-first century. Being a confident orator by all accounts, who was not content to merely sit back and permit other men to do all the debating, Simonds was soon making contributions to the House at large. 'I spake thrice this morning,' he reported proudly to his wife afterwards, '...and at my second speech vouched a record, which not only gave great satisfaction to the House, but ended a weighty and perplexed dispute it was then controverting.'[7]

Thus, the precedent for D'Ewes's conduct in the Long Parliament was tentatively set. On 24 November, Simonds continued with his parliamentary contributions by suggesting, following a move by the Commons to have Catholic leaders removed from military service in northern England, that the king should be notified of the resolution first. Three days later, he spoke again to advise that tonnage and poundage ought to be introduced as an additional consideration of the ship-money committee, branding it nothing more than 'an arbitrary and an infinite tax' without parliament's authority. Upon delivering each of these speeches, Simonds made sure to cite historical legislation or examples from a vast bank of antiquarian knowledge, which is something else that would be characteristic of his time in Westminster – and that would, notoriously, give him the reputation of being a nit-picker. However, what provided the antiquary with the most obvious satisfaction in these early days of the Long Parliament was the total condemnation of a certain levy by the Commons, who unanimously dismissed ship money on 7 December as a scandalous tax that had been illegal from the outset. Simonds wrote gleefully to Anne on 10 December to inform her that 'on last Monday morning, December the seventh, we utterly damned the ship money, and those sheriffs that have been too busy in levying it are likely to be questioned'.[8] The development meant that prosecuting D'Ewes for his failures earlier in the year would now be virtually impossible.

Business turned to the Root and Branch Petition on 11 December, which had been signed by a staggering 15,000 people in London and called for the abolition of bishops within the Church of England. D'Ewes regarded it as 'the weightiest matter that ever was yet handled in the House', though he urged moderation when he was given a voice during the associated debate. 'For the petition before us,' he reasoned in the presence of his fellow MPs, 'it could not be denied but that there was much chaffe in it; as well as wheat, but yet like the good husbandman we should not cast away the wheat with the chaffe but fan away the one and preserve the other.'[9] A bill inspired by the petition would be drawn up and presented to the Long Parliament in May 1641 by Oliver St John, MP for Totnes.

It was only natural that, in entertaining the notion of abolishing episcopacy (which many believed was a popish hangover), members of parliament began to look bloodthirstily towards the head of the perceived monster. On 16 December, Sir John Hotham, MP for Beverley in Yorkshire, voiced what many of his peers were thinking when he enquired 'whether the Archbishop of Canterbury ought not to be charged with high treason'. Of course, such a motion did not just relate to William Laud's continued facilitation of the prominent position of bishops within England's ecclesiastical hierarchy; it was also a delayed parliamentary response to the religious reforms that the theologian had fearlessly overseen in the country throughout the 1630s. To nobody's great surprise, Hotham's suggestion found little resistance in the House of Commons. Two days later, Laud was duly denounced as 'the root and ground of all our miseries and calamities; both in Church and Commonwealth were originally proceeding from him', leading John Pym to set the wheels in motion for the archbishop's impeachment and indefinite imprisonment.[10]

So ended a year bursting with high stakes, disquieting disagreements and constitutional U-turns, the undertones of which were suggestive of something more sinister lurking in the wings. For Simonds, the finale of 1640 managed to bring a touch of familial joy to an otherwise demoralising state of affairs, through the birth of yet another child – the couple's tenth in total. That it was a girl, called Elizabeth, simply encouraged uncharacteristic relief from both the MP for Sudbury and his wife, the latter of whom admitted to her husband that 'though we have failed in part of our hope by the birth of a daughter yet we are likewise freed from much care and fear a son would have brought'.[11] Elizabeth was baptised at Ixworth on 21 December, where she had been born; unusually for the offspring of Simonds and Anne D'Ewes, she would go on to outlive one of her parents.

Chapter 16

STRAFFORD

THE SIGNIFICANT TIME that had now elapsed since Simonds's marital negotiations and wedding – a grand total of fourteen years – was made evident through the sobering confession of one of the undertaking's chief architects, Dame Ann Barnardiston, in January 1641, who mentioned in a letter to D'Ewes that she was facing her 'declining dayes'.[1] The great Suffolk gentlewoman, who had always been the foremost matriarchal figure in her granddaughter, Anne D'Ewes's, life, would die shortly afterwards at a good old age.

Indeed, this was a period in Simonds's political career where he would be concurrently compelled to revisit less pleasant memories. On 8 January, a parliamentary committee, formed to discuss the religious innovations witnessed within the Diocese of Norwich during Charles I's personal rule, convened in Westminster, counting D'Ewes among its participants. On the agenda was a petition from the townspeople of Ipswich, who had complained to the Long Parliament that Bishop Matthew Wren, the instigator and overseer of the diocese's reforms, had commanded in the mid-1630s that communion tables 'in all or most churches' be set up 'altar-wise' – in other words, raised and railed off.[2]

Bishop Wren was a familiar character to Simonds, who had been at least partly caught up in the man's implementing of Archbishop Laud's countrywide amendments to the Church of England. What the MP for Sudbury had seen of the bishop and his policies at this time, he had not liked in the slightest. In 1637, D'Ewes had even inserted his tendentious view in the preface to a work he was writing, entitled *The Primitive Practise*, noting that he was 'then residing in the County of Suffolke, which had newly groaned under the Prelaticall tyranny of Bishop Wren, as did all other parts of his Diocese'. For anybody acquainted with Simonds intimately, or perhaps just vaguely, at the height of the eleven-year personal rule, it would not have been difficult to deduce why he had held such a low opinion of Matthew Wren's general conduct. Aside from enforcing papistical religious reforms that would have horrified any Puritan standard-bearer, the Bishop of Norwich had personally offended the antiquary on more than one occasion. In October 1636, for example, Wren had marched into Stowlangtoft with a chaplain in tow and threatened Simonds with severe punishment if he did not start to take the Laudian programme more seriously.[3]

Then there had been the numerous kindred spirits of D'Ewes in the diocese – in matters of religion, at least – who had been forced out of their livelihoods, or even out of the country altogether, as a result of Wren's policies. 'Mr Mott of Stoake & Nayland standeth suspended *ab officio* et *beneficio* for refusing the new Conformitie, as they call yt,' Suffolk parson Robert Stansby had written to John Winthrop in New England in the late 1630s. 'My selfe was deprived of my parsonage July 18, 1636,' he had continued in his letter, 'by our B., for refusing the old Conformity. Many in Suffolk lost ther [sic] places for feare, & many stand excommunicated, & many suspended, but none was deprived but my selfe.'[4] If any Puritan minister had felt as though they had had no other choice but to emigrate because of Wren's acts of intolerance, in all likelihood they would have travelled to America, where John Winthrop himself had fled to escape religious persecution in the early years of Charles I's reign.

The king remained an elusive presence during the first months of 1641. His French wife, however, made direct contact with the House of Commons on 4 February, using Sir Thomas Jermyn, Comptroller of the King's Household, as her trusted mouthpiece. Queen Henrietta Maria seemed anxious to convey to the House that she had done everything in her power to steer her husband in certain directions when it had come to the governance of his kingdom, including persuading him both to foster a 'good correspondence' with the people over whom he reigned and to summon the Long Parliament. Mindful of the dominant view in Westminster of the place of Catholics in England, the queen also informed the members, through Jermyn, that she was willing to help rid the country of 'such priests and Jesuits as stayed here against the laws of the realm'.[5]

Her words were met with an awkward silence in the chamber. Acting as if Sir Thomas Jermyn had not spoken at all, some members proceeded to fill it by suggesting that the Commons begin with the day's business. It was only Sir Hugh Cholmeley, MP for Scarborough, who felt sheepish enough about the Commons' cold reception to come to the comptroller's rescue, proposing to the House that it should do the decent thing and at least pass on its thanks to the queen for her message. Carefully noting down everything that was being said, Simonds, though no outspoken fan of the royal family, agreed with him. 'I was loath,' he wrote, '[that] the queen's complying with us should receive a neglect from us. I therefore stood up and said... that... we ought to value any message from her as from a queen in her widowhood.'[6] He had, again, relied on past precedent to colour his opinion on the issue.

The future of episcopacy within the Church of England was again debated on 9 February, with one Oliver Cromwell, devout Puritan and MP for Cambridge, challenging the royalist Sir John Strangways' support for bishops by stating that 'he knew no reason of those suppositions and inferences which the gentleman had made that last spake'.[7] Simonds himself merely exhibited regret to the House that episcopacy was being discussed by the Commons at all, for it seemed perfectly obvious to him that it was a component of the church hierarchy that needed to be carefully pruned (though not dispensed with entirely), therefore not warranting further consideration at that time.

There was excitement in Westminster on 17 February. Fleetingly, a barge carrying Thomas Wentworth, 1st Earl of Strafford, sailed past the Lower House on its way from the Tower of London to the site of the House of Lords, causing scores of curious MPs to dash across to the window overlooking the Thames to catch a glimpse. Simonds was not one of those who felt the need to legitimise a man who, like Archbishop Laud, had been accused of high treason. Waiting impatiently in his seat for the commotion and general intrigue to die down, he was only too pleased to join in with the subsequent calls to punish the applicable members for interrupting the proceedings of the House – though, in the end, debating this matter was considered a waste of time in itself.

Originally impeached by parliament on 10 November 1640, the Earl of Strafford's list of supposed crimes was substantial. A mixture of unconfirmed hearsay and credible evidence implied that the royalist nobleman had looked for ways to prevent the summoning of parliament following the king's defeat against the Scots; had made plans to have various MPs arrested for supposedly conspiring with the covenanter party in Scotland; and, at one point, had even raised the possibility with King Charles of employing an army from Ireland to restore discipline in England in May 1640, following the collapse of the Short Parliament. When the earl's defence was finally delivered in the presence of the Commons in late February 1641, Simonds was left feeling disappointed by the performance he observed. '[It] came exceedingly short of my expectation,' he wrote in his journal, 'for I looked from him to have found all things that should *sublime spirare ingenium*; and witness that great and vast depth of wit and judgement that was generally conceived to be in him.'[8] Something D'Ewes did take away from proceedings, however, was an even stronger conviction that Strafford deserved to be held to account.

On 26 February, in further considering Thomas Wentworth's second-rate defence with his parliamentary peers, the privileges of the House of Commons were at the forefront of D'Ewes's mind. He advised against seeking the view of the House of Lords on the answers that the earl had provided, fearing that, in doing so, the Commons' rights would be further thrown into doubt. The MP for Sudbury also worried that involving the Lords would only serve to delay the incarcerated nobleman's trial.

Surprisingly, given the direction in which events were moving, there was a moment of playfulness to be had in the House mere days before this great courtroom drama commenced. Perhaps more surprisingly still, the refreshing interlude originated from the straight-laced Simonds D'Ewes himself. The House of Commons discussing some lands in Fulham held by the Bishop of London on 17 March, the Speaker of the House 'put the question whether it should be committed or not'. When it became clear that there was no undisputed victor out of the confused, echoey clamour of 'Ayes' and 'Noes', Simonds stood up to quip that 'the "Ayes" were the greater number; but the "Noes" were the louder'.[9] Much to his satisfaction, this made several of the MPs in the chamber laugh approvingly.

Many dared to hope that Strafford's trial would conclude relatively quickly. Alas, it was not to be, with the evidence alone taking weeks to sift through and analyse in Westminster. Simonds's exasperation at the handling of the trial was unequivocal. On one occasion, he conveyed his astonishment at 'the many delays' that were plaguing court proceedings; on another, later in April, the MP for Sudbury could not help but complain about the sheer number of hours that had been lost 'on the debate of so few lines'. Working towards a verdict that would find Strafford guilty of high treason, on 5 April, the Commons set about focusing on claims that he had suggested drafting in an Irish army to bring parliament into line during the Second Bishops' War, 'for the ruin and destruction of the kingdom of England and of His Majesty's subjects, and altering and subverting the fundamental laws and established government of this kingdom'. When, annoyingly, the nobleman skilfully parried this latest attack, officials of the court knew that they were running out of options. Thus, on 10 April, Sir Arthur Haselrig's proposal that a bill of attainder be used – which would allow Strafford to be automatically found guilty – was lauded. 'Divers spake whether we should proceed by way of bill of attainder, or as we had begun,' D'Ewes noted, 'but most inclined that we should go by Bill.'[10]

Parliament now had the means to declare Sir Thomas Wentworth a traitor without the need for any trial. King Charles, all too aware of what this meant, consequently made a last-ditch attempt to spare his friend the block by making a personal appearance in Westminster on 1 May. 'On Saturday morning,' Simonds wrote, 'we understood that the king was come to the Upper House and expected us. Some feared a dissolution; but Mr Maxwell came in with his white stick, and looking cheerfully, said, "Fear not; no harm, I warrant you".'

Yet, as far as D'Ewes and the rest of the Commons were concerned, there was plenty to fear. Charles shamelessly used his position of influence that morning to argue to them all that the Earl of Strafford 'was not guilty of treason in his conscience, but of misdemeanours only, and so would not have him suffer death, but only be removed from his places'. It was a move that would keep the MP for Sudbury awake at night over the coming days, in particular provoking him to think tearfully about his wife and children in Suffolk, whose safety he now questioned. Parliament's collective response to the king's argument was not to pursue immediate, additional action against Strafford, but to instead fortify itself against further insurrection. This came packaged as the Protestation Oath, which, in the words of Simonds, advocated 'the defence of the true religion, the king's person, the privileges of parliament and our liberties'.[11]

Ever since D'Ewes had first taken his seat in the Long Parliament in November 1640, he had found comfort in compiling detailed notes on the countless historic sessions of which he had been a part. It felt to him very much like a personal attack, then, when on 5 May, amid emerging details of an 'Army Plot', there were questions raised about the appropriateness of members doing so. Simonds, as ever, had a good deal to say on the subject:

> For my part I shall not communicate my journal... to any man living, and if men shall not be permitted to write in the House you must permit them to do as some have done, that is, to sleep among us or else to go to play as others have done. So in the issue, after some others had spoken, both the said motions of forbidding men to take notes in the House and of delivering in the notes taken of the declaration now in question were laid aside.[12]

There was absolutely no exaggeration here. Sir John Coucher, MP for Worcester, was about 80 years old in 1641, and therefore more likely than most to nod off during a particularly dry parliamentary session. He had been caught fast asleep on his bench by Sir Arthur Haselrig on several occasions.[13]

Backed into a corner, and despite his passionate protestations at the beginning of the month, the king reluctantly assented to the Act of Attainder against Strafford on 10 May, bowing to both parliamentary and public pressure to see Sir Thomas Wentworth's blood spilt on Tower Hill. In giving his blessing, he had sealed the fate of his long-time companion. Not even a last-minute message to the House of Lords, delivered by his son, the Prince of Wales, begging for a reprieve for the earl, could now stop the law from taking its unsavoury course.[14]

Strafford's execution took place on 12 May in London, before a gargantuan crowd of perhaps 100,000 people. Very few present were sad to see the condemned man gingerly climb the scaffold on Tower Hill, so universal was the opinion that he represented the root cause of much of the country's recent battles and trials. Like many prisoners had done before him, Wentworth resorted to using emotional blackmail against his despicable judges in his final moments, though this strategy ultimately fell flat. 'Now I have nigh done, one stroke will make my wife husbandlesse, my deare children fatherlesse, and my poore servants masterlesse, and seperate [sic] me from my deare brother and all my friends, but let God be to you and them, all in all,' he is said to have declared to the masses. Then it was time for the end. Removing his doublet and 'winding up his hair' so that it could be tucked away beneath the white cap he would be wearing, he knelt before the block, laid his neck across the wood and stretched out his hands to signal that he was ready for the axe. His head came off in one, slick swing. Surrounded by shrieks of approval from everybody assembled at the Tower that day, the executioner hastily showed off the severed body part to confirm that Strafford was no more. 'God save the king!' he then bellowed.[15]

Chapter 17

THE STORM GATHERS

PANIC GRIPPED THE House of Commons on 19 May 1641.

Simonds recounted of the event afterwards that, all of a sudden, a loud noise like a *crack!* had torn through the chamber and sent grown men running in absolute terror out of the gallery, where the disturbance had originated from. Those who had been gathered directly below the source of the disconcerting sound had also leapt from their positions in fright, with some falling 'one upon the other', others 'running away out of the House', and yet more sprinting 'amazed through Westminster Hall'. 'Stand like true Englishmen!' 72-year-old MP Sir Robert Mansell had cried to the frenzied members scrambling past him to escape the unknown adversary, the aged man having drawn his sword in readiness for a fight. 'But,' D'Ewes continued, 'no man stayed with him.' The scene had been one of total chaos: Thomas Earle had broken his shin trying to get out of harm's way, while Sir Frederick Cornwallis, his hat covering his hair, had been swallowed up by a cloud of lime dust.

What, then, had really gone on here? It transpired that one Mr Moile, in stooping down to retrieve a piece of paper that he had dropped between the gallery and a window, had destroyed 'a few lathes, which made a sudden noise, much like the fall of some part of a scaffold'.

Heightened anxiety over a popish plot that had not yet been foiled by the House of Commons explained the members' irrational behaviour. However, Simonds himself was at pains to write that he had not been one of those who had decided to charge out of the chamber at the first sign of danger. 'The Speaker, standing up a good while, did first spy the error before any other that stood at the upper end of the House where I was, near my constant place, being there,' he noted, almost proudly. D'Ewes would have been wise not to become too complacent as both this incident and the Earl of Strafford's execution were added to the annals of history. For, by June, the man appeared to be encountering certain personal difficulties, namely of a financial nature. On 3 June, as a way of borrowing money, Simonds entered into an agreement with Arthur Barnardiston of Suffolk (Sir Nathaniel's brother), leasing the manors of Stowlangtoft, Lavenham, Overhall and Netherhall to him at a peppercorn rate for twenty-one years.[1]

Shortly afterwards, the MP was nearly tripped up in the House of Commons itself. The Root and Branch Bill reportedly not on the parliamentary agenda until the following week, which sought to ruthlessly pull up the unwelcome weeds of papistical-inspired Christianity in the country, Simonds believed it perfectly safe to take himself away from the chamber for a walk 'behind the shops, near the Court of

Common Pleas' one day. However, while wandering through Westminster Hall, he was stopped suddenly by one Stephen Marshall, a godly man from Finchingfield, who informed him that parliament was currently 'in agitation about this great business for abolishing bishops'. D'Ewes at first refused to believe that this was possible, given that he was absent from the chamber (how could they start without him?). Even so, it was not long before the antiquary-at-heart was dashing up to his private quarters to look out the painstaking notes he had compiled for the debate. Truly, this represented an act of betrayal in Simonds's eyes. '[It] shows the hollow-heartedness of Mr Pym, Mr Hampden, and those other seeming wise men,' he wrote frustratedly, 'who, though they relied upon me to speak, yet they concealed their intendment from me, that I might do below myself in speaking.'[2]

There was better news to come. On 5 July, parliament, outraged by the horrifyingly unjust activities of both during the personal rule of Charles I, abolished the Court of Star Chamber and the Court of High Commission. Simonds could view the abolition of Star Chamber in particular, named after the starry ceiling of the room in which it sat, as an incontrovertible victory. Not only had he disliked the court generally, stating its irregularities 'had been so extreme as there could be no moderating of them', but, as mentioned, he had been targeted by the legal body personally for his failure to raise his quota of ship money in 1640.[3]

Simonds's involvement in discussions on how best to help the stricken Elector Palatine reclaim his lands on the continent was another step in the right direction for the MP for Sudbury. Being a part of the committee that was in favour of a manifesto published by the king on the subject, D'Ewes was granted a spot in the limelight when he delivered a speech to the House of Commons feeding back on what had been chewed over by its members. Not one to play down his antiquarian skills, he took great care to mention to his colleagues that he had been diligently rummaging through relevant records beforehand. 'I have in those few spare-houres I could borrow yesterday, from the publike service of the House, recollected some particulars, which may conduce to the clearing of this great cause, being drawn out of the Autographs themselves, or out of our Records at home, or out of the Writings of our very Adversaries, and others abroad,' he announced.[4]

Yet further good fortune came Simonds's way on 15 July, in the shape of a baronetcy. The gleaming accolade instantaneously propelled D'Ewes up the social food chain in Suffolk and further afield, to the genuine admiration of many of his closest friends, including Sir William Elliot of Busbridge. 'In the first place I congratulate the addition to your title,' he wrote to his brother-in-law following the conferral, 'and the rather as a reward of merit; and I believe it is all the recompense that sweet and virtuous lady is like to receive from you for a summer's absence, for I hear you mean to tide it out.'[5]

It was true that Simonds had been spending almost all of his time in London of late, attending to the overwhelming business of the House of Commons and the worsening national situation. But when it came to the most significant absences within the D'Ewes family that summer, that of the new baronet would ironically prove to be at the very bottom of the list. A surviving parish record tells us that, on 26 July, Simonds's eldest daughter, Anne, was buried at St Dunstan's church in

Stepney. If this were not bad enough, despondent correspondences written around the same time communicate to posterity that her namesake, Simonds's cherished wife, Anne D'Ewes, also died towards the end of July. The baronet of Stowlangtoft had not been with the sick gentlewoman in her final hours at Stow Hall, as Anne had battled desperately but futilely against a fatal case of smallpox. This was something that he knew he would have to live with for the rest of his life. 'How great your loss is, I must confess, I cannot well tell, because I never had the like; but that it is the greatest that ever you had, I can easily imagine, because it came nearest to you, being part of yourself,' John Stuteville of Dalham soothed in a letter. In a touching nod to the supportive network enjoyed by the Puritan gentry in the county in the mid-seventeenth century, he added that 'all your friends here in Suffolk (of which I myself justly have not the least) do bear a part in it'.[6]

Naturally, Simonds wanted answers in the bleak days that followed his wife's death. Why, for instance, had nobody at Stow told him that she had gone downhill so quickly? And why had Lady Elizabeth Denton, his father's widow, been so insistent in instructing Anne to leave Ixworth Abbey during her sickness, when it had been evident to everybody how unwell she was? D'Ewes simply could not understand any of it through his unbearable grief. 'I demand how you and all the rest I left behind could want so much discretion and conscience as not to send after me when you found my Dearest Joy to grow worse and worse,' he wrote angrily to a servant, emphasising that it would have been more than possible for a messenger to reach him in good time on his return from Stowlangtoft to London.[7] As for Elizabeth Denton's behaviour, he penned the following to the same man, James:

> …it doth infinitely trouble my soul, that I think she was merely cast away as the meanest servant the Lady Denton kept could have been, by her suffering her to depart from Ixworth. My reasons are these: first, my blessed wife told me, that she was all over of a sweat when she came away; and yet, said she, my Lady Denton never offered me to stay. I have since my coming up, in the second place, advised with some skilful in that disease; and they all conclude that removal, being in a sweat, without all question lost her her life; for it is most probable that, being the third day of her being ill, the pox would that night have come out in that sweat, which being checked and retarded by her removal, did never come out naturally afterwards.[8]

Simonds was so riled by Denton's actions that he chose to write to her directly at Ixworth, demanding to know why she had shown such apparent indifference to her stepdaughter-in-law in her hour of need. 'My calamity hath laid me so low,' he started in the letter, 'as should you see me, you would scarce know my mourning countenance.' D'Ewes then proceeded to explore the circumstances surrounding Anne's departure from Ixworth Abbey in detail, ensuring to include his wife's own reservations about travelling with smallpox – albeit for only a short distance. 'I must go whatsoever hurt comes of it, seeing nobody offers me to stay,' she is said to have lamented before entering the coach.[9]

What seems to have upset Simonds the most, out of everything that had happened, was the conviction that he had held, upon leaving Anne for the very last time, that she had been on the mend. Sadly, things had not gone at all the way that he had anticipated they would for his wife. There was to be no funeral observed as such for the Clopton heiress at Stowlangtoft, though her body was interred with great care within St George's church soon after her death, aged only 28. One reason for this surprising omission needed no explaining for those who were familiar with the parish's problems at this time: 'you know who must preach [the funeral sermon]', Simonds reminded his servant, James, in a letter, referring to the vexatious local parson, Richard Danford.[10] D'Ewes was similarly quite certain that nobody who had been fortunate enough to call Anne an acquaintance would need to be reminded of her infinite virtues via a preacher.

⟵⟶

Life somehow had to go on for the bereft Sir Simonds D'Ewes in late 1641; the uncertainty of the times demanded it.

Thus, on 31 August, it was back to religious considerations in the House of Commons, when a committee, in which Simonds took part, convened to debate the nationwide reversal of Archbishop Laud's loathed church reforms. The following day, parliament resolved that all such 'innovations' should be wiped away. This was an instruction that went down well with most long-suffering ministers across England, although some required a little more persuading than others to undo the assiduous work of the last ten years. The reluctant reaction of one parson dwelling near the Nottinghamshire home of future roundhead John Hutchinson is recorded in the man's contemporary biography, written up by his wife, Lucy:

> Within two miles of [John Hutchinson's] house there was a church, where Christ upon the cross, the virgin, and John, had been fairly set up in a window over the altar, and sundry other superstitious paintings, of the priest's own ordering, were drawn upon the walls. When the order for rasing out those relics of superstition came, the priest only took down the heads of the images, and laid them carefully up in his closet, and would have had the church officers to have certified that the thing was done according to order; whereupon they came to Mr Hutchinson, and desired him that he would take the pains to come and view their church, which he did, and upon discourse with the parson, persuaded him to blot out all the superstitious paintings, and break the images in the glass; which he consented to, but being ill-affected, was one of those who began to brand Mr Hutchinson with the name of Puritan.[11]

It would appear, then, that there were those parish ministers who feared – not without good reason, it should be emphasised – that the winding back of the ecclesiastical clock risked pushing religious doctrine too far in the opposite direction.

Many members of the clergy needed absolutely no encouragement to do parliament's bidding, to the point where they might become downright violent in their mission to rid churches of idolatrous fixtures and other alterations introduced under the Laudian programme. Even staunch Puritans like Simonds could not condone such behaviour if it got too out of hand, as indeed it did within St Mary Woolchurch Haw in London in October. Granted, Simonds's love for relics of the past encouraged him to be particularly appalled by the actions of the building's churchwardens, who, 'in obedience to the order of the House of Commons', had proceeded to remove brass inscriptions from tombs and deface any monuments that depicted a person in prayer. 'I spake in effect following,' he wrote of his contribution to the parliamentary debate on 14 October, 'that [the churchwardens'] indiscretion had brought a great scandal upon the House of Commons as if we meant to deface all antiquities. That when we had prepared a statute to pass to this end and purpose for the removing of all offensive pictures yet we had specially provided that no tombs should be meddled withal.'[12]

Nevertheless, D'Ewes was clearly keen for the project in general to be a success, having heard horror stories first-hand – including from his brother-in-law in Surrey – of ministers who continued to shamelessly and aggressively insist on Laudian practice in their respective parishes. Nicholas Andrews, the preacher of Godalming, proved to be the cause of Sir William Elliot's headaches in 1641. '...[Andrews] lately put one from the Communion because his conscience would not suffer him to kneel,' he told Simonds furiously in one letter. 'For afternoon sermons we can have none... he is so great an enemy to preaching and goodness.'[13]

Following a stomach-churning incident in Westminster on 25 October, whereby a derogatory letter targeting John Pym had been delivered alongside 'an abominable rag, full of filthy abominable matter', thoughts pivoted towards the need to reform the very heart of King Charles's corrupt government on 28 October. These ruminations were crafted into the beginnings of a coherent plan of action at a committee meeting held that same afternoon, which, once again, Simonds himself attended. Aimed at preventing 'the mischiefs that may happen to the Commonwealth by the choice and employment of evil counsellors, ambassadors, judges, officers, and other Ministers of State', the resulting Grand Remonstrance (in essence, a very long list of grievances) was narrowly passed by 159 votes to 148 in the Commons on 22 November. Its entrance into the political confusion of late 1641 was followed at the end of the month by widespread demonstrations in Westminster, driven by popular dissatisfaction at parliament's repeated failure – thanks to the House of Lords – to eject bishops from the church hierarchy. Though the protestors claimed to the Commons that they had come in a 'peaceable manner' to air their grievances, a powerful supporter of the king, Edward Sackville, 4th Earl of Dorset, would swiftly dismiss them as simple troublemakers, and was soon ordering a parliamentary guard to fire on the assembled crowds.[14]

'It [is] against the privileges of this House to set a guard upon us without our own consent,' Simonds grumbled afterwards, when the arrangement was made permanent. Only a short time before, he had accompanied other representatives of the House of Commons to Hampton Court Palace to present the ground-breaking

Grand Remonstrance to the king. Charles having listened interestedly to the pressing points raised in the petition, delivered eloquently by Sir Ralph Hopton, his knee-jerk reaction had been to give the impression that he knew nothing about the evil councillors to which the Remonstrance referred. On the assertion that His Majesty was trapped in the middle of a 'malignant party with a design to change religion' in particular, he had merely responded by saying, 'the Devil take him, whomsoever he be, that had a design to change religion'. Nevertheless, Charles had confirmed at the presentation that he would be willing to give the Westminster petition some thought, adding sardonically that 'I suppose you do not now expect an answer to so long a petition.'[15]

Fast-forward to two days before Christmas 1641, and it would seem that, not only had Charles failed to respond to the Grand Remonstrance to the satisfaction of parliament, but he had also apparently confirmed the fears expressed within it by appointing Thomas Lunsford to the post of lieutenant of the Tower of London. '[He is] a man given to drinking, swearing, and quarrelling, much in debt, and very desperate,' D'Ewes remarked in his puritanical way, believing Lunsford to be most unsuited to the role bestowed on him, 'unless there were some dangerous design in hand against us.' Parliament as a whole likewise objected to the man's involvement in the recent Bishops' Wars. The Commons became unsettled enough about the appointment to demand an immediate conference with the House of Lords, to which hereditary body they insisted that 'there had long been a design of the Papists to ruin the true religion, and that the appointment of Colonel Lunsford shewed that the same design was now growing to a maturity'.[16]

Simonds, far from revelling in the festive season of 1641–2, could now feel the floor of the House of Commons giving way beneath him. He wrote of the Lunsford business that:

> ...all things hastened apace to confusion and calamity; from which I scarce saw any possibility in human reason for this poor Church and kingdom to be delivered. My hope only was in the goodness of that God who had several times during this Parliament been seen in the Mount, and delivered us, beyond the expectations of ourselves and of our enemies, from the jaws of destruction.[17]

D'Ewes's instincts served him well. The myriad controversies of the past decade came to an astonishing head on 4 January 1642, when King Charles, ostensibly convinced that five MPs were 'traitorously endeavouring to subvert the fundamental laws and government of the kingdom of England', came to the House of Commons to arrest them.[18]

The five members in question were William Strode, Arthur Haselrig, Denzil Holles, John Hampden and John Pym. Before the king arrived in Westminster that afternoon, each man had been tipped off about the veritable storm heading his way, and so the very first 'parliamentarians' were long gone by the time Charles graced Westminster Hall with his presence. Simonds either witnessed everything for himself or quickly acquired first-hand accounts from others. '[The king's entrance] struck such a fear and terror into all those that kept shops in the said Hall, or near the gate thereof, as they instantly shut up their shops, looking for nothing but bloodshed and desolation,' he wrote. Passing through to the lobby, accompanied by the Elector Palatine and 'divers officers of the late army in the north, and other desperate ruffians', Charles proceeded to enter the rather hushed chamber in which his insubordinate MPs could be found. Every man had retained enough respect for their sovereign to stand and remove their hats upon his coming in, including the Speaker of the House, William Lenthall, who rose before his chair in readiness to receive the royal visitor. After a cordial exchange of bowing between the king and the House at large, Simonds included, Charles asked Mr Speaker if he might be permitted to 'make bold' with this chair.[19]

D'Ewes recounted what happened next in minute detail, knowing full well, at the time, that Pym and the others were already safely away:

> ...he asked for My Pym, whether he were present or not, and when there followed a general silence, that nobody would answer him, he then asked for Mr Holles whether he were present, and when nobody answered him, he pressed the Speaker to tell him, who, kneeling down, did very wisely desire His Majesty to pardon him, saying that he could neither see nor speak but by command of the House: to which the King answered, 'Well, well! 'tis no matter. I think my eyes are as good as another's'. And then he looked round about the House a pretty while, to see if he could espy any of them.[20]

'Well, since I see all my birds are flown, I do expect from you that you will send them unto me as soon as they return hither,' Charles eventually concluded (according to Rushworth), appearing to be hugely incensed at the five members' purposeful absence from the Commons.[21] With nothing left to say to the House – the situation all men found themselves in was now an unspoken one – the king presently made to leave the chamber again.

A great deal can be inferred from the fact that, in the days directly following the monarch's unconstitutional arrest attempt, one of Simonds's primary concerns was ensuring that he had left his last will and testament 'with a third person in trust'.

War was coming.

PART THREE
WAR

'Matters are now grown to a desperate pass'

CHAPTER 18

BROTHER AGAINST BROTHER

THE HOUSE OF Commons was in a state of unconcealed shock on 5 January 1642.

King Charles I's audacious visit to Westminster the previous day had caused most members to feel as though they were now under attack from the very man whom they had sworn to serve. 'It [was] this day declared by the House,' the Commons journal noted, 'that the same is a high breach of the rights and privileges of Parliament, and inconsistent with the liberties and freedoms thereof.'[1]

Accordingly, a committee met at the Guildhall in the City of London the next day to decide what was to be done about the king's latest, but by far worst, escapade. Particularly, parliament encouraged the emergency assembly to discuss the various measures that should be taken to make certain 'the Good and Safety of the City and Kingdom'. Simonds was once more a member of this historic committee; the typically conscientious speech he gave at the Guildhall on the privileges of parliament, moreover, was later printed, and has thus survived to the present day. ''Tis true indeed that upon the empeachment of the House of Commons for Treason or other capitall crimes, they doe Immediately commit their members to safe custody, because it is first admitted that we accuse not till wee are satisfied in the matter of fact, and secondly, it is also supposed in Law that such an aggregate body as the House of Commons is will doe nothing,' part of the document reads.[2]

By 10 January, support for parliament had grown so strong – Pym and his associates were welcomed back to Westminster as heroes – that King Charles and his family were forced to leave London altogether, choosing to head to the relative safety of Hampton Court Palace. From here, on 12 January, they would move again to Windsor Castle. The preliminary drawing of battle lines in the capital was perhaps made most obvious to Simonds himself on 11 January, when the MP for Sudbury decided to take a walk through Westminster Hall between parliamentary sessions. He discovered there an imposing guard of no less than 2,400 soldiers, many of whom were members of London's trained bands, and who, combined, already emitted the unnerving air of an army ready to march into the field. The presence of copies of the Protestation Oath endorsed by parliament, stuck to the top of each man's glinting pike, left little doubt that these combatants had picked their side.

With just a scattering of other trained bands across the country also beginning to be mustered in anticipation of armed conflict between the king and his parliament, D'Ewes's attention was refocused on the dire state of Protestantism in England on 17 January 1642, when William Elliot wrote to him from Busbridge to impart that he had recently been asked by the vicar of Godalming to sign a petition for the retention of bishops. 'These popish and proud clergy were never at a greater height. What hopes they may conceive I know not,' he scribbled hysterically to his brother-in-law.[3] Now that the Commons had at long last started to get on top of the issues plaguing government, this was not a problem that Elliot or D'Ewes would be compelled to contemplate for much longer.

All eyes rolled beadily in the direction of Hull, a strategic port town in the north, as preparations for a war that few wanted continued. Here was kept an arsenal containing weaponry that had been stockpiled for use in the Bishops' Wars, but that would now conveniently furnish either parliament's or the king's faction with a plentiful store of arms. On 20 January, a letter landed in the lap of the Commons that shocked Simonds and the rest of the assembled MPs: a delegation sent to secure Hull for Westminster had been traitorously denied entry to the town. Sir John Hotham, the relater of the bad tidings, blamed the mayor and aldermen for the snub, though he felt confident that the townspeople were more supportive of parliament's cause. Sure enough, just days later on 31 January, Hotham's son and the trained bands of the East Riding managed to take control of the port.[4]

One obstacle after another dropped in front of the House of Commons in early 1642 as combative sides formed and political loyalties were cemented. Sir Edward Dering, shire knight for Kent, only added to this exasperatingly long list of hindrances when he chose to print his defamatory opinions on the Grand Remonstrance, which went down very badly with parliament. Even Dering's fellow antiquary, Simonds, could not stand to let the incident pass without proper punishment. In fact, he believed the more severe the sentence, the better. Discovering upon entering the Commons in early February that Dering had been earmarked for a stint in the Tower and nothing more, Simonds wrote that he was 'very much troubled at it; especially when Sir Ralph Hopton said that we might retain him because of his great parts'. Thus, the Long Parliament ultimately voted in favour of having Sir Edward's book burnt in Palace Yard, Cheapside and Smithfield, so that his disadvantageous words might go up in smoke once and for all.

The MP for Cambridge, Oliver Cromwell, seemed somewhat sceptical about parliament's resolution the following day. Concluding that putting together a reasoned response to Dering's harmful publication might be more beneficial to the Commons in the long term than mindlessly setting fire to it, he nominated Simonds to be the author of the proposed 'confutation'. This was too much to ask of D'Ewes after a long day of debating. '[It] made me presently stand up and answer, that I conceived that the gentleman who last spoke did not dream that it was now near 7 of the clock at night, or else that he would not at this time have made such a motion as he did,' Simonds wrote. He suggested, instead, that Cromwell draft the reply himself if it was so important to him, after which 'the subject dropped'.[6]

A moot point discussed at some length over the following weeks in the House of Commons was who exactly should have overall control of England's haphazard patchwork of trained bands. This was despite the fact that a handful of proactive men on both sides of the developing schism had already taken it upon themselves to commence mustering regiments. Technically, such control rested with the king – and the king alone – under existing law. On 2 March, amid seasonably cold weather, D'Ewes sat in a chilly chamber that was 'full of sadness and evil augury, all conceiving that, whether we sat still or did proceed to settle the militia by authority of both Houses, matters were now grown to a desperate pass'.[7] Three days later, with many of those harbouring royalist sympathies having abandoned Westminster to join Charles somewhere outside of London, the Militia Ordinance was approved by both the House of Lords and the House of Commons, giving parliament total authority over the country's only recognisable – albeit poorly organised and scattered – army.

A figure from Simonds's distant past, Richard Holdsworth of the University of Cambridge, decided to focus on promoting peace, not preparing for war, on 27 March. Preaching at the church of St Mary the Great in Cambridge, and carefully directing his words towards King Charles himself, the theologian advised 'princely clemency and patience' before his congregation, as well as conveying his hope that 'happiness... howsoever it be now eclips'd, may again shine forth in full strength, through Your Majesty's great prudence'. The sentiment to which Holdsworth alluded was certainly in short supply in London into April 1642. On 14 April, D'Ewes and Sir Beauchamp St John were sent on behalf of parliament to profusely apologise to the diplomat Alessandro Antelminelli, who had recently been threatened with violence and verbally abused by men claiming to represent Westminster. '[They] haled his servants to prison,' the Commons journal records, 'and gave him railing words, calling him and his servants Traytors, Rogues, and Papist Dogs.' Simonds reported to the House the next day that Salvetti had taken 'the respect very kindly; and will acquaint his master, the Grand Duke of Tuscany, therewith'.[8]

King Charles, another figure who probably wasn't too familiar with the sentiment of happiness at this time, had decided to establish his court in York towards the end of March. From here, a failed attempt was made on 23 April to take back the Hotham-controlled Hull from parliament, such was the recognised value of the arsenal kept there. Back in the capital, D'Ewes found himself pledging the large sum of £50 a year 'to the relief of Ireland, so long as the war lasts' on 27 April, 'without expecting any part of the rebels' lands in that kingdom'.[9] The rebellion in Ireland, erupting in 1641 and fuelled by valid concerns that events in England and Scotland might provoke further discrimination against Irish Catholics, is not within the scope of this book, though it is, of course, worth mentioning that Simonds felt a curious amount of sympathy for those unlucky enough to be embroiled in the conflict across the Irish Sea.

Parliament's calculated Militia Ordinance of 5 March did exactly the opposite of keeping the king away from the country's trained bands. On 6 June 1642, Charles breezily persisted in his hostile attitude towards both Houses by issuing the first commissions of array to gentry leaders throughout England, which obligated them to begin officially recruiting soldiers for the uncertain times that lay ahead. With preparations for war now agonisingly visible in both camps, Simonds's anxieties were becoming palpable in the Commons. The House debating on 8 June the need to begin formally defending itself through pledges of money, plate and horses from all who were able to provide them, D'Ewes advocated caution to his fellow MPs, arguing that sending out an effective call to arms might only succeed in filling 'men's hearts with the fear and expectation of a civil war'.[10] In any case, Simonds appeared in no doubt that parliament was already in the better position by the start of summer, citing its control of the navy, its occupation of Hull, and the allegiance of the Scots to the government as reasons to be optimistic.

The current crisis had become deeply and uncomfortably personal for D'Ewes in recent weeks, a fact that he was reminded of in late June, when his little brother, Richard, wrote to him from the court in York to emphatically urge that his sibling join the king's cause in the north, as he had done. Concerted efforts to keep Captain D'Ewes safe on his hurried journey from London are recorded in a warrant issued by the 2nd Viscount Falkland on 9 April, which survives today as part of the Harley Collection:

> Whereas the bearer hereof Captain Richard D'Ewes is to make his speedie repaire to York about His Majesties especiall affaires these are to will and require you, and every of you, forthwith upon sight hereof to furnish unto him three sufficient and able posthorses, and a guide, with sufficient furniture, at the usuall and accustomed prices. Faile not hereof, as you will answer the contrary at your perills. Given at Westminster.[11]

There is no question that Richard was cognisant of his older brother's difficult position in his letter. 'I daily understand how you stand affected, and what your opinions are, and out of that sincere affection I bear you, I heartily wish you fortunate in their continuance,' he made clear. However, as stated, the captain likewise pushed for Simonds to see sense in these darkening days of adversity, and to allow the brothers to stand together. 'If your other occasions will dispense and give place to my hopes, I can in some measure accommodate you with horses for your journey. 'Tis but sending a note under your hand to Sir Henry Newton for a grey gelding and a bay mare to be left at his house,' he continued.[12]

That Simonds had failed to reply to an earlier correspondence sent by his royalist brother shows the conflicting emotions felt by the MP with regard to Richard's choices. 'For mine own part,' he conceded in a reply written on 21 June, 'I have often repented my being of this Parliament; having ... been much interrupted in my precious studies by it.' 'But,' he went on, surely to Captain D'Ewes's eternal disappointment, 'I bless that higher Providence that gave me courage to speak freely, and if mine own heart deceive me not, I could be willing to redeem the reunion of His Majesty and the two Houses with my dearest blood.'[13] In essence, there was simply no way that Simonds could now abandon his seat within the Long Parliament.

This great scandal authored by Richard was accompanied by another of equal impropriety the same month, of which his brother was again to bear the brunt in London. On 17 June, the Middle Temple parliament revealed that a bastard child had lately been found abandoned within its revered halls. An innocuous enough happening in itself, though treated with due exasperation by the Temple authorities, it was claimed that the infant had in fact been fathered by none other than the royalist absconder, Captain D'Ewes. 'The Masters of the Bench, by reason of Mr Dewes' absence, were forced to take care of it, and committed it to be kept at the charge of the House till they had procured it to be settled in the parish where it was born,' the parliament records assert. An order was given post-haste during the sitting to have Richard's chamber at the Middle Temple 'seized and disposed of, unless sufficient cause be shown to the contrary at the next Parliament', while care was also taken to have Sir Simonds, already humiliated by his younger brother's behaviour, informed of the insalubrious development at his lodgings in Westminster.[14]

Perhaps it was a blessing in disguise for D'Ewes that events around him surged on with such unstoppable speed in the tumultuous summer of 1642. Indeed, many things happened in quick succession in July: on the second, the navy declared for parliament, therefore turning against the king; on the third, Charles moved his court to Beverley in eastern Yorkshire, where a swelling army of royalist soldiers was also to be quartered; on the fourth, parliament established a Committee for Safety, made up of ten men from the Commons, and a further five from the Lords; and, finally, on the twelfth, a crucial decision was made by parliament to set about mustering its own exclusive army, commanded by the Earl of Essex, Robert Devereux. All of the above, furthermore, were to play out against the backdrop of the king's cutthroat rejection of parliament's attempt at a negotiation, the Nineteen Propositions, which had been put to him in early June.

Oliver Cromwell, according to Simonds, would let no man hold him back in his determination to gather an army to represent his constituency. '[He] moved that we might make an order to allow the townsmen of Cambridge to raise two companies of volunteers, and to appoint captains over them,' D'Ewes remarked on 15 July, which can only have reassured the House now that a full-blown war was so close at hand. Simonds's own conduct would actively displease the Commons just a week later, when the opinionated baronet strongly objected to the manner in which a committee had presented its answer to 'declarations and messages from His Majesty, that lay imputations and aspersions upon both Houses of Parliament'. Particularly, D'Ewes accused members of the committee of using 'bitter and irreverential language towards His Majesty'; he also insinuated that each of them intended to 'make fierce and hot preparations for a civil war'. Moreover, the Commons journal would record that Simonds had brusquely declared that there 'were many things in this declaration, that were taken out of other men's pockets and budgets, and before printed'. The under-fire MP had no choice but to apologise for the sudden outburst. To make the whole episode even more embarrassing, D'Ewes went on to receive a telling-off from the Speaker of the House, who warned him that he should be 'more careful of his expressions hereafter; and to be careful hereafter not to lay any imputations upon any particular Member; much less upon any Committee'.[15]

Simonds was left so red-faced by the events of 23 July that he decided not to reappear in the chamber until the end of August. While the antiquary licked his wounds in private, having exhibited an early manifestation of his clear preference for a peaceful settlement over continued fighting, gentry families across the length and breadth of the country – some supporting parliament, others loyal to the crown – continued to publicly muster local trained bands for imminent military service. The disgraced Richard D'Ewes was one of those orchestrating recruitment drives in towns and villages in August 1642, having now been made a lieutenant colonel in Colonel Richard Bolle's regiment of foot. Far away from the contemplative Simonds, Staffordshire in the Midlands was the soldier's principal territory; wherever the rhythmic beating of drums or shrill cry for volunteers could be heard in the county, Richard was likely to be nearby.[16]

Regiments of soldiers had begun marching by mid-August. Nehemiah Wharton, part of the sixth company of the Volunteers of the Metropolis, which would eventually join up with the Earl of Essex's army, wrote the following to his master in London on the sixteenth of the month:

> On the 8th August we marched to Acton, and being belated were constrained to 'lodge on beds whose feathers were above a yard long'. The next day, Tuesday, several of our soldiers sallied out to the house of one Penruddock, a Papist, and, being basely affronted by him and his dog, entered his house, and pillaged him to the purpose. This day also the soldiers got into the church, defaced the ancient and sacred glazed pictures, and burned the holy rails...[17]

The behaviour of Wharton's company was alarming, and certainly did not bode well for the future. He continued:

> Saturday morning our companies overtook us, and we marched together towards Aylesbury, and after we had marched 4 long miles, for so they are all in this country, we came to Wendover, where we refreshed ourselves, burnt the rails; and accidentally one of Captain Francis's men, forgetting he was charged with a bullet, shot a maid through the head, and she immediately died.[18]

CHAPTER 19

EDGEHILL

AFFORDED A BREATHER from the endless business of the House of Commons, August 1642 turned out to be a fruitful month for Simonds. Enough time had passed now for the baronet to begin considering marrying again, which is precisely what he decided to put his mind to in these precious weeks of quasi-freedom. D'Ewes, it must be remembered, was still without a son and heir – war or no war. On 1 August, he wrote to Sir Henry Willoughby of Risley in Derbyshire, seeking to convey his interest in the gentleman's eligible daughter, Elizabeth. 'She is, indeed, your youngest by birth, but her growth and stature retain their full proportion in respect of her years; and her rare discretion, with other inward endowments, striving to outshine nature itself, which hath enriched her with many outward beauties, doth frequently set my admiration and wonderment on work,' Simonds gushed, though he hardly knew the family, let alone Elizabeth herself. With a good word or two likewise being put in by Sir John Potts of Mannington Hall in Norfolk, a kinsman of the Willoughby clan, it seemed probable by the month's close that the marriage would go ahead.[1]

The same John Potts would bring an uplifted Simonds D'Ewes back down to earth again on 19 August, upon writing to tell his friend that, thankfully, all was currently quiet in Norfolk. 'Whensoever necessity shall enforce us to make use of the multitude I do not promise myself safety,' he added ominously, the man clearly keen to avoid any kind of military entanglement. This dreaded day of 'necessity' appeared destined to arrive in the county sooner than Potts had anticipated. The Commons journal tells us that, on 24 August, Sir John Hobart of Blickling Hall was sent back to his native Norfolk laden with 'five case [sic] of pistols, three carabines, and two little short pieces of brass', a move that came in the wake of a premature engagement fought at Marshall's Elm in Somerset some weeks before.[2] Principally, though, it constituted a panicked response to the raising of the royal standard outside Nottingham Castle. The country was now formally at war.

Immediately, reports besieged the House of Commons from across England of violent reactions to the news. On 23 August, the mayor of Colchester wrote to parliament to inform its members that the house of Sir John Lucas, a royalist sympathiser, had been looted for its horses and arms by those loyal to 'the Commonwealth', and the proprietor and his wife imprisoned for treason. This, naturally, sat well with the Commons members, who were always pleased to hear of acts carried out in their honour. So, too, did information received from Kent, where the residence of Sir Edward Dering had been plundered. From champions of heritage and tradition, however, such as D'Ewes himself, there was undoubtedly an altogether less positive response to additional intelligence received that Canterbury

Cathedral had been vandalised. Soldiers keen to uphold Protestantism in its purest form had destroyed the organ there, wrenched up the communion rails, ruthlessly cut out an image of Christ woven into a tapestry, and proceeded to use a stone depicting the same as target practice in the cathedral grounds.[3]

King Charles proclaimed the Earl of Essex, commander of parliament's newly formed forces, to be a traitor following the raising of the royal standard in Nottingham. In turn, parliament briskly moved to declare its intention to protect the loyal earl in any way it could, via a conference held jointly by the Commons and Lords in late August 1642. The Commons went even further in their demonstration of allegiance to Essex when MPs eventually returned to their own chamber. Closing the door so that 'no one could go out', the 'hot spirits' of the House proceeded to demand that all men personally declare whether they were willing to 'hazard their lives and fortunes with the Earl of Essex, Lord General'.

Seemingly, there was no patience for political hesitancy that day. When the aged MP for Coventry, William Jesson, begged that he be given some time to consider the matter properly, he was met with pointed looks from his fiery colleagues that pushed him into making up his mind there and then. The answer he provided – 'Noe' – was not the response they had been looking for. 'When the poor man,' D'Ewes reported, 'terrified with the displeasure he saw was taken against him, would have given his "Aye", they would not permit him to do that neither.'[4] The disturbing scene encouraged other MPs to give their own 'Ayes' irrespective of the views they held, including Sir Guy Palmes and John Fettiplace, the latter of whom would eventually join the king's ranks.

Simonds purposefully avoided giving his own answer to the Commons until he could dodge the action no longer. At last being made to declare in front of the House, he noncommittally announced that 'I saw the particulars for the defence of which I was to declare myself were all conjoined, and therefore I might very well give my "Aye" to it, which I did.' Again, some among him were not satisfied. Mr Speaker, William Lenthall, however, was for once with D'Ewes in his declaration, quieting the baronet's critics by asserting that '[Simonds] had answered as fairly and fully as possibly could be desired, and that he himself had given his "Aye" in the same notion'.[5]

The 'hot spirits' in parliament were right about one thing: the time for decisive action had well and truly come. On 2 September, one of the first episodes of siege warfare in the country began at Sherborne Castle in Dorset, which had been garrisoned by a royalist army led by William Seymour, Marquess of Hertford. The Earl of Bedford, William Russell, intent on dispersing the force billeted there, was behind the act, having arrived at the property with thousands of rowdy men who had taken up arms for parliament. It was a depressingly ugly scene by the end. Beaten back into the castle by Bedford's large party, nine men on Hertford's side were killed, including one Captain Hussey of Dorset, who met a very undesirable fate before being slaughtered by his opponents. 'Whilst they had him at their mercy,' a contemporary account reveals, 'they most barbarously cut off his members.' Even before this, some sixteen combatants fighting for Bedford had been scalded and hideously disfigured by two barrels of powder catching fire and exploding. 'God turne our swords into sythes, that leaving all acts of hostilitie, we may peaceably receive the fruits of the earth,' the same account beseeched.[6]

Back in Westminster, Simonds watched as the Earl of Essex triumphantly departed for the Midlands on 9 September. Alas, much like the Earl of Strafford had done when defending himself in the House, the great statesman let D'Ewes down in his attempt at eloquence at the crucial moment. 'My Lords,' he uttered in the Painted Chamber, in the presence of both the Lords and Commons, 'you have employed me about a service which I am very willing to undertake, and therefore I desire to know what you will please to command me.' The earl then donned his hat and spoke no further. 'The company soon after departed,' Simonds recounted later, 'thinking this message somewhat ridiculous' – for its length, but also because Essex had chosen only to address the House of Lords.[7]

The earl was parading through London on horseback by mid-afternoon, guarded by hundreds of faithful pikemen and musketeers, who lined the streets from Essex House to Bishopsgate. Upon reaching Islington or thereabouts, the site of Simonds's former townhouse, he got off his horse and entered the coach that would take him to Dunstable, and then on to Northampton. It was planned that the commander would oversee a military rendezvous here, and, indeed, on 14 September, Essex could be found rigorously reviewing parliament's assembled army in the town, which at that time numbered around 20,000 men. Captain General Devereux (Essex) was under no illusions about the perilousness of the task that soberingly hung over him in the autumn of 1642. To that end, he had insisted that a coffin, winding sheet, and 'ready drawn' funeral escutcheons travel up with him to Northampton, in case the worst should occur.[8]

Simonds enjoyed another passing modicum of happiness on 20 September. This day, he married for a second time, to the young heiress Elizabeth Willoughby, whose father he had corresponded with in August. '[In my] new, most delightful wife I heartily esteem all those very rare gifts which were in my former wife,' the knight wrote afterwards, somewhat emotionally, to Johannes de Laet. Richard D'Ewes had heard about the union on a coincidental march through Risley in Derbyshire, learning via Henry Willoughby himself that Sir Thomas Aston, husband of Elizabeth's sister, had insultingly branded Simonds 'an owlde decrepit man' who was both 'blinde' and 'deaph'. Certainly, more than one Willoughby family member had reservations about the considerable age gap between the girl – one of their own – and her new spouse.

Yet there were no extended periods of elation in times of civil war. All too soon, D'Ewes was in the tense House of Commons once more, seeing off an attack from his fellow MPs over his brother's detestable betrayal of parliament. Intelligence had recently been received, via an interrogation, that Richard had been recruiting for the king's army under Colonel Bolle in Staffordshire that summer. Simonds might have gotten off relatively lightly, had it not been for the antagonistic comments of 'fiery spirit' Henry Marten, who seemed determined to run the MP for Sudbury into a corner. '[He] stood up and desired,' D'Ewes wrote irately, 'that I, being brother to him who raised men against the parliament, might declare what I would do for the defence of the parliament.' The initial answer Simonds gave Henry – that he could not be blamed for his brother's shortcomings, just as Marten could not be held accountable for the actions of his own siblings – was not deemed a satisfactory one by other 'fiery spirits' such as Sir William Armine, MP for Grantham. Thus, a financial contribution of some kind to the parliamentary war effort appeared the only viable way forwards. D'Ewes, in fact, had been in the Commons so consistently since November 1640 that he did not know how much money he could pull from his estates in Suffolk, where things were still rather quiet. Willing to give a down payment of £40 in the meantime, he conveyed as much to the House, requesting that he be granted leave to return to Stow Hall to see to his affairs. Mr Speaker thought it a perfectly reasonable ask considering Simonds had only lately been married to 'a fair lady', though for now the request was 'neither granted nor rejected'.[9]

While Suffolk was left well enough alone in September 1642, Powick near Worcester was not. Close by to the village bridge on 23 September, a parliamentarian force, which included officer and devout Puritan Nathaniel Fiennes, smashed headfirst into a royalist cavalry commanded by Prince Rupert of the Rhine, who had travelled from mainland Europe to aid his maternal uncle, King Charles, on the battlefield. Rupert, already a skilled military leader with an impressive track record, almost immediately gained the upper hand in the skirmish, leading him to give chase to Fiennes and his startled men as far as Powick itself, before he halted the charge and claimed a victory for the king. By around 10 October, the prince was to be found riding furiously with his forces in the direction of Wolverhampton, pre-empting Charles's daring plans to march on London.[10]

The following day in the House, Sir Gilbert Gerard, MP for Middlesex, at last secured Simonds permission to go into the country for a month, the helpful parliamentarian having renewed the motion amid 'some of the fiery spirits being absent'. Before leaving for Suffolk, D'Ewes declared that he would willingly give £100 to parliament – out of his own pocket – for the defence of the realm, with half to be paid presently, and the other half to be settled once he had enquired after his estates in East Anglia.[11]

Just over a fortnight later, and with Simonds absent from the Commons for the time being (he would travel as far afield as Derbyshire), the Speaker of the House received a significant letter signed by Denzil Holles, Philip Stapleton, Thomas Ballard, William Balfour, John Meldrum and Charles Pym. It concerned a great battle that had recently been fought between the royalists and parliamentarians near Kineton in Warwickshire:

> Sir, we should do our army a great deal of wrong, and not discharge our duty of thankfulness towards God, if we took not the first occasion to declare his goodness, in giving so great a blessing, as he hath now done to the resolute and unwearied endeavours of our soldiers fighting for him in the maintenance of his truth, and for themselves and their country, in the defence of their liberties and the privileges of Parliament; this makes us give you now a narration of a blessed victory which God hath given us upon the Army of the Cavaliers, and of those evil persons, who upon Sunday the 23rd of this instant, engaged His Majesty in a dangerous and bloody fight against his faithful subjects, in the army raised by authority of Parliament, for the preservation of his crown and kingdom.[12]

This was the Battle of Edgehill, the first major engagement of the First English Civil War. 'Their forces appeared to be much greater than we could possibly have conceived them to be by the confession of the prisoners we have taken,' the letter continued, with its endorsers describing how the king's army, overseen by King Charles and Prince Rupert, had torn down Edgehill and clashed with the Earl of Essex's men at the bottom.[13]

Enclosed with the message was a 'George', plucked from the field by a common soldier, which had been presented to the House of Commons as 'one of our trophies, that you may see it'. In reality, there had been no clear victor at the conclusion of the engagement, though Holles and the rest were at pains to emphasise the virtuous – and indeed victorious – actions of parliament's army. The night following the main part of the confrontation had seen Essex's men almost 'starved with cold' in the exposed Warwickshire countryside, according to the letter; yet, early the next morning, the courageous soldiers had reassembled, in the face of adversity, to see the king's forces off from their position on the hill. This is the version of events that Simonds himself, in all likelihood, would have been fed upon his return to the House of Commons in mid-November. It was one that would be further propagated by contemporary commentators loyal to parliament, including the Eastcheap chronicler and ardent Puritan Nehemiah Wallington, who seemed particularly hellbent on painting the royalist army in a bad light in his writings. He wrote of the aftermath of the battle that the Earl of Essex left behind 'about 200 of his wounded soldiers in Kineton to be cured there, who were all most inhumanely slain by Count Rupert and his troopers'.[14]

Of course, the royalists had their own story to tell concerning the events of 23 October. On 27 October, Sir Edward Sydenham wrote to Ralph Verney of Middle Claydon to relate both the triumphs of Charles's army and the valiant behaviour of its members in the thick of savage fighting:

> For all our great victory I have had the greatest loss by the death of your noble father that ever any friend did, which next to my wife and master was the greatest misfortune that by death could have fallen to me: he himself killed two with his own hands, whereof one of them had killed poor Jason, and broke the point of his standard at [the] push of [a] pike before he fell, which was the last account I could receive of any of our own side of him.[15]

The minister Richard Baxter, while a Puritan man, offers perhaps the most authentic account of the peculiar atmosphere surrounding the Battle of Edgehill, being but a curious bystander to proceedings. 'As I was preaching [in Alcester] the people heard the cannon play,' he recollected, 'and perceived that the armies were engaged.' The sun dipping below the horizon later in the day, Baxter had seen runaway soldiers racing – panicked and confused – through the town from the battlefield, crying that 'all was lost on the Parliament side, and the carriage taken and waggons plundered before they came away'. An even grimmer spectacle had greeted the minister when he had gone to inspect the site of the engagement for himself. He noted that he had 'found the Earl of Essex with the remaining part of his army keeping the ground, and the king's army facing them upon the hill a mile off; and about a thousand dead bodies in the field between them'.[16]

CHAPTER 20

AN UNHAPPY CHRISTMAS

ANXIOUS CALLS FOR a truce between the warring monarch and his parliament were made in the House of Lords on 29 October 1642. These were at once echoed by the poet and MP Edmund Waller – a known royalist sympathiser – across the way in the House of Commons, effectively establishing the peace party to which Simonds D'Ewes would be drawn as an objector to continued violence in the country.

Anybody believing that armed conflict could be eradicated at this point in time, however, can only have been in a dreadful state of denial. Edgehill had set the tone for the war when the battle had been aggressively fought at the end of October, meaning that subsequent confrontations were now practically unavoidable. Hence, the Commons received another letter composed haphazardly in the field on 13 November, informing them that a parliamentary force had, the previous day, been set upon by an army commanded by Prince Rupert at Brentford. Simonds still being in Suffolk, the remaining members of the House were swift in their response to this latest atrocity, which had seen a number of Denzil Holles's men drown as they had attempted to swim across the River Thames to escape their pursuers. Parliamentary representatives were to be dispatched with all speed to question 'the prisoner that is taken of the king's army'; Sir Thomas Dacres and one Captain Fuller were to go to the Committee for Safety to see what should be done with him; and a delegation, including Sir John Bampfield, were to organise provisions, munitions and surgeons for employment by parliament's compromised forces.[1]

A second standoff at Turnham Green that same day, 13 November, would help to restore a sense of optimism in the House of Commons, which until then had been steadily evaporating. Here, King Charles's irrepressible desire to bear down on London was thwarted when a 24,000-strong force led by the Earl of Essex prevented him from marching any closer to the capital, thus forcing him to retreat towards Oatlands Palace in Surrey. Simonds's brother-in-law, William Elliot, though no fan of the royalists as a Puritan gentleman and supporter of parliament, believed it his responsibility to greet the defeated king and his nephew during their short stay at the royal residence. The encounter was relayed to D'Ewes via a letter dated early December, in which Elliot also revealed that he had lately come across a familiar figure from both their pasts. 'My brother, Lieutenant Colonel D'Ewes, was well on Tuesday last, and is quartered at Reading, where he was visited by one you know,' he wrote, confirming that Richard was alive and well.[2] Because the war had now become so very uncivil, any concrete news of his royalist younger brother was surely considered good news by Simonds, who had not allowed their differences in political opinion to wholly divide them as brothers.

One more individual from D'Ewes's rather crowded personal history, Bulstrode Whitelocke, who, like Simonds, had attended the Middle Temple in the 1620s, would be a direct victim of soldierly violence early in November 1642. Prince Rupert pillaging his way to Henley-on-Thames as part of the king's aforementioned advance on London, Whitelocke's country seat, Fawley Court, was identified by the military leader as a target for requisition, being the mansion of a repugnant parliamentarian. Its occupants were well aware of the horrors bound to come their way when Rupert's men arrived at the property. Consequently, Whitelocke's children were swept away from the house by a concerned tenant, to be passed off as his own grandchildren; valuables and personal treasures were taken and hidden where they could not be found; and anything metal that might be melted down and employed by the enemy was thrown into the moat, all before the royalist Byron brothers, Sir John and Sir Thomas, showed up at Fawley with their military orders.

Though the honourable Byrons themselves were willing to show restraint at the last minute, the mob of common soldiers accompanying them had other ideas. The once-proud house was utterly ransacked. There was not an ounce of respect shown for Whitelocke's personal possessions as the royalist invaders pulled down curtains, emptied mattresses of their feathers, smashed apart items of furniture, kicked down fences, burnt books, and slaughtered most of the deer grazing in Fawley's park. There was even littler concern shown for modesty. William Cooke, the tenant who had possessed the quick thinking to take Bulstrode's children off the property to safety, could not believe his eyes when, hobbling around the estate trying to put an end to the ruckus, he caught some of the king's men behaving inappropriately with members of the opposite sex.[3]

Simonds returned to the House of Commons on 19 November, immediately noticing that, whereas before there had been a determination to promote conflict, there was now a greater inclination towards reaching a peaceful settlement with the king. A better update there could not have been: for the knight was wrongly told that day that Richard, his brother, had been slain at Edgehill. Fined £10 by the Middle Temple on 25 November for 'not reading' (he no doubt had more pressing matters to attend to that morning), on 28 November, D'Ewes decided to write to Sir John Potts to convey his dismay that 'you begin already in Norfolk to send for commanders', with the baronet appreciating that 'the face of things begin to look after an hostile manner amongst you'. Three days later, on 1 December, Simonds's older sister, Johanne, felt a similar need to contact her brother to relate to him that her dear husband, Sir William Elliot of Busbridge, had made himself ill worrying about the present troubles. The gentlewoman also hoped that D'Ewes and his new wife might join them for Christmas in Surrey that year, owing to the fact that it was sure to be a very subdued festive season in the war-torn country generally.[4]

On 25 November, the Middle Temple, where Simonds and his brother were now but notorious ghosts, had decreed that its own Christmas was to be a substantially stripped-back affair over 1642-3, 'without any music, gaming, public noise, or show, whereby company may be drawn into the House'. These measures, the

Temple parliament had specifically noted, were 'in respect of the danger and troublesomeness of the times'.[5] Both phenomena were present in equal measure in Winchester in mid-December, upon a band of parliamentarian soldiers commanded by Sir William Waller breaching the city's defences and coarsely relieving the royalist leader Lord Grandison of his post there. Heavily biased towards the king's cause, *Mercurius Rusticus* detailed the ensuing violence directed towards Winchester Cathedral as follows:

> The doors being open as if they meant to invade God himself, as well as His profession, they enter the church with colours flying, their drums beating, their matches fired, and that all might have their part in so horrid an attempt, some of their troops of horse also accompanied them in their march, and rode up through the body of the church and quire, until they came to the altar; there they begin their work, they rudely plucked down the table, and break the rail, and afterwards carrying it to an alehouse, they set it on fire, and in that fire burnt the books of Common Prayer, and all the singing books belonging to the quire; they throw down the organ, and break the stones of the Old and New Testament, curiously cut out in carved work, beautified with colours, and set round about the top of the stalls of the quire; from hence they turn to the monuments of the dead, some they utterly demolish, others they deface.[6]

To the unquestionable abhorrence of D'Ewes, the soldiers then purportedly proceeded to yank up the bones of the deceased persons whose memorials they had shattered, throwing them across the floor with bloodthirsty delight.

And so the First English Civil War kept on going. On 20 December, in the shadow of Christmas Day, Simonds was routinely dispatched to the House of Lords, in order that a motion to raise further 'dragooners' in Cambridge might be passed by them.[7]

Chapter 21

RICHARD'S FAREWELL

ELIZABETH POLEY, SIMONDS'S younger sister, wrote in 1643 of the marked anguish felt by members of the Suffolk gentry affected by the civil war. Many feared that they would never see their loved ones again, with husbands, sons and servants all mourned for even before any information on their current whereabouts had been established. One woman, Elizabeth indicated, had drowned herself out of dread that she would never be reunited with her relations.[1]

Tidings like these were exactly why D'Ewes himself categorically opposed, in February 1643, the 'preposterous' proposition put forward by John Pym and others in the House of Commons to have the armies touring England disbanded before any kind of a treaty was contemplated.[2] Simonds knew that a disbandment without a settlement in place first would be nigh on impossible to achieve in the present climate; thus, to take this course of action was in effect to render peace itself an impossibility, and in turn to allow the acute suffering of families, noted by Elizabeth, to continue indefinitely.

Indeed, the prevention of peace would also have various consequences in terms of D'Ewes's personal life. His tenants would continue to blame the war for their rent arrears, as John Bunn did in March, the man claiming that 'we have no trading but at poor rates'; his beloved antiquarian studies would be further heaped on the back burner, though records suggest that Simonds was defiantly paying professionals to do work for him by the summer of 1643; and any hopes of reconciling with his brother, Richard, would be more or less scuppered.[3]

Sadly, this last consideration was to become an irrelevance two months later. First receiving word that one John Bewdith of Chardstock had 'entered upon certain lands' of his in Dorset, which was irksome enough given everything that was going on, Simonds then learned a terrible truth around 21 April: his little brother, Lieutenant Colonel D'Ewes, had been killed. The location of Richard's death was Reading, where the courageous lieutenant colonel had been taking part in a bloody siege orchestrated by the Earl of Essex and his forces, who were in the process of hacking a route through Berkshire and Oxfordshire to reach the royalist headquarters at Oxford. Fighting for the king until the very end, 27-year-old D'Ewes had originally been wounded on 18 April, when he had been hit in his left thigh by a hurtling cannon ball. Taken to a surgeon to have the gaping puncture dressed, he had then perished following a fever brought on by the wound becoming infected.[4]

Richard had already been buried in Reading Minster by the time his brother discovered that he had passed away in service. One of his coffin bearers had been Nathaniel Moyle, a soldier in Sir Thomas Lunsford's regiment.[5] In later years, the lieutenant colonel's demise would not be overlooked by those contemporaries chronicling the great events of the First English Civil War, which just about spared him the obscurity that ultimately befell the vast majority of the conflict's combatants. Edward Hyde noted in his famous *History of the Rebellion*, concerning a particular moment during the siege of Reading, that:

> The approaches advanced very fast, the ground being in all places as fit for that work as could be, and the town lying so low, that they had many batteries, from whence they shot their cannon into the town and upon their line at a near distance, but without any considerable execution; there being fewer lost by that service than will be believed, and but one man of note, Lieutenant-Colonel D'Ewes, a young man of notable courage and vivacity, who had his leg shot off by a cannon bullet, of which he speedily and very cheerfully died.[6]

'Cheerfully', we must assume in this case, meant 'religiously' and 'willingly', which is not hard to believe when one contemplates the devout upbringing Richard had received at the hands of Paul D'Ewes, whom he had now joined in God's eternal mansions.

The rough-and-ready nature of the siege of Reading in April 1643 cannot be understated. An officer in Essex's army, Sir Samuel Luke, reported that the parliamentarian offensive began on 15 April with shooting on both sides, followed by a prolonged, cacophonous 'battering' of the town by the earl's men, and then, to fittingly round off the first days of the siege on 18 April, an explosion in parliament's ranks that killed as many as four soldiers, caused by several barrels of gunpowder being set alight by enemy fire. Rousing news reached Essex's encampments around Reading on 19 April that the royalist commander Sir Anthony Aston had either been mortally wounded or shot in the neck, although this intelligence turned out to be false. In reality, when a cannonball had ripped through the roof above him, Aston had been hit squarely on the head by a falling tile, sinking him 'almost to the ground before Colonel Lunsford and another officer caught him by both arms, held him up, brought him into the guard-house, [and] put him into this chair'. 'My head's whole, I thank God,' Aston had quipped, before lying back speechless.[7]

With the situation having grown desperate inside Reading's walls by 25 April – two men from the town had insisted on 23 April that most civilians were now being forced to eat horse flesh to prevent them from starving – a white flag was displayed by the king's forces to bring a merciful end to the siege. Articles of surrender were subsequently agreed on, and the hostilities paused. 'In the interim,' Sir Samuel Luke continued in his diary, 'upon Cawsham hill, unexpected to us, came His Majesty's forces, under the command of General Ruven and Prince Rupert, consisting of about 40 colours of horse, and nine regiments of foot, with ordnance and other ammunition'. Essex's troops managed to beat back this surprise assault, with rumours later implying that 500 of Rupert's men had been wounded severely enough to warrant being tended to in a barn 5 miles away. As for the individual who had surrendered Reading in the first place, Colonel Fielding, he was to be court-martialled by the king for his disgraceful behaviour, after which he 'never recovered the misfortune and blemish of this imputation'.[8]

It was not long before the House of Commons got wind of the passing of Richard D'Ewes. Shaken by recent events, Simonds was still made to publicly answer for his dead brother in Westminster in mid-May, with some 'hot' MPs unequivocally demanding the sequestration of his estate to help with the war effort. It seems that the money given by Simonds at the end of the previous year was now regarded as quite insufficient. The MP for Sudbury, however, was not about to go down without a fight in the chamber, such was his increasing distaste for those parliamentarians who seemed fixed on continuing the conflict that had brought utter ruin to England. Stating for the record that he was 'newly clad with a sad and mournful habit', Simonds then argued that, because Richard had died in his own bed, he had technically not perished in the service of the king. Furthermore, he deftly informed the members that 'if you will take his property from me by force and violence, so you may deprive me also of the rest of my estate'. Remarkably, this counterattack seemed to persuade the Speaker of the House that no more should be said on the matter – a lucky escape indeed for the baronet of Stowlangtoft, had one Gurdon not afterwards shrieked that he still considered Lieutenant Colonel D'Ewes 'a traitor to the parliament'.[9] The outburst left Mr Speaker with no choice but to refer the business to the sequestration committee after all, where Simonds played its members once more until the controversy was dropped entirely.

What made the saga pointless from the very beginning was the pitiful amount of 'ready' money Richard had actually had to his name when he had died in Reading: no more than 15 shillings, according to Simonds. The rest of his fortune – totalling perhaps £4,000 or £5,000 – had been spent on travelling the continent long ago. Such a disappointing deficiency in Lieutenant Colonel D'Ewes's wealth was somewhat countered in the young man's last will and testament, which had originally been drawn up in August 1640 in preparation for his involvement in the Second Bishops' War, before being added to in the lead-up to his death. Here, there were to be found riches aplenty, manifesting both as bequests of capital and as touching inferences of love and loyalty. Richard desired that his surgeon, Captain Mollais, receive £20; his 'two men', Robert Goulsborough and Luke Jones, £4 each; his 'other servant', Paul Man, 40 shillings; five more servants, 40 shillings each; his lieutenant in the field, Lionel Watson, his 'best horse and saddle'; his 'ancient' servant, Richard Willis, 'the next horse and saddle'; and his regiment's chaplain, Doctor Johnes, a further £10. The multiple references Richard made to Simonds in his will, meanwhile, which read affectionately in places, show a fondness between the brothers that had never truly gone away. 'Dear brother,' the young colonel finished, dictating from his deathbed, 'I pray fail not to see these legacies performed, it is the last desire of your loving brother Richard D'Ewes.'[10]

Within the immediate family, Richard's memory would live on, despite the unpalatable decisions he had made in the final years of his short life. As late as the 1660s, William Poley of Boxted Hall, Suffolk, included the following in his own will:

> ...my loving wife, to whom I give the same diamond ring I had in legacies from her brother Richard D'Ewes, esquire, to preserve the memory of us both.[11]

Chapter 22

'THESE MISERABLE CALAMITIES AND CIVIL WARS OF ENGLAND'

WITH RICHARD D'EWES becoming just one of thousands of war dead, the conflict with no end raged on.

At Wardour Castle in Wiltshire, parliamentarian forces led by Sir Edward Hungerford arrived to commandeer the property from the royalist Arundells on 2 May 1643, in yet another provocative act. Lady Blanche Arundell refusing to give up her beloved home, having been left to face the castle's attackers alone in the absence of her husband, Hungerford ordered that it be besieged until she yielded. While there was little damage done to the place initially, save for the destruction of a 'chimney-piece, by a shot entering at a window', a week's worth of hard sieging saw the 'roundhead' commander resort to blowing up the castle walls with gunpowder to bring the stalemate to a close. 'The threatening of the besiegers to spring the other mine, and then to storm it, if it was not surrendered before an hourglass, which they had turned up, was run out, so terrified the ladies therein, whereof there was a great number, that they agreed to surrender it,' Colonel Ludlow's memoirs describe.[1]

There were similar stories of heroism and strife almost everywhere in England, though, naturally, not within the sheltered halls of Westminster. On 13 May, the business of the day in the House of Commons included the reading out of an ordinance for 'calling an Assembly of Divines', which merely served to confirm most MPs' preference for theoretical discussion and debate over muddy battlefields and besieged mansions.[2] The assembly in question would later grow into the famous Westminster Assembly of Divines, commissioned by parliament in the summer of 1643 to re-evaluate the structure and precise creed of the Church of England, the ambiguities of which were viewed, even then, as a primary cause of the war. King Charles officially forbade attendance of the great synod on the grounds of its unlawfulness; regardless, many of his discontented subjects came to recognise the potential benefits of throwing their hats in the ring where such an initiative was concerned. At its height, the assembly consisted of thirty men from parliament – twenty from the Commons, and a further ten from the Lords – and roughly 120 members of the clergy.

For the time being in May 1643, members of the Commons were in agreement that there were other ways of dealing with the religious problem. At the end of the month, Simonds recorded in his parliamentary journal that preliminary discussions were under way in the House to have all Catholics fighting for the king denounced as traitors, including, rather astoundingly, Queen Henrietta Maria herself. However extreme, there seemed to be no stopping this particular train of thought from developing once it had been introduced into the collective psyche of the House of Commons by MP Henry Darley. A decision was soon reached, through formal means, that the papist queen should obviously be impeached for her role in providing her husband with arms and soldiers. The baton was therefore handed over to a committee on 24 May, which included D'Ewes and Pym, to prepare an impeachment of high treason against her.[3]

An additional, though somewhat less radical, ecclesiastical fortification came in June 1643, with the passing of John Pym's profound 'Vow and Covenant'. Ostensibly deemed necessary because of a recent plot dreamt up by Edmund Waller to take London for the king, the covenant demanded of anybody who took it that they communicate their conviction that parliament continued to act, among other reasons, 'for the defence of the true Protestant Religion'. Simonds himself 'covenanted' on 6 June, before publicly criticising parliament's military tactics at the end of the month, specifically those of the Earl of Essex. D'Ewes believed that the man had squandered far too much time in the wake of Reading's surrender in April, which had allowed the king's dispersed, near-mutinous forces to regroup and rebuild, and thus go on to secure a victory at Chalgrove Field on 18 June. The baronet, pessimistic and suspicious as he was, suspected that there might be ulterior motives behind such a strategy. 'It is probable,' he wrote, 'that most of the commanders in the said earl's army desired not an end of the war, but a continuance thereof, receiving great and continual pay thereby; so as in the issue the commonwealth must of necessity be exhausted and destroyed by exactions, oppressions, and payments, besides the plundering and other violences of the armies.'[4]

Even so, Simonds remained aware that there was an enemy to bring to heel in 1643. Reacting to news delivered to the Commons, at the end of June, of an attempted uprising in Scotland supported by a Catholic army from Ireland, he commented:

> The discovery of this plot... did more work upon most men than anything that had happened during these miserable calamities and civil wars of England, because it seemed now that there was a fixed resolution in the Popish party utterly to extirpate the true Protestant religion in England, Scotland, and Ireland.[5]

D'Ewes was usually more than willing to pay attention when it came to matters of religion, and, further, to act in his capacity as a member of the Long Parliament if necessary. This even extended – within reason – to stepping in to help out Protestant ministers who found themselves in trouble, including the obstinate Richard Danford, sometime parson of Stowlangtoft, who wrote to Simonds in July 1643 to complain about the abuse he was receiving from a parliamentary committee operating in Suffolk.[6]

The month of July saw many of the men who had battled alongside Richard D'Ewes in Reading forming those regiments of Prince Rupert tasked with taking Bristol, which had been maintained until then by a parliamentary garrison. The royalists began the assignment on 24 July, in the following manner:

> Thus have you all our Tertias lodged at their designed posts, where they were to fall on afterwards, where from this time forward they were incessantly plied with great shot, case-shot, prick-shot, iron drugs, slugs, or anything, from all the works and along the curtain, with all which we received but little harm, our men as cheerfully repaying them again with leaden courtesies. Night coming on, the enemy lay very quiet till about midnight, at which time, upon a signal of two cannons, shot off from my Lord Grandison's quarters, those in the work by Prior's fort were roused by a hot alarm. The enemies answered it with case-shot as well as muskets, for they feared a storm presently. It was a beautiful piece of danger, to see so many fires incessantly in the dark, from the pieces on both sides, for a whole hour together.[7]

In fact, this was considered by royalist leaders to be an altogether soft beginning to proceedings. On 25 July, a council of war held in the vicinity of Bristol's walls, attended by Princes Rupert and Maurice, agreed that it would be best to henceforth 'assault' the city, instead of merely 'approaching' it.[8]

The ensuing offensive, commencing on 26 July 1643, was one of great fury and energy. Lord Grandison's men, some 250 of them in total, charged towards a double ravelin and threw nine grenades into its depths in an attempt to break through the enemy's defences. When this failed to have the desired effect, the commander set his sights on 'Prior's fort' itself, ordering his soldiers to wade across the ditch surrounding the structure and scale its walls using ladders. Yet, upon reaching the site, it was discovered that there *were* no ladders, and so the royalist troops were forced to retreat again. Later returning to the ditch, where some parliamentarian men had begun to cautiously descend the fort's walls to meet their attackers head-on, Lord Grandison was shot in the leg, and Colonel John Owen, Welshman and passionate supporter of King Charles, wounded in the face.

Fellow royalist Colonel Henry Wentworth, meanwhile, had better luck during his own furious charge on the city. The commander's forces quickly broke into a key area of ground between the forts of Brandon Hill and Windmill Hill, from which position, protected by the lowness of the terrain, they were able to 'fling down the work with their hands, halberds, and partisans, as they could, to let in their fellows'. This success was made decidedly more theatrical by the flickering form of Lieutenant Colonel Edward Littleton on horseback, who rode up and down 'the inside of the line' with a flaming pike clutched in his fist, clearing the way of parliament's defenders.[9]

Realising that Prince Rupert and his army had penetrated the city walls and were now marching towards Bristol Cathedral, parliamentarians sheltering in houses along the route proceeded to fire down on their foes from open windows. One of these shots hit the bar on Lieutenant Colonel Thelwell's headpiece, bounced off it, and drove itself into the arm of a nearby captain. Bullets raining down from commandeered buildings similarly impeded Colonel Bellasis and Sir Arthur Aston's advance on Frome Gate, which was on the urban river of the same name. The fight here 'grew hard' in the face of Bristolian resistance, with Colonel Henry Lunsford being shot through the heart and killed instantly, and Colonel Bellasis likewise receiving a nasty wound to the forehead.[10] Nevertheless, Bristol had soon been taken by the cavaliers, leaving the man who had lost it, Colonel Nathaniel Fiennes, to answer for his perceived incompetence at a parliamentary court martial.

The court martial, when it occurred shortly afterwards, unearthed further disturbing details pertaining to the storming of Bristol, none of which were particularly successful in painting Fiennes in a valiant light. Reports gathered from the event in July even spoke of civilians stepping up to defend the city where soldiers, terrified of losing their lives, had shrunk away: of women 'stopping up' Frome Gate with mounds of earth and sacks of wool to prevent the royalists from gaining entry, for instance, and children offering to stand in the way of cannons. As for the actions of the humiliated colonel himself, it was determined that he had gone against the wishes of his regiments by surrendering Bristol so willingly, which had, at the time, provoked many a man to holler angrily that 'they would never serve the Parliament more'. Therefore, Fiennes was to be dismissed at once from the army as a coward (a decision D'Ewes was inclined to agree with), though his life was, mercifully, to be spared.[11]

Simonds, now firmly set on the idea that the present conflict had to be stopped using any reasonable means, again urged the Commons in Westminster to find a route towards a peaceful settlement in July. Once again, however, he was to be let down by his fellow members of parliament, a few of whom appear to have deliberately derailed, in early August, certain 'propositions the Lords' House was… preparing to be sent to His Majesty for adding [*sic*] of peace to his kingdom' – namely by tracking down the Earl of Essex and persuading him that the war must continue. These proposals for a settlement were formally rejected by the Commons on 7 August, though narrowly, by a majority of seven votes.[12]

The wilful thwarting of peace by MPs such as John Pym angered not only the likes of Simonds D'Ewes within the House of Commons, but also run-of-the-mill Londoners outside of it. Following parliament's vote against pursuing a settlement with Charles I, a group of agitated women wearing white ribbons in their hats appeared in the streets of Westminster to seek an end to the war, demanding that Pym and others show themselves so that they might be thrown into the Thames. To ensure that someone – anyone – would listen to their grievances, they fell to banging on the Commons door for an entire hour, before clashing with the guards who had been sent to disperse them. The women's subsequent harsh treatment at the hands of William Waller's horsemen was noted by Simonds in his parliamentary journal:

> No man can excuse the indiscreet violence of these women, but the remedy used against them by the procurement of John Pym

and some others, who were enemies to all kind of peace, was most cruel and barbarous; for, not content to have them suppressed by the ordinary foot guard, which had been sufficient, there were divers horsemen called down, who hunted the said women up and down the back Palace Yard, and wounded them with their swords and pistols with no less inhumanity than if they had been brute beasts, of which wounds some of the poor women afterwards died; and one of those horsemen, being a profane fellow, and bearing an old grudge to a religious honest man, named John Norman, who sold spectacles without Westminster Hall gate on the east side thereof, did shoot his daughter to death as she was peaceably going upon an errand, for which wilful murder the said father could never to this day procure justice to be done upon the malefactor.[13]

It would seem that the patience of the 'hot' MPs in particular was now wearing perilously thin when it came to being ordered about by people who possessed no authority over them.

Almost two months later, the Speaker of the House received a letter whose general content should have been familiar to him by this point in the war. Composed by one Mr Baldwyn, secretary to the Earl of Essex, it told of a 'fight on Wednesday last at Newbury'. This was the First Battle of Newbury, fought on 20 September 1643 in Berkshire between Essex's regiments and those of Prince Rupert, the latter of whom had been chasing his enemy eastwards in the direction of London from Gloucester. While neither side would walk away indisputably victorious from the smouldering, corpse-ridden battlefield, the Commons felt encouraged enough by Baldwyn's dispatch to organise the sending of a committee to Newbury to congratulate Essex on 'the great service done' to parliament. The House likewise wished to reassure the earl that it was doing everything it could to 'send additional forces for the prosecution of this opportunity, to the perfecting of the work'.[14]

The realities of the battle for anybody taking part in it on that late summer day were described by a parliamentarian soldier to his friend in London. The two sides engaging within clear sight of King Charles, still reeling from the collapse of the recent siege at Gloucester, and Queen Henrietta, facing charges of treason from her own subjects, the resultant fight was reported to have been 'long and terrible', lasting from the morning of 20 September until the early hours of the next day. 'Many men were killed on both sides, but God be praised wee won the field of them, and beat them into the Towne,' the roundhead wrote in his letter. He had been devasted by the state of the battlefield on 21 September, upon which had lain at least 500 bodies (locals had informed him that '60 cart loads of dead and wounded men' had already been removed before his inspection).[15] The man, furthermore, reflected that he had never heard so many feeble voices calling out for a surgeon in unison.

When 'hot tears' leaked from Simonds's own eyes in the Commons on 25 September, it was not in response to the terrible number of casualties at Newbury, but rather out of a hope that thousands more lives might yet be spared. For it was on this day that an important letter was received from the General Assembly in Scotland confirming its acceptance of the Solemn League and Covenant, and thus commending it to the parliament in Westminster for implementation. The game-changing piece of legislation had been passed by both the Commons and the Lords a week earlier, on 18 September. In effect, the covenant represented a mutually beneficial agreement between England and Scotland, both of whom had urgent needs at the close of 1643 that could not be fulfilled autonomously. Under its terms, Scotland would be willing to part with some 20,000 men for the English parliament's cause south of the border, in exchange for the English parliament agreeing to oversee national church reforms that would better accommodate Scottish Presbyterianism.[16] Indeed, such an arrangement would prove crucial in turning around the fortunes of the flagging parliament side in England; hence, Simonds, along with the rest, took the covenant submissively on 25 September within St Margaret's church, Westminster.

Where religion specifically from the point of view of the English was concerned, targeting traitorous Catholics remained a top priority into October, on top of the business of the Westminster Assembly of Divines. D'Ewes himself, for example, was given a warrant on 20 October to inspect the property of a suspected papist in London, one Morgan, though, surprisingly, he was urged to show respect and civility towards the Duke of Gelderland, who currently resided there. Perhaps the duke's links to a Dutch region that featured prominently in Simonds's own ancestral line made the undertaking all the easier. In any case, the baronet would have no qualms about the next task assigned to him on 2 November, which involved perusing 'all such books and manuscripts, records, and other monuments of antiquity, as have been, or shall be, sequestered', and ensuring that none of them were 'sold, or any way embezzled or defaced'.[17] This kind of work was made for a diehard antiquary.

In a development that was distressing for some and distinctly gratifying for others, including D'Ewes, anti-pacifist and political grandee John Pym died of cancer on 8 December. His reign in the Commons ended quietly and stoically by all accounts, with an 'evenness of spirit which he had in the time of his health'. Curiously enough, some of his last words were supposedly given over to praying for the king and his heirs, as well as for 'the parliament and the public cause'.[18] The MP's state funeral took place on 15 December in the capital, his corpse carried to Westminster Abbey from Derby House on the shoulders of ten of his greatest allies in politics, including Denzil Holles, Oliver St John, Gilbert Gerard and Arthur Haselrig, all of whom were dressed in sombre mourning.

Countless other members from both Houses of Parliament, similarly garbed in black, were also in attendance to see Pym safely into the ground.

Chapter 23

MARSTON MOOR

THE CLOSE OF 1643 had seen Simonds turn 41 years old.

Clearly, he was no longer a young man in his prime upon the arrival of 1644, as he had been in the 1620s and even 1630s. This fact was probably increasingly obvious to the seasoned MP now that the civil war had begun to take its toll on him as well, with D'Ewes having revealed miserably to the Commons in December that he had only spent eight days in Suffolk over the preceding three years.[1] Whether such a claim was quite true is open to speculation. Nonetheless, there remained a genuine willingness within the baronet of Stowlangtoft in the first months of the new year – a steady fire of sorts, one might argue – that was not about to be extinguished while there was still work to be done for the good of the nation.

With covenanter soldiers from Scotland now pouring into the north of the country as per the stipulations of the Solemn League and Covenant, parliament set about replacing the Committee for Safety with a new, inclusive body in February 1644, which was to be referred to as the Committee of Both Kingdoms. Closely following this great business was more good news received in the House of Commons from the Elector Palatine, who wished to communicate, among other things, 'a good affection to this kingdom, and to the cause'.[2] D'Ewes was subsequently selected to be a part of the committee tasked with considering the prince's message, which, no doubt, he agreed to with a sense of characteristic duty. Surely by now, Simonds's meeting with the Elector Palatine in Newmarket in February 1636 had come to feel like little more than a dream from a past life, as opposed to a real event that had taken place only eight years previously.

The blurred lines between fact and fiction were ever-present at the beginning of 1644, with D'Ewes himself accused of being somewhere that he was not in the first months of the year. 'Sir Symond D'Euce appearing in the Parliament House in Westminster upon Friday, was here at the Oxford, riding all night, upon Saturday morning,' it was asserted anonymously upon the opening of the Oxford Parliament summoned by King Charles, which had attracted a substantial number of MPs from London. This was not true in the slightest, as the reporter himself would concede later in his correspondence. 'The news of Sir Symon D'Euce is nothing for there is no such man in Oxford,' he wrote.[3]

The need for immediate and effective strategic action by parliament was once again highlighted midway through March, when awful reports surfaced that, after taking Hopton Castle in Shropshire from his roundhead enemies, the royalist Sir Michael Woodhouse had ordered the cutting of the defenders' throats in a 'cellar unfinished, wherein was stinking water, the house being on fire over them'.

Simonds's thoughts were on religion at the end of April, through his involvement in a committee created to discuss 'taking away, and demolishing all superstitions and illegal matters in the worship of God', but they were in all likelihood refocused on such military intelligences on 27 May, upon the Commons' receipt of a letter from York.[4] The sender was Sir Thomas Fairfax, a distinguished parliamentary commander, who had written to ask for money and arms to reinforce the siege that had unfolded around the city. On this occasion, it was the parliamentarians doing the sieging, with the crucial aid of the Scottish covenanter army, which had now marched down from the border to honour Scotland's side of the Solemn League and Covenant.

The siege of York in 1644 was arguably not as devastating as others across England had been, or would be, but its occurrence certainly let the city know that it had been dragged back into the war after a period of relative calm. One of the besiegers wrote the following of his experiences:

> Yesternight, being June the fifth, they have caused a work to be raised for a battery upon a hill near Walmgate, where there are four pieces of battery already planted, that have played all this afternoon upon the castle, tower, and town: and they from the town have sent us at least 100 bullets from several platforms in the town, but they have done us very little hurt... But we are getting more pieces up to our new work, which we know hath already put them into a very great fear, for this day they have fired most part of the suburbs, and drawn their people into the town; our men fall into the suburbs, and beat them in when they sally out either to fire houses or fetch in goods; but whilst they skirmish, the fire consumes the houses, they will not suffer our men to quench it, for if the houses could have been saved, they would have been a great shelter for our men in their approaches. And the suburb without Bootham, where there were many fair houses, being fired, the Earl of Manchester's men nevertheless entered, and beat in the enemy this morning, and have saved much of the houses from the fire, and do gallery through them close to the walls.[5]

Ten or so days later, an explosion rocked York when a mine was sprung beneath St Mary's tower by the Earl of Manchester, causing huge slabs of rock to tumble outwards and open up a gap in its defences. This rendered parliament's access to the city instantaneously easier. 'Some at the breach, and some with ladders, got up, and entered to the number of 500,' Sir Henry Slingsby of the royalist garrison there recalled. 'Sir Philip Byron, that had the guard of that place, was unfortunately killed as he opened the doors into the bowling green, where the enemy had gotten.'[6]

Parliament would learn of the outcome of the siege in early July. Following Prince Rupert of the Rhine's famous liberation of York at the end of June, an epic battle had been fought on a lonely piece of Yorkshire ground known as Marston Moor, a few miles outside of the city. The largest engagement of the civil war by far, incorporating parliamentarian, royalist and covenanter armies, there had been perhaps 46,000 men involved in the historic confrontation. On the parliamentarian and covenanter side, proceedings had been overseen, among others, by Sir Thomas Fairfax and Oliver Cromwell; as for the royalist regiments, these men had been guided by the likes of Prince Rupert and William Cavendish, Marquess of Newcastle, who had been acting as leader of the York garrison. When the business of fighting had concluded and the weapons of all parties laid down, parliament had found itself the clear victor of the battle, in what would transpire to be a huge blow to the already haemorrhaging royalist cause in the north.[7]

Thus, parliamentary members felt the need to celebrate in London on 18 July in response to the favourable update they had been given. 'The acknowledgement, oblation, and due thanks to God for his mercy and goodness to us,' a parliamentary newspaper read, 'was in every parish church and chapel within the jurisdiction and power of the Parliament humbly offered; the minister of every such parish that day serving the cure relating some certainties... of the undoubted victory.' That afternoon, meanwhile, after a service had been delivered in the presence of MPs by Scottish preacher Alexander Henderson, cannon fire rent the air 'from every fort about the cities of London and Westminster', complementing 'one of the colours won and brought from the enemy' that had tauntingly been displayed atop St Paul's steeple.[8] It appeared that inviting the Scots to join the war had been one of the best decisions the Commons and Lords had made since 1642.

D'Ewes and the rest of the Commons, much like in the immediate aftermath of Edgehill some years earlier, were without question offered a doctored version of the events of the Battle of Marston Moor on 2 July. Cromwell's clean, vainglorious letter of 5 July to Colonel Valentine Walton was probably typical of the general account that those in Simonds's position in Westminster were acquainted with (though, of course, the MP for Sudbury and many others around him knew better):

> It's our duty to sympathise in all mercies; and to praise the Lord together in chastisements or trials, that so we may sorrow together. Truly England and the Church of God hath had a great favour from the Lord, in this great Victory given unto us, such as the like never was since this War began. It had all the evidences of an absolute Victory obtained by the Lord's blessing upon the Godly Party principally. We never charged but we routed the enemy. The Left Wing, which I commanded, being our own horse, saving a few Scots in our rear, beat all the Prince's horse. God made them as stubble to our swords. We charged their regiments of foot with our horse, and routed all we charged. The particulars I cannot relate now; but I believe, of 20,000 the Prince hath not 4,000 left. Give glory, all the glory, to God.[9]

So, too, the royalists were guilty of promoting – and also printing – rose-tinted assessments of the battle in the weeks and months after it had been fought, even though they had lost at Marston Moor. Scoutmaster-General Lionel Watson, for instance, recalled:

> We came down the hill in the bravest order, and with the greatest resolution that was ever seen. The Earl of Manchester's foot began the charge against some of the bravest of Newcastle and Rupert's foot, Colonel Frizeall and his dragoons acting their parts admirably, and driving before them the musketeers in the ditch.[10]

It was only natural for both sides to want to harvest only the best moments from the battlefield, and moreover to advertise to the country at large that their army was the superior force of the all-consuming civil war.

Winner or loser, however, the Battle of Marston Moor was no uninterrupted performance of chivalry and military daring. Most soldiers would have been terrified as they ducked and dived their way through the savage fight erupting around them, feverishly praying, when they had a second to spare, that they would somehow avoid being shot in the head or speared with the end of a pike. Indeed, one combatant from the king's forces wrote the most extraordinary account of a particularly hopeless moment on the moor, which involved all sides:

> I could not meet the prince until after the battle was joined; and in fire, smoke, and confusion of the day I knew not for my soul whither to incline. The runaways on both sides were so many, so breathless, so speechless, so full of fears, that I should not have taken them for men but by their motion, which still served them very well, not a man of them being able to give me the least hope where the prince was to be found, both armies being mingled, both horse and foot, no side keeping their own posts. In this terrible distraction did I scour the country; here meeting with a shoal of Scots crying out, 'Wae'us! We're a' undone!' and so full of lamentation and mourning, as if their day of doom had overtaken them, and from which they knew not whither to fly.[11]

Into this scene of utter chaos eventually leapt the Marquess of Newcastle, William Cavendish, who soon spied vast numbers of men running from the field in a state of panic and shock, having apparently ignored the shrieks of their superiors to stand firm and fight.

One disturbing aspect of a civil-war battle that always tended to be kept at arm's length from those not directly involved in the fighting, including parliament, was its resultant sea of dead bodies. Given the sheer volume of troops who had taken part in the decisive engagement on 2 July, Marston Moor's offering was particularly bad. Corpses lay everywhere, and hung limp over everything. These remains did not just consist of deceased humans, but mangled horses, too, and even one confirmed dog: Boye, the beloved poodle of Prince Rupert, which had scampered from its master at the first sign of danger, right at the beginning of the deadly encounter. Worse still were the reports of soldiers who, when inspected by locals preparing to bury them, were found to be 'not altogether dead'.[12]

For soldiers who miraculously survived the violence on the moor, not much better awaited them. Water from wells ran out quickly the first night after the battle, forcing desperately thirsty combatants to drink out of ditches and puddles instead. Food was scarce, too, which meant that most men went hungry, or had to make do with a penny loaf. Any veteran of Marston Moor thinking that the answer to all their problems rested in nearby York, still recovering from the siege of the previous month, was sorely mistaken. When Sir Henry Slingsby presently rode towards the city – incidentally, having lost a nephew and kinsman himself – he was greeted by the sight of a street 'thronged with wounded and lame soldiers; which made a pitiful cry among them'.[13]

CHAPTER 24

THE WRATH OF RELIGION

'ALL RIGHT AND property must cease in a civil war... and we know not what advantage the meaner sort may take to divide the spoils of the rich and noble among them,' Simonds had cautioned in the uncertain days of 1642.[1]

Regrettably, popular plundering was now quite the reality in the anarchical England of 1644. On 5 August, the House of Commons laid the groundwork for a routine exercise in damage control pertaining to an especially brutal instance of pillaging that had taken place in Bolton in May, following Prince Rupert's storming of the parliamentarian town. The event had been so terrible that it was even referred to contemporaneously as the 'Bolton massacre'. Royalist soldiers had allegedly looted on an unprecedented scale upon gaining entry to the place, and when they had run out of things to loot, they had taken to murdering instead. 'At their entrance, before, behinde, to the right, and left, nothing heard, but kill dead, kill dead was the word,' a pamphlet described, 'in the Town killing all before them without any respect, without the Town by their horsemen, pursuing the poore amazed people, killing, stripping, and spoiling all they could meet with, nothing regarding the dolefull cries of women or children.'[2]

The pamphlet, undeniably pro-parliamentarian in its leanings, went on to list specific townspeople whom Rupert's men had personally violated during the plundering. One William Boulton had been 'fetched out of his chamber' and killed in front of his pregnant wife, who had first thrown herself over him in an attempt to save his life. Seventy-two-year-old Katharine Saddon, having no money to donate to the assailants, had been stabbed in the heart with a sword. One Elizabeth Horrocks, witnessing her own husband's murder, had subsequently been bound in ropes and dragged up and down until she had provided the troops with information on where they could locate plate and other valuables. And Alice Greg, minister's widow, had been indecently 'stripped to her smocke' by the royalists, after which she had been provided with 'scarce old rags to cover her nakednesse'.[3]

Westminster knew that the unruly behaviour exhibited by soldiers from both sides of the schism had also extended to mutinous activity by the summer of 1644. On 6 July, Sir William Waller wrote to the Committee of Both Kingdoms to assert that, while parliament's recent victory at Marston Moor was to be commended, there was nonetheless trouble afoot in terms of soldierly discipline. 'The meeting with Major-General Browne, which I thought would have proved an addition of strength to me, has very much weakened me,' he elaborated, 'for my London regiments immediately looked upon his forces as sent to relieve them, and without waiting for further orders are most departed. Yesterday 400 out of one regiment quitted their colours.' Major-General Richard Browne himself had been dealing with worse, however. His men, comprising a mixture of members of the trained bands of both Essex and Hertfordshire, had become so 'mutinous and uncommandable' of late that they had recently gone as far as wounding their commander in the face. Waller understandably took a dim view of such unacceptable conduct. 'Such men are only fit for a gallows here and a hell hereafter,' he declared to the committee.[4]

Where required, Simonds stepped up to the plate in Westminster among these unnerving reports. On around 16 August, he joined a committee instructed to look into the damaging effects of a decision taken by the parliamentary garrison at Hull to drown certain swathes of land for the protection of the town. Then, on 17 August, D'Ewes threw his lot in with another Commons committee tasked with considering the latest round of peace proposals to be dispatched to the king, which, obviously, would have been an easy ask for a moderate. Additionally, in September, the baronet seemed to feel it his duty to send Lord Fairfax, father of Sir Thomas Fairfax, various intelligences to York from London, with the commander in turn writing a letter to his 'friend' to thank him on 27 September. 'I cannot return you anything from hence of moment, we being in a very sad condition for want of monies and clothes for the soldiers; neither am I able, upon their discontent, to act much upon an enemy,' Fairfax relayed.[5]

For Simonds particularly, it was time once again to see to religious business in December. Parson Ambrose Copinger (who had preached Paul D'Ewes's funeral sermon back in 1631) having lately died and left the benefice of Lavenham vacant, there was an ecclesiastical position now up for grabs that D'Ewes – being lord of the manor – was required to fill. One William Gurnill (or Gurnall) was ultimately chosen as the man for the job; 'learned', 'godly' and 'orthodox', the Commons displayed no hesitation in confirming his appointment on 16 December, allowing him to 'continue rector and incumbent of the same church, for and during the term of his natural life'.[6]

On the last day of the year, the theme of faith continued in Simonds's life (though, really, it was ever-present) with the receipt of a petition from George Carter, holder of the livings of Whatfield and Elmsett in Suffolk, who, having been articled against by his parishioners in Elmsett, earnestly craved the help of an individual with local influence and standing. Carter's situation had arisen, in the first place, following the formation of two religious committees in wartime Suffolk, whose main interests lay in hunting down and holding to account 'scandalous ministers' – or, more accurately, members of the clergy who harboured royalist sympathies. 'Noble knight,' the rector began, 'your happy inclination [and] disposition to workes of mercy & charity (whereof I have heretofore had good experience) encourage mee in this tyme of my urgent misery to repayre unto your worshipp for shelter in a storme.'[7] Detailing his plight, he then asked that his petition might be passed on to the Earl of Manchester, who wielded even greater levels of authority than D'Ewes did.

Simonds had already proven his genuine preparedness to assist ministers who had fallen victim to the parliamentary committees in operation in Suffolk in the 1640s, specifically through his dealings with the parson of Stowlangtoft, Richard

Danford. Yet, when it came to the great architect of so many of the country's religious woes, the imprisoned Archbishop William Laud, the MP for Sudbury drew the line. Surrounded by evolving Protestant doctrine wholly foreign to the archbishop, which was, in January 1645, set to be complemented by a Directory for Public Worship, Laud had witnessed his fortunes nosedive in the latter months of 1644. His trial having opened in March 1644, parliament had come to the conclusion by autumn that, if it could not find a legitimate reason for a guilty verdict, it would resort to passing a bill of attainder instead, just like it had done with the Earl of Strafford in 1641. It could then do what it wanted with its prisoner, held for now in the Tower of London. Beforehand, Simonds had been one of those flexing his (probably quite stiff) legal muscles as part of a committee of lawyers that had convened to consider the feasibility of condemning Laud without the need for an attainder.[8]

Inevitability dictated that an attainder bill had been read for the first time on 16 November, had been read again on 22 November, and was read for a third time on 4 January 1645, where it finally received the assent of the House of Lords. Simonds was certainly pleased by the development, but the baronet was no monster. Indeed, when Laud had appeared in parliament in early November to hear the charges that had been brought against him, D'Ewes had admired the fact that the accused had written 'all the while without spectacles reasonable fair, he being about 70 years old' (he had poor eyesight himself). He had likewise noted that Laud had maintained a praiseworthy confidence once the deliverer of the charges, Samuel Browne, had concluded his speech. This Bedfordshire man, arguably unremarkable and lacking in independence of thought, Simonds had been far less impressed by, referring to him in his parliamentary journal afterwards as nothing more or less than 'the solicitor's ape'.[9]

William Laud's attainder read as follows:

> Whereas the knights, citizens, and burgesses of the House of Commons in this present Parliament assembled have, in the name of themselves and of all the Commons of England, impeached William Laud, Archbishop of Canterbury, for endeavouring to subvert the fundamental laws and government of the kingdom of England, and instead thereof to introduce an arbitrary and tyrannical government against law, and to alter and subvert God's true religion by law established in this realm, and instead thereof to set up Popish superstition and idolatry, and to subvert the rights of Parliament and the ancient course of Parliamentary proceedings, and by false and malicious slanders to incense His Majesty against Parliaments. For which the said Archbishop deserves to undergo the pains and forfeitures of high treason, which said offences have been sufficiently proved against the said Archbishop upon his impeachment.[10]

Its content spelled the end for the vilified archbishop and his religious reforms of the 1630s, with the incarcerated man now poised to walk in the footsteps of the Earl of Strafford and meet his doom on Tower Hill. The verdict was to constitute another significant loss for King Charles I, whose tenuous hold over the war was fast slipping.

Laud's date of execution was set for 10 January. The archbishop refused to surrender to fear in his final days at the Tower, choosing to spend his time either in quiet prayer or in preparing his soul for the next world with a chaplain. As one account had it, the night before his beheading, he slept soundly. 'The fatal morning being come,' a pamphlet commented, 'he first applied himself to his private prayers and so continued, till Pennington, and other of their public officers, came to conduct him to the scaffold.' Clinging to his resolute outlook on what was about to happen, Laud climbed the wooden structure erected on Tower Hill calmly, the block having to be cleared of excitable members of the crowd before he could get close to it. 'God's will be done, I am willing to go out of this world; no man can be more willing to send me out of it,' he said, before lowering his neck for the waiting axeman. The archbishop stopped in his tracks, though, upon spying through the gaps in the floorboards yet further swarms of eager spectators, who had gathered beneath the scaffold to get a better view of the execution. 'He called on the officers for some dust to stop them, or to remove the people thence, saying it was no part of his desires, that his blood should fall upon the heads of the people,' the pamphlet continued, ever concerned with portraying its subject favourably. Once they had been cleared, there was nothing left to delay the inevitable.[11]

Laud's head rolled after a single flourish of the axe, sending blood spilling through the floorboards and onto the now-vacant patch of ground below them. His countenance was reported to have been 'fresh and cheerful' that morning, even in the face of death; such an observation might well tally with that made by Simonds, who had previously described the late archbishop as 'a little, low, red-faced man'.[12]

CHAPTER 25

NASEBY

IN 1645, SIMONDS organised for the publication of a work he had written on the suppression of 'heresie and schisme', which sought to recommend ways the Church of England might continue to resist both obstacles in the coming months and years. Entitled *The Primitive Practise*, this was the essay that D'Ewes had originally penned in the late 1630s, mentioned in a previous chapter. 'My many present imployments, both publike and private, did scarce permit mee to supervise it, and to amend it in some few places,' the MP for Sudbury fretted in its opening section, 'which puts mee almost out of all hope ever to transmit to posterity any one of those severall great and more necessary Works I had in part collected and prepared (for the good and benefit of this Church and Kingdome) in the time of my leisure and freedom.'[1]

It goes without saying that Simonds knew plenty about heresy, and even more about schisms, by the start of yet another civil-war year. Schisms in particular were an education that D'Ewes would continue to embark on into 1645, to include a familial matter that concerned his second wife's sister, Lady Anne Aston. Her royalist husband, Sir Thomas Aston, dying in Stafford, the baronet would be required to set aside his political feelings to assist the gentlewoman in receiving a part of his estate for the maintenance of herself and her children, via the Committee for Sequestration in Cheshire. 'She is very exemplary for her goodness and piety,' Simonds stressed to William Brereton, a powerful figure in those parts, 'and deserves as much from parliament as any distressed lady in the country.'[2]

Spurred on by recent successes in the field, but aware that there was still a fair way to go before overall victory could be secured, parliament concentrated on re-evaluating its military set-up in early 1645. On 17 February, one 'Mr Knightly' was sent to the House of Lords to confirm to its members that the Commons had voted in favour of certain amendments to the 'Ordinance concerning the New Model'. This was the beginnings of the New Model Army, a vision of maximum martial efficiency cooked up by the Committee of Both Kingdoms, with particular inputs from Oliver Cromwell and Sir Henry Vane the Younger. The New Model would wipe the slate clean in terms of parliament's existing forces. In place of collections of trained bands commanded by politicians or 'great magnates', which might be bound by local ties, irregularly paid or armed, and hampered by complicated attitudes towards the war, there was instead to be a centralised army controlled directly by the Commons and Lords, which was to be reliably remunerated and equipped, freed from connections with specific regions or localities, and led by full-time, professional soldiers who did not bring political agendas or unhelpful theatrics to the battlefield.[3]

The promise of such an advanced body of soldiers obviously caused great excitement in the House of Commons. 17 February, the day on which the initial agreement was made between the Commons and Lords regarding the New Model, saw the following ordered:

> That no Member do presume to go over the seats, or cross the House, or discourse, or whisper, during the sitting of the House, to the disturbance of the House; or read any printed book in the House; and that such Member, as shall so offend, shall pay 12 pence to the box, for the use of the poor.[4]

On 3 April, an unequivocal move towards the organising of parliament's new, consolidated army was achieved through the passing of the Self-denying Ordinance, which obligated current roundhead commanders-cum-politicians (or -magnates), including the Earls of Essex and Manchester and Sir William Waller, to relinquish their positions with immediate effect to make way for fresh blood.

Sir Thomas Fairfax, uninhibited by direct political associations, and a man who had proven himself at Marston Moor as a worthy soldier, was to be appointed the lord general and commander-in-chief of the emerging New Model. His role would involve directing the movements of around 22,000 men, consisting of ten companies of dragoons, twelve foot regiments and a further eleven horse regiments. Accordingly, in early April, it was to his headquarters in Windsor that all remaining parliamentary commanders and officers were ordered to make their way, the summons being published 'by beat of drum, and sound of trumpet'. Soon, the greater part of the New Model Army had been gathered here for mobilisation. The body's first task, given to it at the close of the month, was to march westwards to Somerset to lift the royalist siege currently crippling Taunton.[5]

Even though the New Model was lauded by MPs on the whole, there nevertheless remained one or two reservations among members of the Commons. Simonds himself reacted cautiously to proposals put forward in May 1645 that the Eastern Association, which included Suffolk, should furnish Fairfax's war machine with an additional horse regiment, declaring to the House that the counties of East Anglia were desperately overburdened as it was. In early June, he equally could not condone parliament's plans to pass a conscription ordinance, which would force men to join the New Model Army whether they wanted to or not – unless they had £10 to spare to buy their way out of service. Of course, most common soldiers did not have any money at all to give away, let alone the princely sum highlighted above. 'The burden would lie upon the poorer sort,' D'Ewes, quite correctly, argued.[6]

Impressment, unfortunately, was passed into law irrespective of Simonds's feelings. One negligible consolation for any conscripted soldier was that the New Model Army was at least a better-structured military entity than anything that had come before it in the First English Civil War, with pains taken to ensure a level of comfort and protection for each combatant. On 21 March, for example, the House of Commons had resolved that 'each common soldier… shall be furnished with a coat, breeches, a shirt, a pair of stockings and shoes, and snapsack, by the several committees of the several counties'. On 29 April, it had further ordered that a thousand 'saddles, bridles, and furniture', a thousand pairs of pistols and holsters, and 500 spare holsters be sent at once to Fairfax in Windsor.[7]

4 June witnessed Simonds taking issue with one more development related to the New Model Army in Westminster. A petition being received by the Commons to have Oliver Cromwell made 'lieutenant general of the horse', which would mean the man presiding over those units of the New Model linked to the Eastern Associations, D'Ewes, along with other moderates, came to the uneasy conclusion that the proposal constituted 'a breach of privilege'. Alas, given Cromwell's instrumental involvement in the New Model's creation and subsequent facilitation, his appointment to the role seemed inevitable. A few days later, Fairfax and 'divers of the chief officers of his army' sealed the deal in writing to parliament from Sherrington to request that their comrade be awarded the post, after which parliament itself voted for the lieutenancy to go to Oliver 'if [Fairfax] think fit'.[8]

D'Ewes, as ever, was concurrently caught up in religious matters at this time. On 30 May, the minister of Elmsett in Suffolk, George Carter, reached out to the distinguished knight and baronet to ask him once again to engage with the Earl of Manchester regarding his dire predicament. 'I doe further desyre your worshipp to move my Lord of Manchester to call for all the examinations of my late wittnesses,' he wrote.[9] Little did Carter know that Sir Simonds's interventions on his behalf would, in the end, amount to absolutey nothing: for, on 23 July 1646, Westminster would go ahead and deprive him of the living of Elmsett.

⟵⟶

The good effects of the New Model Army were indicated to the House of Commons as soon as the evening of 14 June 1645, when the Speaker of the House received word, via seventeenth-century news correspondent John Rushworth, that parliament had secured a monumental victory at Naseby earlier that day.

Sir Thomas Fairfax, who had been at the battle, fleshed out the particulars of the Northamptonshire confrontation in a follow-up message delivered to Mr Speaker on 15 June:

> I thought fit to send this bearer, Mr Boles, who may more particularly inform you, concerning the abundant Goodness of God to this army and the whole kingdom in the late victory obtained at Naseby-Field, the whole body of their foot taken and slain; such a list of the prisoners as could be made up in this short time, I have sent. The horse all quitted the field, and were pursued within three miles of Leicester; their ammunition, ordnance and carriages all taken, amongst which there were two demi-cannons, a whole culverin, and a mortar-piece, besides lesser pieces. We intend to move to Leicester, as soon as we have taken order with our prisoners and wounded men. All that

> I desire is, that the honour of this great, never to be forgotten Mercy, may be given to God in an Extraordinary Day of Thanksgiving.[10]

As with Marston Moor in July 1644, the Lords and Commons needed no encouragement to joyfully celebrate parliament's latest triumph. The Commons initially giving the lucky messenger who had brought them Rushworth's letter the generous sum of £10 (enough to get him out of New-Model conscription if it came to it, no less), both Houses then duly acted on Fairfax's suggestion for a day of public thanksgiving across London. This was to be followed on 27 June by a nationwide observance of the victory.

The New Model Army's performance at the Battle of Naseby was certainly worthy of praise. Made up of roughly 15,000 men, the substantial force easily outnumbered its royalist opponents, who perhaps could boast no more than 10,000 soldiers between them. Both armies first faced each other, tensely and amid swirling fog, on opposing ridges close to Naseby village, before Prince Rupert, at about 10:00 am, broke the ominous stillness that had settled on the moor by charging with his determined cavalry towards an equivalent parliamentary body. While such a daring enterprise succeeded in definitively scattering the said roundhead cavalry, and even culminated in a three-mile chase across the Northamptonshire countryside, it ultimately failed to safeguard the royalist units left exposed on the ridge, whose commanders included the king himself. At the mercy of Cromwell's deadly regiment of horse, the remaining cavalry and infantrymen were battered into near-oblivion. Charles's army was finished.[11]

Again, however, it was not all fearless warriors, their noble steeds, and courageous rushes across moody, provincial moors to gain the upper hand over one's foes. There were uncomfortable aspects of the fight at Naseby that D'Ewes and everybody else in parliament were not readily told about – though nobody in England could be truly ignorant to the realities of war, now that the country was so far into one. 'I saw the field so bestrewed with carcasses of horse and men as was most sad to behold, because [they were] subjects under one government,' a 'gentleman' from Northampton wrote to his friend.[12] Speaking also about the royalist waggons commandeered by parliament, he continued:

> ...there was many of [them] laden with rich plunder, and others with arms and ammunition, about 50 loads of muskets, pikes, powder, match, and bullets, abundance of trunks, which the soldiers soon emptied, as they did the waggons that carried the middle sort of ammunition whores, who were full of money and rich apparel, there being at least 150 of that tribe, the gentiler sort in coaches, whereof I only saw 7 coaches with horses taken stuffed with that commodity, and the common rabble of common vermin on foot, 500 of them at least being taken and kept with a guard, until order was taken to dispose of them and their mates, many of these were Irish women, of cruel countenances, some of them were cut by our soldiers when they took them...[13]

These were the sorts of details that might just do more harm than good to parliament's cause in the long run.

The minister Richard Baxter, who seemed to give such a raw, almost incidental, account of the Battle of Edgehill in 1642, did the same with regard to the immediate aftermath of Naseby in June 1645. 'Naseby being not far from Coventry where I was, and the noise of the victory being loud in our ears,' he recorded, 'and I having two or three that of old had been my intimate friends in Cromwell's army, whom I had not seen of above two years, I was desirous to go see whether they were dead or alive.' This feat he managed to achieve, happily finding his companions very much alive and well, and moreover optimistic about the present condition of the New Model Army. All the same, Baxter was uneasy about the conversations he overheard during his short stay in the parliamentary camp. There was, he recalled, shocking talk of subverting church and state, of altering the constitution even, beyond anything that the minister could have imagined back in Coventry, where 'we were unfeignedly for King and Parliament'. He recognised that he was in the company of some honest men, unquestionably, but Baxter additionally observed among parliament's representatives 'proud, self-conceited, hot-headed sectaries [that] had got into the highest places, and were Cromwell's chief favourites, and by their very heat and activity bore down the rest'.[14] Such men were reminiscent of the activists whom Simonds had also feared for so long in Westminster.

Several days after the Commons had received glad tidings of the Naseby victory, D'Ewes made his feelings plain about a recent parliamentary loss, deeming it to have been wholly unnecessary. The storming of Leicester by Prince Rupert at the end of May 1645, in fact, had caught both Houses of Parliament completely off-guard when it had occurred amid an explosive array of other sieges further south in the country. The episode had been typically brutal, even from the point of view of the royalists themselves. 'All the evening was a general preparation to assault the town, and a little before 12 of the clock in the night this violent storm began, and continued till after one,' Richard Symonds, a soldier fighting for King Charles, noted in his diary.[15] He further relayed some specific details pertaining to the engagement, with no intention of holding back on unpleasant information:

> They set the prince's black colours on the great battery within. Earl of Northampton's horse about one of the clock were let in at the ports, and they scoured the line and town. In the meantime the foot got in and fell to plunder, so that ere day fully open scarce a cottage unplundered... More dead bodies lay just within the line far than without or in the graffe. I told 30 and more at the breach, as many within as without. Every street had some. I believe 200 on both sides were not killed. We lost Colonel St George. Major Bunnington, gentleman pensioner, shot in the eye just as he was on the top of the ladder. About day, about 10 of the enemy got out and escaped by the riverside; were followed.[16]

An account that probably found its way into parliamentary circulation merely confirmed Richard Symonds's comments. It reported that '[the royalists] stormed the town in five several places at once, but the fiercest assault and most desperate service was at the beforementioned breach in the new-work wall, where they came to push of pike, and Colonel St George of the king's side, in a gallantry came up almost to the mouth of a cannon, and was by it shot to pieces'.[17]

Neither Simonds D'Ewes nor any other MP in the Commons could be too glum about Leicester in June 1645. The fruits of parliament's breakthrough win at Naseby continued to settle satisfyingly at each politician's feet as the month progressed, with the House, on 18 June, organising for the thousands of royalist prisoners captured during the battle to be escorted down to London, where they were to be further dealt with by the resident authorities. Passing through St Albans on their way to the capital, a pamphlet informs us that the king's incarcerated men, having been herded into a church for the night to quarter, 'pulled downe the pewes, and did much hurt there, as men set upon mischiefe, as indeede all the broode of them are, most desperately given to wickednesse'.[18]

Once in London, parliament chose to treat its captives fairly, if not a little derisively. Several orders were made in the House of Commons on 25 June concerning the royalist men who had amassed at the artillery grounds in Tothill Fields. Surgeons were to be sent for to dress the injured and tend to the sick, handpicked by the Company of Surgeons; officers guarding the prisoners were to forbid any passers-by or visitors from having 'any intercourse or speech with them'; all Irishmen and parliamentary deserters within the dishevelled ranks of soldiers were to be rooted out and made to face martial law; and, lastly, those detainees left within the artillery grounds were to be forced to listen to periodic sermons delivered by Protestant preachers approved by the Westminster Assembly of Divines.[19]

Meanwhile, the force that was responsible for the royalist prisoners' current confinement, the New Model Army, marched on to further victories. Wiping the floor with the last remaining regiments of the king's disintegrating army, Fairfax and his troops first defeated Lord Goring at the Battle of Langport on 10 July, and then, exactly two months later, successfully stormed a wasted and vulnerable Bristol, leading Prince Rupert to humiliatingly surrender the port city that had been under cavalier control since 1643. Simonds, obviously nowhere near Bristol during these late summer days of 1645, indirectly contributed to any future successes Fairfax might enjoy through his participation in a Commons committee, whose aim was to furnish the lord general with additional units of 500 horse and 500 dragoons respectively.[20]

Chapter 26

1646

SEVERAL PROMINENT FEATURES of D'Ewes's life thus far had quietened as a result of the terrible conflict between king and parliament. The Middle Temple, a place that Simonds had vacated long ago, was certainly not its usual self when the institution's parliament met on 31 October 1645. 'Through the troubles and distractions of the times, by reason of these unnatural civil wars,' it was noted during the sitting, 'there has been no reading in this or any other Inn of Court for three years, so that the number of Benchers is grown very small.'[1]

Something else that had slowed because of the war, as previously mentioned, was the baronet's pursual of all things antiquarian. Yet, this adored hobby of Sir Simonds D'Ewes had far from disappeared altogether. In recent times, the man had effortlessly proven that he remained committed to the intellectual world by developing an intense interest in the work and general presence of Anna Maria Van Schurman, the Dutch painter, scholar and philosopher. He had even written to her in Holland to introduce himself in early 1645, in which (rather forward) letter he had further asked for advice on how best to instil an appetite for learning in his surviving daughters, as well as requesting that Schurman send him some of her exceptional portraits. Anna Maria had not been best pleased by the unsolicited communication she had received from England. Corresponding with one Frédéric Rivet afterwards, the artist had complained, 'a letter from that English baronet arrived; I cannot see how to respond appropriately to him, since it seems neither advisable nor safe to have communication with those I don't know.'[2]

Having still heard nothing back from Schurman by October 1645, Simonds probably believed that that particular ship had well and truly sailed. On 31 October, however, Anna Maria at last composed a response to the 'English baronet' in Suffolk, apologising for the letter's nine-month delay (in a flourish of perfect Latin) and assuring D'Ewes that she had heard all about his aptitude for study and his gentlemanly dignity. Five self-portraits also eventually arrived for the MP and his family. Simonds kept one back for himself, gave his two daughters, Isolda and Cecilia, and wife, Elizabeth, a portrait each to admire, and saved the last 'for a son, who maybe will still be born (if I read the signs correctly)'. Sadly, D'Ewes's youngest daughter from his first marriage, also Elizabeth, had died in June 1645. Succumbing to convulsions at Albury Lodge, the knight wrote of his offspring's passing that 'this sad augury made me afraid that in the end God would take all my daughters from me and not grant me any issue of my second wife'.[3]

Simonds could not afford to spend much of his time inspecting the many culturally significant portraits that he owned. In early November, his parliamentary obligations again took over in Westminster, in the form of yet another miserable committee, which had been assigned the delicate task of discussing how best to pension off those unfortunate servants who had formerly enjoyed employment in the households of King Charles's children. November 1645, it should be noted, also saw D'Ewes suddenly abandon the parliamentary journal that he had kept up since first entering the House of Commons as an MP in November 1640. This the baronet decided to do one day out of sheer, unadulterated exasperation at his fellow parliamentarians, who had lately demonstrated that they were more interested in putting forward proposals for by-elections than restoring peace to the fractured kingdom.

Into the spring of 1646, thankfully, D'Ewes was back in more familiar territory. On 19 March, the House of Lords put his name forward as a worthy candidate to 'settle and regulate the Office and Officers of Arms', which had been abused of late by 'divers persons' who had either assumed coats of arms in error, or, more likely, consciously appropriated them.[4] The gratifying selection was followed by additional good news for parliament as a whole at the end of the month: the very last of King Charles's field armies, commanded by Sir Jacob Astley, had been defeated at Stow-on-the-Wold, Gloucestershire, by Sir William Brereton. Such was the significance of the defeat that Oliver Cromwell and Sir Thomas Fairfax felt justified in processing through Plymouth in Devon to observe the concluding of the war on 25 March, claiming an overall roundhead victory.

Conversely, there was only familial despair and sadness for Simonds in mid-April, upon discovering that his older sister, Johanne Elliot, had died in London. The bereft brother would later write to his nephew, Johanne's eldest son, William, to convey his appreciation for the 'sacred' way the young man continued to keep his dear mother's memory alive, mentioning, at the same time, that he himself was still deeply mourning her loss. D'Ewes also begged for forgiveness that he had not been at his sister's side in her final days, when she undoubtedly would have found most comfort in his company. He cited his wife's welcome pregnancy, and the need to look after his two young daughters, as the primary reason for his absence.[5]

All seventeenth-century men, including Simonds D'Ewes, knew that in the midst of life they were in death. It was a reality that would have been more apparent than ever now that the country had been hauled through a civil war, and one with a notably high fatality rate to boot. Thus, in the spirit of this mantra, the business of living went on in the House of Commons in May 1646. On 6 May, there was a rumbling of approval, and perhaps even restrained cries of relief from the sea of benches in the chamber, when a message was received by the Speaker of the House relating that, in light of his heavy losses and the certain fall of Oxford to Fairfax's besieging troops, the king had handed himself in to the covenanter army at Newark the previous day. Parliament had their man at last. 'The question was propounded, whether it should be desired of the Commissioners of the Parliament of Scotland residing with the Scots army before Newark, and also of the general of the Scots army there, that the person of the king may be disposed of to such place within this kingdom, as the two Houses of Parliament shall appoint,' the Commons journal continued.[6] After some debate, Warwick Castle was chosen as a suitable holding pen for the monarch in the short term.

The day that the burden of war itself was effectively lifted from Simonds's buckling shoulders, another weight of considerable substance disappeared from his private life. The Middle Temple parliament announced at its latest sitting in the capital on 6 May 1646, in business-like fashion, that 'at the request of Sir Simondes D'Ewes... the chamber of his brother, Mr Dewes, deceased, in Elme Court, shall be sold'. The proceeds from the sale, when Richard's debts to the Temple had been paid off, were to go to 'Sir Simondes' himself.[7] It was poignant, some might argue, that the official decision to erase one of Richard D'Ewes's remaining material assets in the country was made at the very moment that the conflict that had prematurely killed him in 1643 – the First English Civil War – drew to a close.

On 23 June, the anxious House of Commons was informed in person by Sir Thomas Fairfax's chaplain, William Dell, that the royalist garrison at Oxford was to submit to parliament's forces, and that therefore the First English Civil War was over. The unassuming bearer of such extraordinary news had appeared quietly at the door of the chamber clutching a letter from the lord general himself, with a copy of the articles that had been drawn up for the city's surrender also on his person, which parliament would need to authorise. Its authorisation duly given, the next day, the royalists capitulated.

Tentative hope for the future now trickling through England like the tributaries of a glittering river, this was surely the opportune time to bring new life into the world, being something that Simonds had desperately desired ever since his marriage to Lady Elizabeth Willoughby in September 1642. As if on cue, sometime before mid-July 1646, a daughter was indeed born to D'Ewes and his wife. She was called Mary, the namesake of Simonds's younger sister, who had married Sir Thomas Bowes of Much Bromley. Records compiled and kept by St Margaret's church, Westminster, indicate that her christening took place within its walls on 7 July, being just a stone's throw from her father's second home, the bustling House of Commons. Though Mary was Elizabeth D'Ewes's first biological child, the Derbyshire-born gentlewoman had by no means behaved aloofly towards her existing stepdaughters during her first years of marriage to Simonds. In fact, if the latter's observations are to be believed, then she had instinctively been the model mother figure to Cecilia, Isolda and, until her death, little Elizabeth.[8]

The month of July, then, was a cautiously happy one for the Suffolk baronet and his rejuvenated family. Of course, nothing lasted long in the volatile England of the 1640s. Soon enough, Simonds found himself cast back into the depths of the nation's misfortunes, receiving the following letter from Conyers Darcy on 30 July:

> Sir, I am got thus far on my journey towards you upon the order for the first of August to present to the House, by way of petition, the miserable condition my Lord and my father are in, being destroyed by the Scots' army, and yet under their power... Sir, I humbly beseech you to advise this bearer, and befriend him, how he may possess the House of their condition, and they may be considered accordingly.[9]

The questionable actions of the covenanter army in England would quickly come to the attention of parliament that summer, predominantly through the Scots' apparent willingness to use the king, whom they still had in their custody, as a bargaining tool to negotiate a pay-out for their involvement in the war. In September 1646, the Lords and Commons finally agreed to part with £400,000 to satisfy their recalcitrant associates, on the proviso that they left the country promptly and handed King Charles over before doing so.

The problem of organised hostilities had providentially gone away by the summer months of 1646, but the issue of what exactly was to be done with the sovereign had not. For moderates like Simonds, arranging a peaceful settlement that would hopefully put to bed the horrific events of the last four years seemed the obvious way forward, as it had always done to those men who proudly made up the peace party in the House of Commons. Accordingly, Charles was sent the basis for a treaty with parliament as early as July, known ambiguously as the Newcastle Propositions, because it was in this city that the monarch was being held by the covenanter army when he received them. The propositions were a long shot, and perhaps asked too much of him, too soon. Several of the points of contention that had caused a rift to develop between the Stuart king and his parliament in the first place appeared once again in the latter's latest list of demands, including the removal of bishops from within the Church of England, the taking of a hard line against Catholic worshippers, and the granting of additional powers to parliament itself. There were also brand-new requests from Westminster that the king could not get on board with. Its wish for the English church to be reformed so that it embraced a Presbyterian core baffled Charles in Newcastle, who deemed the move compromising, incomprehensible in regard to what exactly it sought to achieve, and to the detriment of all in his kingdom.

The king therefore had no intention of agreeing to parliament's terms. On 1 August, he gave an initial, third-person answer to Westminster that was deliberately evasive:

> The Propositions tendered to His Majesty by the commissioners from the Lords and Commons assembled in the parliament of England at Westminster, and the commissioners of the parliament of Scotland... do import so great alterations in government, both in the church and kingdom, as it is very difficult to return a particular and positive answer, before a full debate, wherein these Propositions and the necessary explanations, true sense and reasons thereof, be rightly weighed and understood.[10]

Parliament would vote to abolish episcopacy anyway. As part of the movement, the sale of land owned by bishops was authorised, leading to D'Ewes sitting in a committee in early November that had been tasked with considering 'a fitting maintenance to be allowed to such bishops as have remained and continued under the Power of the Parliament, and for such other bishops as have deserted the Parliament'.[11]

While it was certainly still interested in crafting a peaceful settlement with the king, parliament demonstrated on 26 December that its main focus remained on extracting him from the Scots. This day, D'Ewes and others were instructed to iron out the finer details of Charles's imminent removal to Holdenby House in Northamptonshire, where he was to become a captive of the Commons and Lords. Specifically, the committee was to:

> ...consider of a clause to be added to the vote passed, concerning the king's person, touching both kingdoms employing their joint endeavours with the King, after he shall be come to [Holdenby], and that the Scots Forces shall be gone out of this kingdom, to procure his assent to the propositions agreed by both kingdoms; and in case of refusal, to express their resolutions to maintain the union between the kingdoms.[12]

CHAPTER 27

THE KING'S ESCAPE

KING CHARLES I HAVING been delivered into the hands of parliament on 30 January 1647, the devastation inflicted on the antiquarian world as a result of the war he had waged with his roundhead enemies was hinted at in a letter sent on 6 March, from antiquary Roger Dodsworth to D'Ewes. Dodsworth was at Skipton Castle in Yorkshire at the time of writing, complaining to his research associate – whom he sometimes referred to as 'the beast' – that certain ancient 'evidences' relating to the Tempest family had been plundered by a royalist force at Bolling Hall back in 1643, and were now therefore irrecoverable.[1]

Simonds's nickname of 'the beast' probably referred to his well-known puritanical leanings. While these did not come to light when D'Ewes empathetically presented a petition to the House of Commons on 9 April, which detailed the struggles of the 'late Bishop of London', William Juxon's, tenants in the wake of episcopalian annihilation, they can only have surfaced upon the MP sitting in a parliamentary committee that was to 'provide for the suppressing and punishing of incest, adultery, and whoredom', as well as 'drunkenness, profane swearing, cursing and blasphemy'.[2] Such vices had appalled Simonds since his university days, during which period he had witnessed them all in abundance, save perhaps for the particularly unnatural act of incest.

The king was moved from place to place during much of 1647, amid swelling rumours that rescue attempts were being planned. The chief engineer of such designs was thought to be the 'Presbyterian' faction of parliament, which had grown out of the existing peace party and was so called because of its gradual gravitation towards the Scottish Presbyterians, who had begun to show a genuine interest in treating with Charles. Indeed, its bitter rivals in the House of Commons, the 'fiery' Independents (formerly making up the war party so detested by Simonds), were soon under the impression that a concerted effort to restart hostilities was under way. These fears were not entirely unfounded. Eleven suspect MPs having already been singled out for their suspicious conduct, on 26 July, a mob of common Londoners identifying themselves as Presbyterian supporters used violence to force their way into the Commons chamber itself, demanding that the king be immediately invited to return to London to reclaim his position at the head of government.

Increased levels of parliamentary infighting had been inevitable in light of the political stalemate that had developed in Westminster. As far as Simonds was concerned, however, there was only one calamity worth mourning on 9 September: the death of little Mary D'Ewes, the sole child of the baronet

140

and his second wife, Elizabeth, in Camberwell in modern-day south London, aged just 'one year, two months, and some days'.[3] Though undeniably a painful personal loss for the D'Eweses, at the same time, it cannot have come as a complete surprise, given the numerous infantile deaths that had occurred in the long, difficult years before it. Mary was buried in St George's church, Stowlangtoft, on 12 September 1647, joining her paternal grandparents, her father's first wife, and her older half-brother, Clopton D'Ewes, who had passed away at a similar age.

Simonds chose to console himself through vigorous study the next month. Records suggest that he checked out an Anglo-Saxon manuscript from the Bodleian Library, Oxford, on 19 October, entitled *Chronica Burgi Sancti Petri*, which he noted was 'for a public use'. 'I do faithfully promise to restore [it] again whensoever it shall be demanded,' D'Ewes continued in the diligent check-out note he penned for the library's administrative records. One aim of borrowing the document from the university was possibly to aid the antiquary in his putting together of an Anglo-Saxon dictionary. It does not seem likely that Simonds merely wished to print the work for widespread consumption, as the manuscript's original donor, William Laud, had anticipated would happen when he had originally gifted it to the Bodleian in June 1639.[4]

Another political entity in the Commons by late 1647, 'the Army', which had accidentally emerged out of parliament's New Model Army of 1645, brought additional trouble to the chamber door in October, its representatives seeking swift redress for the soldierly arrears that had amassed since the conclusion of the First English Civil War. On 22 October, Simonds was one of those asked to consider the matter in a committee created for that purpose. The Commons knew very well that, if not properly dealt with, the problem could quickly and dramatically escalate, with foreboding signs of unrest among troops having already been relayed to Mr Speaker. Around this time, Major General Poyntz wrote the following from Worcester House:

> Honoured Sir,
> The 15th of this instant, a surgeon of Colonel Copley's regiment marched with the aforesaid colonel's own troop through Leeds to a rendezvous, where some few of other troops met them, upon the moor near Leeds, where they made a halt: the chirurgeon drew some papers out, and read to the soldiers, and told them, that the army in the south desired they should join with them, and that they desired nothing of the parliament but their arrears, and an act of indemnity; and if they had not an act of indemnity, they should be most of them hanged when they were reduced: and, for an example, told them, the judges have hanged fourteen soldiers already, which took horses by order from their officers.[5]

While composing the letter, Poyntz was also made aware of 'a second rendezvous' organised by the surgeon, which had seen double the number of soldiers attend as the first. Men had supposedly walked away wearing blue and white ribbons in their hats on this occasion, 'as tokens of their engagements'. The additional meeting encouraged Poyntz to fear the worst. 'I do believe that, under the covert of [Pontefract] castle,' he warned, 'they do intend to raise a body of horse and foot, if not prevented.'[6]

This was, however, nothing compared to the pandemonium that engulfed the House of Commons on 12 November, upon Mr Speaker receiving a somewhat icily worded letter from Oliver Cromwell, by now an immensely authoritative figure in the New Model Army. Its content announced that the king, at that stage kept comfortably under lock and key at Hampton Court Palace in Surrey, had made a successful bid for freedom the previous evening. 'The manner is variously reported,' Cromwell remarked coolly in his correspondence, 'and we will say little of it at present, but that His Majesty was expected at supper when the Commissioners and Colonel Whaley missed him.'[7] Charles's cloak had reportedly been found abandoned in a private gallery, which intimated to those in the know at the royal palace that he had escaped via the river. Letters written in the king's own hand had similarly been discovered on a table in his withdrawing room, one of which had been earmarked for parliament.

Simonds's former tutor at Cambridge, Richard Holdsworth (who had risen to become personal chaplain to King Charles), had been cautiously optimistic about the future of the country until his dramatic abscondence. 'The little spark of hope that seemed to appear, is in some danger of being extinguished by the king's withdrawing of himself on Thursday night,' he wrote to an acquaintance, further observing that the whole affair had 'put all into amazement, not knowing what to think'.[8] The theologian had heard on the grapevine that certain individuals had advised Charles before his stunning escape that he was no longer safe within the confines of Hampton Court Palace, and that he would be better off elsewhere, away from the New Model Army and its scheming affiliates.

Before the Christmas holidays arrived, an apparently securer location was to be found for the king on the Isle of Wight, specifically Carisbrooke Castle, where he was taken in mid-November by the island's governor, Colonel Robert Hammond. In reality, it turned out to be no safer than Hampton Court Palace on the mainland. Willing to show the monarch respect where respect was due, and in general proving to be a courteous and amenable host, Hammond nevertheless proceeded to inform parliament in London about the guest he had acquired. Carisbrooke Castle became Carisbrooke Prison at the stroke of a pen.

As a result, for both the king and many of his subjects, Christmas 1647 was to be another bad one. The reason it passed so unfavourably for Englishmen and Englishwomen at large lay in the simple fact that a recklessly puritanical government, which now energetically controlled most aspects of the country's organisation, had decreed beforehand that it should not pass at all. As the famous phrase goes, Christmas had been effectively 'banned' by parliament. A move that sought to suppress a period of joviality and celebration, particularly in the middle of England's slow recovery from one of its bloodiest ever decades, was never going to go down well with the activists of society. And, as expected, it did not.

The king's escape

On 28 December, Westminster was made aware of a diabolical Christmas riot that had erupted in Canterbury, with further insurrections taking place in Oxford, Ipswich, Bury St Edmunds, Norwich and London itself. The Canterbury disorder began on 25 December, when a mob of townspeople, determined to observe the Christian festival, appeared in the city's streets and demanded that those who had opened up their shops for the day close them again. This performance was then followed by a game of football among the 'rabble', before the mayor and aldermen of Canterbury intervened and attempted to carry the players off to the nearest gaol. Their attempts were violently thwarted by the wider 'multitude', who 'beat the mayor and aldermen into their houses, and then cried "conquest"'.[9]

The next day being Sunday and thus peaceable, on the morning of 27 December 1647, the mayor woke to the belief that it would be necessary to station soldiers around the city to prevent any further violence. 'Till noon they were quiet,' a contemporary pamphlet describes of the rioters, at which point a one-on-one confrontation caused the disaffected demonstrators to take up clubs and other weapons to defend themselves. Eventually, they headed for the mayor's own house, smashing his windows and 'pulling up his posts' in their indefatigable rage.[10]

Chapter 28

COLCHESTER FALLS

SIMONDS STRONGLY OPPOSED the latest plan of action debated in the House of Commons on 3 January 1648, believing that it would only serve to enhance the royalist agenda in the future. In short, the Independents and representatives of the Army had proposed that negotiations should be cleanly broken off with the king, and any further attempts at a settlement abandoned, intelligence having been received that he was now actively treating with the Scots from Carisbrooke Castle on the Isle of Wight.[1]

It was a tense day for members of the Long Parliament. As the Vote of No Addresses prepared to receive its preliminary count, the outer room was cleared, no MP was permitted to leave the chamber without authorisation, and candles were brought in to improve visibility amid the wintry gloom. The results of the vote, when they came, were not as conclusive as members like Oliver Cromwell, who was now a firm critic of King Charles, might have hoped for: 141 'Yeas' and 92 'Noes'.[2] Thus, it was thought sensible to also procure the agreement of the House of Lords in the matter. Frustratingly for those in parliament who had come to the end of their tether regarding the king's behaviour, the Lords decided that they could not readily accept the Commons' scheme, on the grounds that its undertones of a constitutional overhaul threatened their own uncertain position in government in the late 1640s.

However, the time for sitting back and merely accepting when things did not go a particular way was long over. The startled Lords having been veritably cowed into submission by the timely arrival of a band of Fairfax's soldiers in Whitehall, orchestrated by the Commons, the Vote of No Addresses went on to pass on 17 January. The following day, Simonds's unique antiquarian skills were sought out when arrangements were made to have the problematic monarch's 'books, manuscripts, and other antiquities' housed at Whitehall moved to St James's Palace across the way, until they could be taken elsewhere. The antiquary was to oversee the operation, along with John Selden, a scholar of some note, and Patrick Young, Keeper of His Majesty's Libraries.[3]

There was further disorder in the country in the middle of spring, which pointed to dark times ahead. On 27 April, the following was ordered by the House:

> ...that all such persons who have been aiding, acting, or assisting, in the late tumult in the city of Norwich, be disabled to have any vote in the election to be made, on May Day next, of the mayor of the said city of Norwich; and that no person who hath had any hand in the said tumult, be elected mayor of the said city.[4]

These April riots in Norwich had, once more, been in response to parliamentary policies and actions. The great drama had kicked off on 22 April, when a messenger from the Commons had arrived in the city to request that the mayor, John Utting, accompany him back to London to answer for his belligerent behaviour in recent months. Word had reached the House that the man had allowed the Christmas season of 1647 to be observed in Norwich; had authorised the appointment of a royalist alderman to one of its wards; had permitted royalist members of the clergy to practise in local churches; and, most terribly of all, had sanctioned celebrations to mark the accession of the king on 27 March.

Such a summons had soon caused mass demonstrations in support of Utting, which had, in turn, become violent, forcing parliament's messenger to flee the city a little less confidently than he had entered it. On 24 April, the pro-royalist, 1,000-strong mob had proceeded to plunder roundhead houses, before, in a move that demonstrated that these people had not been messing around, they had taken control of the building containing the county magazine. It was a decision that was to cost Norwich dearly. A fight between forces commanded by parliament and the determined rioters breaking out around the magazine, the barrels of gunpowder stored within it had caught fire and occasioned an explosion powerful enough to kill 40 of the insurgents outright, injure perhaps 120 others, and completely shatter the windows of nearby houses and churches.[5]

Hints of a remobilisation continued into May 1648, with more pro-royalist demonstrators in Bury St Edmunds – a Suffolk town that Simonds knew particularly well – seizing its respective county magazine. The House of Commons was notified of the development on 13 May:

> On Friday last here began a great Combustion in this Town about setting up of a maypole, which grew to that height, that by Saturday 6 or 700 Men were gotten into Arms, some of them cried out, 'For God and King Charles'; and began to lay hold on some soldiers which were in Town, and set Guards in several places, pretending they were in fear that the Soldiers would come in upon them and disarm them; some of those which stood for the Parliament were forced to leave the Town and their Goods, to shift for themselves and go away to Friends in the Country. To appease this Combustion, some Troops of Horse which were Quartered in these parts, were drawn before the Town; and finding the Townsmen well armed, and in a posture of Defence, they kept in a body before the Town all that Night: The next day many Country Foot joined with them; by reason whereof they in the Town were kept in on every side; and when they perceived they had brought themselves into a straight, and had no means to recover themselves, but by submission, desired a Parley, which was granted.[6]

Indeed, these activities reintroduced a personal dimension to the nation's troubles for D'Ewes, being especially the case because Bury St Edmunds was so close to the safe haven of Stow Hall, which had, as yet, been practically untouched by the overarching conflict.

'By reason of some extraordinary occasions and through the troublesomeness of the times,' Simonds found himself struggling with his finances again in May. Hence, he was forced to enter into another agreement with Arthur Barnardiston, brother of Sir Nathaniel Barnardiston, to keep his head above water on 16 May. The baronet was then further reminded of the impact that the war had had on almost everybody on 1 June, having been required that day to deliver a petition to the Commons from 'the reduced officers and soldiers, as also of the widows and orphans of such as have lost their lives in the Parliament's service'.[7]

Around this same time, parliament could breathe two temporary sighs of relief. The first related to tidings of a parliamentarian victory at Maidstone in Kent, which had succeeded in stemming the royalist advance that had inevitably grown out of the discontent seen in those parts. During a night of heavy rain on 1 June, Fairfax's forces had confronted and then defeated a motley crew of soldiers led by George Goring, 1st Earl of Norwich, with perhaps 6,000 men fighting for control of the town in its very suburbs, streets and alleyways. The battle, though nowhere near as large as those witnessed at Edgehill, Marston Moor or Naseby, had nonetheless been every inch as brutal as any one of them. Even years later in the 1660s, royalist servicemen would continue to come forwards pleading incapacitation as a result of their involvement in the affray. These veterans included one Abraham Reeves, who in 1662 revealed that he had lost a finger in June 1648, as well as one Thomas Ginder, who in 1665 made it known to King Charles II himself, through a desperate petition, that he had lost his right hand at the Battle of Maidstone.[8] Victory or not, however, that a battle had been fought at all was simultaneously bad news for parliament, for it formally confirmed that the country had entered a follow-up period of armed conflict – now known as the Second English Civil War.

Still, the Commons could similarly heave a second sigh of relief at intelligence acquired on 2 June via Colonel Robert Hammond, who, while disclosing that King Charles I had recently plotted another escape from Carisbrooke Castle, went on to reassure the House that the design had epically failed. 'Through the corruption and naughtiness of two gentlemen attending the king, Mr Osborn and Mr Dowcett,' the governor wrote, 'three soldiers were suborned and dealt with, to assist in this escape, who were to be on duty at the king's window at the time appointed.'[9] He continued:

> Mr Dowcett, who was to be accommodated with cords, to convey him down the castle wall, and then the outline, after he had let himself down through his window to the prepared sentinels, was to be his guide to his horse, which were ready provided, and laid at a convenient place within musket-shot of the works; and Mr Osborn and one Mr Worsley, of Gatcomb, a young gentleman of this island, who were to conduct him to a creek, where also at the same time lay ready a boat to transport them to the mainland, to a place where (as is confessed by one whom I have apprehended) there were horses to convey the king whither he pleased. This design hath been long in hand, but kept from me until yesterday, when two of the soldiers who

had been dealt with came to me, and acquainted me with the whole business.[10]

Upon Colonel Hammond confronting the king and finding that the bars on his window had been applied with nitric acid, the governor had thought it proper to announce that he had entered the room merely 'to take leave of Your Majesty, for I hear you are going away'. Presently, Colonel Hammond was to be sent £100 by parliament as a token of its appreciation, which was to be distributed to 'such personas as made the discovery of the design for the king's escape'.[11]

With another war now undeniably on their hands, both the Independents and Army representatives in parliament had no choice but to reassess the unbending position that they had taken regarding settling with Charles. By mid-July, the metaphorical negotiating table in the House of Commons had been dragged back out from its storage place, with new propositions soon tentatively being drawn up around it. One of the first conditions to be dropped by parliament in the interests of securing a successful settlement, by a margin of eight votes on 28 July, was the establishment of a Presbyterian church structure in England.

Yet, this had all come much too late in the day for the disconsolate townspeople of Colchester, with events there coming to the attention of D'Ewes and the Commons at the end of August. 'Sir, the last night about ten of the clock the Articles were signed by the Commissioners on both sides,' Rushworth informed the Speaker of the House, 'which were to this purpose: that all horse with furniture should be delivered this day by ten of the clock; that all private soldiers and officers, under captains, shall have fair quarter, and render themselves prisoners; that the lords, and all superior officers and gentlemen be drawn together in the King's Head Inn, with their clothes and baggage, by eleven of the clock, and there to render themselves to the mercy of the Lord General.'[12]

Rushworth's report marked the end of the bloody siege of Colchester, the most significant military episode to occur during the Second English Civil War, and one that had more or less begun where the Battle of Maidstone had left off. Following his defeat by Sir Thomas Fairfax on 1 June, the Earl of Norwich had initially made to retreat to London, where he had hoped for a royalist rendezvous at Blackheath. When such a gathering had been frustrated by the London Militia under parliamentary officer Philip Skippon, however, the royalist leader had instead chosen to cut across the Thames and head in the vague direction of Essex. Here, he had been joined by reinforcements eager to support the king's cause, including civil-war veterans Sir George Lisle and Sir Charles Lucas, as well as apprentices from London. All the while, a parliamentary army had been in hot pursuit of Norwich's party, finally catching up with his scurrying troops just short of Colchester. With Sir Thomas Fairfax reliably on the way to support Colonel Edward Whalley, the royalists had found themselves cornered and vulnerable. The unassuming town of Colchester, at the same time, had become accidentally caught in the crossfire.[13]

Accounts of the physical siege of Colchester usually start at this point in proceedings. A royalist commentator recorded that, on 13 June, the opposing sides violently clashed for the first time to the south-east of the town, near Lexden.

While the king's army got off to a reasonably good start, its members were quickly forced to retreat within Colchester's old walls against heavy fire. Later regaining the upper hand, the parliamentary insurgents realised that they had underestimated the combined skill of this 'new and scarcely fleshed army of countrymen' in storming forwards to continue their offensive. It was a preliminary encounter that left the stench of blood, guts, suffering and death hanging thick in the air. 'Here you might see the limbs of men, horses, fire, [and] dust confused together in one horrid Chaos,' a report suggested in the skirmish's aftermath. As for the disposal of the dead, it seems parliament, who had apparently come off much worse, resorted to unwholesome measures to clear up the mess that their men had made on the roads. 'Many of their dead bodies they threw into wells, some they buried in ditches, many they carried off,' royalist Matthew Carter remarked, with a tone of unconcealed revulsion.[14]

The cavaliers, though in a stable position for the time being in Colchester, became concerned when Fairfax's army, instead of dispersing, proceeded to surround the town and commence the slick construction of strategically placed fortifications. Consequently, in readiness for a protracted standoff that might last many weeks, frenzied preparations were made within the settlement itself to stock up on provisions and ammunition, including corn, wine 'of all sorts', salt, fish and gunpowder.[15] Defences were similarly shored up and gaps in the walls plugged with anything suitable that the men under Norwich, Lisle, Lucas and the rest could get their hands on. It was noted:

> Whilest we were thus active for prevention of all dangers that might happen, by strengthening the walls of the town, and fortifying where no wall was, by casting up rampires and counterfcarfs, as a very great part of the town required, the Enemy was as busie without, in running their trenches, making their approaches, and casting up Forts and Batteries against us, still earthing themselves, and we as diligent and laborious within, as in truth not without much necessity on our part, the Towne being in all places very weak, neither had it any more than one Flanker about it, and that very bad too, which was called the Old-Fort.[16]

Clearly, the royalists lacked confidence in the strength of the place that they had, purely by chance, commandeered as a garrison.

Sure enough, the summer siege did not go at all well for those trapped helplessly in Colchester. By the beginning of July, provisions had all but run out, Fairfax's soldiers had attacked the town's defences at multiple points, royalist reinforcements had failed to materialise, and morale had become low. The townspeople were especially disgruntled by the situation with which they were faced, complaining of extreme hunger, battle fatigue and maltreatment by the king's men – all for a cause that few of them believed in.

On 14 July, General Fairfax sought to close in ever more on the foundering garrison by ordering his soldiers to bring down Sir Charles Lucas's own house, which lay only a few hundred yards outside of Colchester's walls. This the effective troops did willingly, first concealing two demi-cannons behind a cluster of old walls and buildings nearby to get a good view of their target, before successfully battering Lucas's gatehouse until one side of it collapsed noisily to the ground in a cloud of fragmented stone and dust. The roundheads were particularly pleased to observe, as the cloud settled, that the wall had fallen into the space where a band of enemy musketeers had been firing from only moments previously. Barely giving the cavaliers time to compose themselves, Fairfax's men proceeded to launch as many as three additional grenadoes at the gatehouse. The defenceless mansion beyond was now practically theirs for the taking.

Details recorded of what happened next may be the product of simple royalist rhetoric, though soldiers from both sides certainly had form when it came to the mindless plundering and destruction of property that did not belong to them. Sir Charles Lucas's house having fallen to the enemy, Fairfax's combatants purportedly set about combing the building from top to bottom, searching for familial valuables and ready money to loot. Being disappointed in the treasures they came across, accounts describe them then turning their attentions towards the adjoining St Giles's church, where several bodies of the Lucas family were interred. The corpses themselves, we are told, immediately came to be viewed as objects in their own right to be defaced. Accordingly, Fairfax's men snatched up the sinewy remains of Charles's mother and sister, Lady Lucas and Lady Killigrew, pulled off each corpse's arms and legs, tossed them into different corners of the vault, and walked away from the vandalism they had committed with bits of the women's hair worn as trophies in their hats.[17]

Sometime after 8 August, the House of Commons was provided with an update on the situation unfolding in Colchester. Things were not good. Reports leaking from the place suggested that the enemy had become quieter than usual due to its continued suffering, that soldiers had been obliged to eat maggot-riddled horse flesh as a result of a lack of alternative nourishment, and that 'the bloody flux is among them, by reason of their bad diet'.[18] Other accounts given at the same time alluded to the forced consumption of cats and dogs, too. It is difficult to know exactly what Simonds was thinking as he was apprised of the horrible information being soberly delivered to the chamber in Westminster. Perhaps he daydreamed of the days he had spent in Colchester in peacetime, when the town had been unblemished and free from death, decay and ruin, and he himself a youthful, eligible man in the throes of courtship, enjoying the innocent company of his good friend, Mr Littlebury. Perhaps he even thought of the woman he had been courting, Jemima Waldegrave, his first real love interest as a young barrister.

At the tail end of August 1648, a paper kite was flown over Colchester by Thomas Fairfax with a message urging the royalist garrison that the game was up. To emphasise that the lord general meant what he wrote, he ordered a follow-up volley of shots to be fired around the parliamentary leaguer, which would hopefully convey to the Earl of Norwich and others that they were insurmountably outnumbered. Finally, on 27 August, after an unsuccessful bid to escape into rural East Anglia, a royalist council of war convened in the wrecked town and admitted defeat. 'There was no refuge, nor remedy left, nor anything to trust to, but what conditions the enemy would give,' its members all agreed with heavy hearts.[19]

When the Commons learned of the surrender on 28 August 1648, there remained a few loose ends to be tied up in Colchester before the siege could – at least in the short term – be set aside. The ordeal of the last two months was not over for Sir Charles Lucas and Sir George Lisle in particular. Confined to the King's Head inn, where Simonds had, twenty-seven years earlier, partaken in a pleasant meal with Mr Littlebury and 'held much discourse' with him, the two royalist officers had been informed that they were to be taken to a spot beneath the walls of Colchester Castle and executed by firing squad for heinous crimes against the benevolent English parliament. Two more men had been given the same sentence, though for different reasons they were to dodge the menacing ends of the roundheads' musket barrels on the evening of 28 August. Colonel Henry Farre had already escaped into the surrounding fields by the appointed time of the execution, so could not be shot; Bernard Gascoigne, meanwhile, was granted a reprieve at the last minute, owing to the fact that he was a Florentine mercenary representing a formidable overseas power.[20]

For Lucas and Lisle, however, time was up at 7:00 pm. Shepherded into the castle yard alone, Sir Charles was the first of the officers to be executed by a duty-bound, three-row-deep party of musketeers. The royalist was reportedly inclined to arrogance in his final moments, though this was possibly interpreted by some as an admirable exhibition of resolve. Praying on his knees, getting back up again, unbuttoning his doublet, bearing his chest, and putting his hands by his sides, he then said to his executioners, 'See, I am ready for you. Now rebels, do your worst.'[21]

Lucas's lifeless body had scarcely slumped down onto its own, ever-increasing pool of blood before Sir George Lisle was brought into the yard to receive the same punishment. Understandably, he found the mutilated corpse of his fallen comrade very difficult to stomach; in fact, Lisle chose to kneel and kiss Lucas's bloodied skin delicately before attending to the task of preparing himself for the end of his own life. Pulling five pieces of gold out of his pocket, he gave one to parliament's musketeers, who probably did not expect such a gesture, and the remainder to a former servant, which was to serve as a legacy for some friends in London. He then mentioned his parents, both of whom were still living in 1648, before addressing those who were at the castle:

> Oh! how many of your lives here have I saved in hot blood, and must now myself be most barbarously in cold? But what dare not they do that would willingly cut [the] throat of my dear king, whom they have already imprisoned; and for whose deliverance, and peace to this unfortunate nation, I dedicate my last prayers to heaven, and now, traitors, do your worst.[22]

The 'traitors' in question did do their worst, and swiftly. In seconds, following a deafening round of gunfire that bounced off the stone walls of the castle, Lisle's corpse had joined that of Lucas on the floor of the yard, where both officers' blood proceeded to mingle.

CHAPTER 29

PURGED

THE SECOND ENGLISH Civil War was over.

Into September 1648, Simonds witnessed parliamentary commissioners preparing to leave Westminster for the Isle of Wight, where further negotiations with the king were expected to take place in Newport. Even though both parties eventually went into discussions willing to forge a peaceful settlement under the right conditions, it rapidly became clear that there remained serious differences in opinion between the camps that would prevent any significant progress from being made in the immediate future. Something that still could not be agreed on, for example, was the place of episcopacy in the long-term structure of the Church of England. Parliament wanted bishops kept out of the country's Protestant faith permanently; Charles did not.

This perpetual state of deadlock, which many believed would carry on and on and have no end, encouraged petitions to be sent to parliament from Newcastle, York and Taunton on 10 October, their inhabitants calling on its members to change tack regarding their handling of the sovereign. As one, the impatient citizens' own advice was to reprimand the king, instead of simply trying to accommodate his return to London.[1] They were not alone in entertaining this line of thinking.

D'Ewes had cause to believe that King Charles was still actively anticipating a settlement towards the end of October, when he and Patrick Young, Keeper of His Majesty's Libraries, received a royal request to begin working their way through the various collections that made up the monarch's library, moved on the orders of parliament to St James's Palace at the beginning of 1648. The communication from Charles read:

> Charles R.
> Whereas we have remaining in our library at St James's divers medals and ancient coins, Greek, Roman, and others. We do hereby authorise, constitute, and appoint, our trusty and well-beloved Sir Simonds D'Ewes of Stow Hall... and Patrick Young, keeper of our libraries, to sort and put ye said coins and medals into their series and order, and to lay aside to be disposed by us all duplicates among them which are genuine and true... All which said pieces so separated and divided, are to remain in our said library at St James', in the custody of the said Patrick Young, until our further pleasure be known. And that ye said Sir Simonds D'Ewes have free liberty from

time to time to take into his own custody and keeping, such and so many of them as he shall have occasion to make use of.[2]

This was in many respects thrilling news for Simonds, who would not need telling twice to help himself to some of the ancient artefacts held by the royal family. Less agreeable, having seen certain members of parliament adopting a much more aggressive stance of late, was the baronet's knowledge of where the optimistic king believed things currently stood in respect of his return to the fold.

Indeed, egged on by their political figurehead and champion, Henry Ireton, the extremist proponents of the Army in the House of Commons were once again of a mind to abandon treating with Charles in late autumn. The justification for the proposed withdrawal was explained in painstaking detail in a document entitled *A Remonstrance of His Excellency Thomas Lord Fairfax*, written up largely by Ireton himself. Initially presented to the Commons on 20 November 1648, the *Army Remonstrance* was found to contain many dangerous and unsettling republican ideas upon being consulted, as well as plans to bring the king to trial for his treacheries. Because there were still, at this time, those moderate MPs holding out for a successful settlement between king and parliament on the Isle of Wight, the whole scheme was ultimately shelved until further notice, before being rejected by the Commons on 30 November.

Even so, during the long night of 4–5 December, the House vociferously debated whether there were sufficient grounds to continue negotiating with Charles in light of the most recent answers he had provided. By a vote of 129 to 83, its members decided that there were. This, again, was not the outcome supporters of the Army had been hoping for, the aggressive forces of which were now bearing down on the capital and poised to take matters into their own hands, if and when ordered to do so. A contemporary of these days recounted:

> Some more forces of the Army came to London this day and yesterday, they still quarter in the suburbs, none in the City; the private soldiers quartered in great houses lie upon the boards, and have no beds, and but a little, if any firing, which is very hard this season. The General has sent to the City to provide bedding, to be allowed out of the arrears, or otherwise quarters to be provided for the soldiers in the City. No money paid yet from the City to the Army.[3]

With the king having already been taken into the direct custody of the Army and escorted back to the mainland, events had begun to move towards an uneasy conclusion.

On the morning of 6 December, Simonds was met by a solemn-looking Colonel Thomas Pride, flanked by soldiers with equally hard looks on their faces, on his usual way into the Commons chamber. The Army representative had in his hand a lengthy list of names, expectantly inclining his ear to the doorkeeper stood with him as the MP for Sudbury approached. The doorkeeper confirming that Sir Simonds D'Ewes was one of those men featured on the paper, Pride at once barred him from proceeding any further, instead ordering that he be conducted securely to the Queen's Court, along with perhaps forty-one other members of parliament who had similarly been arrested. In this place, the targeted MPs were closely watched by armed officers, with each captive wondering nervously why their quotidian routine had been disrupted. 'It [is] the pleasure of the House that they should forthwith attend the service of the House,' the sergeant-at-arms soon announced, having arrived to call the members away.[4] The Army officers, however, held fast, refusing to release D'Ewes and the others upon strict instructions from a higher, invisible power.

This shocking event, in which Simonds had been so suddenly diverted from the political chamber that had become like a lodging to him, was part of Pride's Purge. Tired of certain MPs – D'Ewes clearly among them – derailing endeavours to fully drop negotiations with King Charles and pursue a harder line against the monarch's actions instead, the politicised Army had decided to simply get rid of the repeat offenders to clear the way for a vote that would go in its favour. The following morning, on 7 December, a second batch of men was prevented from entering the Commons and duly arrested under the same operation. Dozens more, though not taken into custody, were similarly stopped from resuming their seats in the chamber over the two days of merciless purging.

As a result, Army grandee Oliver Cromwell returned home from campaigning to a considerably reduced House later on 7 December, receiving a hero's welcome from the MPs who had managed to survive Pride's Purge. 'The House considered of the great and faithful services performed by Lieutenant-General Cromwell to the two kingdoms of England and Scotland, and ordered the hearty thanks of the House should be given to him for the same; he being then present, Mr Speaker gave him thanks accordingly,' it was recorded.[5]

Simonds, distressed and dishevelled, and no doubt longing for the sanctuary of Stow Hall in Suffolk, appears to have been released by the Army on 14 December, a whole eight days after his ordeal in Westminster had begun. By this time, the principal aim of the purge that had cost him his place in the Long Parliament had already been met: a day earlier, on 13 December, the Commons had voted with ease to break off all negotiations with the king.

Chapter 30

'A HAPPY HOUR'

THE LONG PARLIAMENT, now technically the 'Rump' Parliament since Pride's Purge of December 1648, was no longer Simonds's concern into the new year. In the early days of January 1649, it would only have been natural for the ex-MP to feel conflicted about this turn of events as he attempted to move on with his life in a manner that he deemed most appropriate. On the one hand, he was now blissfully free of the endless burdens and demands placed on him as a Commons member, which had consistently meant that his antiquarian work had suffered, as well as the important relationships that he had shared with certain members of his family. On the other hand, he was a political influencer no more. The fate of the country henceforth rested in the palms of, probably as D'Ewes saw it, lesser individuals, and, worse, extremist men who were not likely to put the interests of the country before their own agendas. There must have been a niggling feeling in the back of Simonds's head that his career in politics had all been for nothing.

Active parliamentarian or not, the baronet of Stowlangtoft continued to engage in discussions on the national situation throughout January 1649, as is evidenced in a letter sent to him at his abode in Westminster on 20 January by William Dugdale. 'As this dealing towards ye King is no doubt the great wonder of Christendom, so must it needs be the shame of the English Nation to this and future ages,' the antiquary wrote soberly.[1] He continued:

> I know full well that the great hand of God is eminently in this work, though the immediate causes and ends therein are not to be discerned by us, and I am no less satisfied that all my sorrowing for it avails him... I now expect nothing but to hear of his death, in which I doubt not but that, as in all other his afflictions he hath done, he will perform his part to admiration.[2]

On 9 April, John Stuteville of Dalham in Suffolk kept the conversation on the unfortunate sovereign going in his own correspondence with D'Ewes. 'Certainly, Sir, our particular and national sins are come to so great a height,' he scribbled, in an especially God-fearing manner, 'that the greatest of temporal judgements – war, pestilence, and famine – even all the plagues of Egypt, we may expect and look for. Nay, I fear, a spiritual judgement; the removal of our candlestick, the glorious (which hath shined so clearly amongst us for many ages together), to some other nation, which will bring forth better fruit than we have done.'[3]

Stuteville was here referring to the adverse effects of King Charles I's ultimate fate, which had been decided for him earlier in the year, on the country as a whole.

For, in January 1649, parliament had tried and then proceeded to behead the imprisoned Stuart ruler for crimes against the subjects whom he had promised to defend. Though Simonds was not in a position to be able to witness the activities of the House of Commons in the immediate aftermath of such an extraordinary show of violence, it is nevertheless worth describing the steps that were taken by its members once the king's head had hit the scaffold floor in Whitehall. The very first item of business conducted in the chamber following the execution – that same afternoon, in fact – concerned a parliamentary act 'prohibiting the proclaiming [of] any person to be King of England or Ireland, or the dominions thereof'. This was soon qualified by a resolution that 'the Commons of England, in Parliament assembled, do declare, that the People are, under God, the Original of all just Power', and 'do also declare, that the Commons of England, in Parliament assembled, being chosen by and representing the People, have the supreme Power in this Nation'.[4] The House had absolutely no intention of replacing one monarch with another. It would also make clear that it had had quite enough of its political neighbour, the House of Lords, which it would duly abolish in March 1649.

D'Ewes was able to dedicate himself to antiquarian pursuits, his old love, in these months. In the same letter from William Dugdale written on 20 January, the learned man mentioned Ælfric's *Grammar*, a compendium of Old English that Simonds was preparing for publication, as well as D'Ewes's work-in-progress Anglo-Saxon dictionary – both of which the Suffolk baronet would fail to see through to print. This was not for want of trying. In the late 1640s, Simonds appears to have enlisted the help of two eminent antiquaries to aid him in his labours, researches and meticulous compiling. The first was the royalist sympathiser William Somner, who would go on to successfully take a revised version of the Anglo-Saxon dictionary, entitled *Dictionarium*, to press in the late 1650s. The second was the Dutch scholar Francis Junius, sometime librarian to Thomas Howard, Earl of Arundel, who, through a shared enthusiasm with D'Ewes for rigorous study, ended up spending months on end at Stow Hall in Suffolk in the company of Simonds and his family. On top of these associations, it should be noted that D'Ewes had been in regular contact with an Old English expert, the Dutchman Johannes de Laet, since the early 1640s. All such work led antiquary Robert Vaughan to complain in May 1649 to James Ussher, Archbishop of Armagh, that 'I have not been satisfied by Sir Symon D'Ewes, who, as it seems, being troubled with weightier affairs, had no time to perform what he promised you.'[5]

There were painful callbacks to the past as the year went gradually by. Simonds seemed doomed to forever be reminded of the part his late brother, Richard D'Ewes, had played in the civil war, entering into a bond on 21 May for the payment of £157, which was the remainder of an outstanding fine imposed on him for Richard's unacceptable 'delinquency' in the early 1640s. Then came the sad news of the death of Henry Hastings, the teenage son of Lucy, Countess of Huntingdon, in June. His passing evidently struck a chord with Simonds – undoubtedly bringing back memories of the premature losses of his own boys – for he wrote a letter of consolation to the noblewoman just a few days after its occurrence, under the Latin name Simondsius Deuuensius. In the autumn, meanwhile, D'Ewes's financial problems seemed to resurface, with records suggesting that the Suffolk manor of Abbot's Hall was sold to a clothier from Mildenhall called Robert Canham for £1,400 on 1 October.[6]

A 17th Century Knight: The Life and Times of Simonds D'Ewes

Antiquarianism was front of mind for Simonds once again in January 1650, as it had been intermittently since he had first come across the Tower of London's ancient records in 1623. Indeed, fellow antiquary William Dugdale wrote devotedly to his studious colleague in Westminster on 2 January, anticipating an update on D'Ewes's various projects:

> I hope you have received the book I sent you by carrier. I much long to hear how ye press goes on with Ælfric. I hope now that you have ye advantage of that honest man, Mr Sumner [Somner], his help, you will speed ye impression of your Saxon Lexicon and the Laws. Those no doubt will go of much better, though the times be bad, than Beda, which you know was printed in the heat of the war.[7]

Dugdale betrayed the ugly tendencies of intellectual obsessives like himself and Simonds D'Ewes in his latest letter. While calling Simonds out for 'censuring me a little too rashly concerning my comparing of Domesday for Mr Leicester', the man likewise revealed his own propensity for stuffiness in imploring D'Ewes to make sure that his servants did not 'blot' or 'soil' the precious books that he had allowed them to borrow. Antiquary Roger Dodsworth had added an ounce more substance to this curious world of bickering and backbiting when, in corresponding with Dugdale in November 1649, he had laid into D'Ewes by declaring haughtily, 'I know sufficiently the nature of the beast.'[8]

On 26 January, John Stuteville, son of the late Sir Martin Stuteville, was also back in touch with Simonds on intellectual business:

> Sir – I have, according to your desire, delivered out to be sent you up these books following, viz. – Dyar's Reports, and the Quadragesimes of E. Z., as also Henning's Genealogies in three volumes (which you mistook to be but in two); with the Cambridge printed Bible; but as for the other, which in the note is called Vuesuerus his Descent of Genealogy, I doubt it is misnamed, for I can find none such on the sudden.[9]

He further disclosed that D'Ewes should expect to receive two cakes with the parcel of choice literature he was sending, made by his sister, Susan, which he hoped 'may come seasonably for "groning cakes" for your lady, to whom we all of us wish a happy hour for her safe delivery'.[10]

For Elizabeth D'Ewes, Simonds's second wife, was pregnant again by early 1650. This was exceptional news in itself, but became a veritable answer to the baronet's prayers when the new arrival turned out to be a baby boy. At last, after a decade of little hope that the family name would ever be carried on following his death, D'Ewes had an heir once more. He called this miraculous son Willoughby, after Elizabeth's family, continuing the longstanding tradition within Simonds's personal history of using maiden names for male children. On 7 March, 'Willowby Dewes', son of 'Sir Symon Dewes', was christened at St Margaret's church in Westminster, with nothing to suggest that he was in any way unhealthy.[11]

Epilogue

IN THE END

LONDON. ENGLAND. 18 APRIL 1650.

On this day, in this place, Sir Simonds D'Ewes died. He was 47 years old, and left behind a young son, two daughters and a widow in her twenties.

What exactly killed Simonds has not been recorded for future generations, though antiquary William Somner intimated in a letter written in April that the baronet had sickened relatively suddenly. Thus, one historian has concluded that either a stroke or heart failure was responsible for D'Ewes's death, which seems highly plausible.[1]

Because nothing is known about Simonds's final moments, it is impossible to ascertain for sure what the man was thinking and feeling as mortality claimed him in Westminster. We can, however, speculate – with a level of caution, of course. Logic would dictate that the vast number of important people whom he had lost over his reasonably short tenure on the planet swam before his failing eyes at some point, each of them, in turn, reminding him of the variable life he had led. Perhaps Richard Simonds, the grandfather whom D'Ewes had so idolised as an energetic boy in Dorset, made an appearance in the phantom crowd, together with his spouse, the long-dead Joan; perhaps Lady Anne Clopton, Simonds's first wife and evident soulmate, and all the unfortunate children whom the couple had buried in the 1630s and early 1640s, joined them. It would have made sense for Paul and Cecilia D'Ewes, the antiquary's parents, to show their faces, too, as well as poor Richard D'Ewes, his younger brother, who had died in 1643 in the middle of war, and whom Simonds had continued to love until the very end, despite their political differences. A personal assurance of salvation would have made any strange thought or notion in the extreme twilight of his years easier to bear.

D'Ewes's career in politics, and naturally the civil war itself, possibly crept into his mind alongside these visions of deceased relatives. Had he really done enough for his constituents, for his *country*, between 1640 and 1648? Had he made any kind of a difference as a moderate among extremists, even though such extremists had eventually gotten their way and killed a king? Would he leave a lasting impression, or was he to be forgotten altogether, to be cast into the oblivion of the past? Fortunately, Simonds left so much written material when he died, including his autobiography and parliamentary journals, and such a divisive personality within them, that it would have been almost impossible for him to become invisible to posterity. That this book has been written at all is a testament to the fact that Sir Simonds D'Ewes, knight and baronet of Stowlangtoft in Suffolk, continues to be remembered.

Nevertheless, there is no evidence to suggest that D'Ewes's presence carried on being felt in the House of Commons in the years after his expulsion. On the date of his death, for instance, there were merely signs of militaristic vigour on display in the chamber. 'Sir Henry Vane junior reports from the Council of State, that £50,000... be disposed of by the Council of State, for the setting out of the train of artillery, and other necessaries for the marching army, and for other exigents of the Commonwealth,' it was reported.[2]

Unlike the event itself, reactions to Simonds's death have survived, largely from the antiquary world. 'Our friend of Westminster is dead, which is an unsupportable loss to us,' Dodsworth informed Dugdale on 19 April, which proves that there had been genuine affection shared between the three men all along. Yet, one cannot overlook Dodsworth's simultaneous selfishness in response to the news. 'My cousin [Rushworth wisheth your] Saxon Dictionary gotten out, and I wish you had your other books,' he stressed in the same letter to Dugdale. '[As for] the silver and gold coins, I am confident they will be sold according to their weight. Send [word what you would have] done in your particular for your books.'[3]

Writing to a correspondent in Amsterdam in May 1650, Dutch scholar and librarian to the English nobility, Francis Junius, who had recently stayed with Simonds and his family in Stowlangtoft, revealed the same concern for the antiquarian loot that had become available upon D'Ewes's unexpected demise in the capital. 'There remains another desired business, which has now been brought to our attention, which it is of your interest to know,' he began cryptically, before announcing, 'it is about twenty days, or more, since here among us the knight Simondsius D'Ewes passed away, leaving behind an immense treasure of Greek and Roman coins.' Junius had heard that the extremely valuable coins were to be put up for sale by 'the people who have accepted the care of his children', which, he wrote, had encouraged him to personally urge them to think carefully before offloading the hoard onto the first buyer who came along.[4] Mercifully, he seemed to acknowledge the inappropriateness of his actions so soon after Simonds's widow, son and daughters had lost the head of their little family unit.

It was to be more than a month before D'Ewes began his last journey from London to Stowlangtoft, where there were plans to bury him alongside his close kin within St George's church. On 29 May, Dodsworth finally reported to Dugdale that 'your friend at Westminster's corpse [was] privately carried out of town this day'.[5] His funeral and interment, which occurred nine days later on 7 June, do not appear to have been described in any great detail (for Simonds was the chief orator of his own life), leaving us to piece together the day from the instructions that the baronet left in a draft of his will, dated 1639:

> I desire my body... may be decently buried in the daytime without all vain and superstitious pomp, a godly minister preaching my funeral sermon. Where my body shall be interred I have not yet resolved, but desire my faithful wife, if I shall not appoint a place before my decease, to cause the same to be entombed in the same place where she doth intend to be buried herself; and that she cause a marble stone

to be laid upon the place, with the epitaph engraven on a piece of brass and fastened to the stone... I bequeath to the poor of Lavenham £20, of Stowlangtoft £20... of Chardstock... £10... And I only give mourning apparel to my said wife, brother, and executors, together with my dear children and household servants.[6]

Admittedly, most of these directives were long out of date by the time June 1650 arrived.

Activity in the House of Commons – now the supreme authority in England, and under the influence of Oliver Cromwell – marched ever forwards in Westminster on 7 June, as if Simonds D'Ewes, with his Puritan but strictly moderate views, had never been there. Some items of business, to be sure, he would have approved of. For example, it was ordered in the chamber that a 'bill against swearing and cursing be reported on this-day-sevennight', and further commanded that 'an act against the vice of painting, and wearing black patches, and immodest dresses of women, be read on Friday morning next'.[7] Other items, however, would have left Simonds fearing for the future, to include an order authorising either the sale or dispersal of the late king's personal goods, some of which were to be kept back to furnish parliament's halls like a palace.

The days of the Interregnum had begun.

APPENDIX 1

D'EWES FAMILY TREE

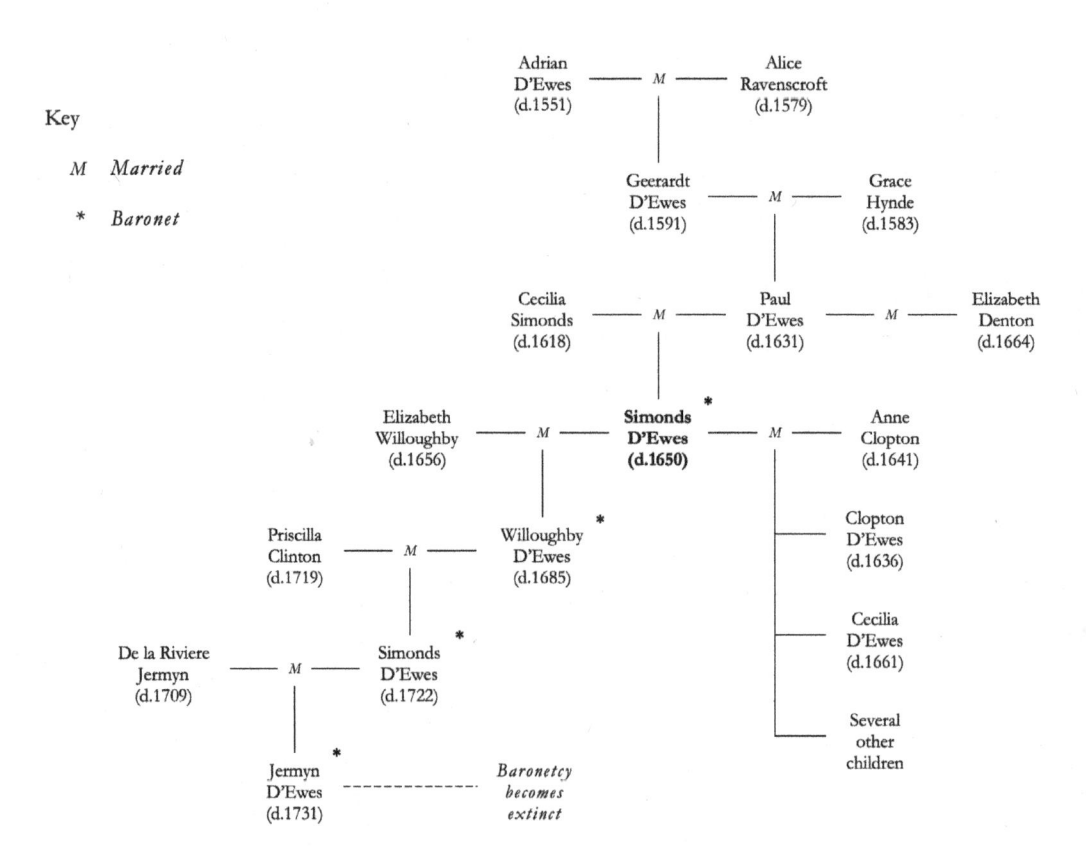

Key

M *Married*

* *Baronet*

- Adrian D'Ewes (d.1551) — M — Alice Ravenscroft (d.1579)
  - Geerardt D'Ewes (d.1591) — M — Grace Hynde (d.1583)
    - Cecilia Simonds (d.1618) — M — Paul D'Ewes (d.1631) — M — Elizabeth Denton (d.1664)
      - **Simonds D'Ewes (d.1650)** * — M — Anne Clopton (d.1641)
        - Elizabeth Willoughby (d.1656) — M — Willoughby D'Ewes (d.1685) *
          - Priscilla Clinton (d.1719) — M — Simonds D'Ewes (d.1722) *
            - De la Riviere Jermyn (d.1709) — M — Jermyn D'Ewes (d.1731) * — — — — *Baronetcy becomes extinct*
        - Clopton D'Ewes (d.1636)
        - Cecilia D'Ewes (d.1661)
        - Several other children

160

APPENDIX 2

BARNARDISTON FAMILY TREE

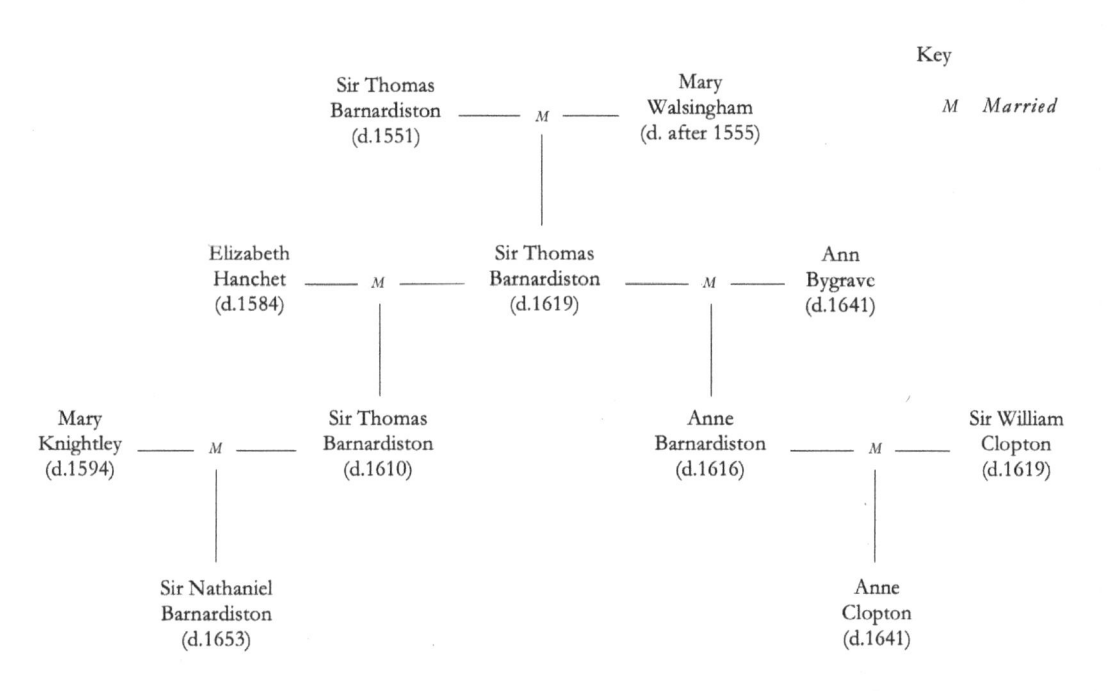

Key

M Married

Sir Thomas Barnardiston (d.1551) —M— Mary Walsingham (d. after 1555)

Elizabeth Hanchet (d.1584) —M— Sir Thomas Barnardiston (d.1619) —M— Ann Bygrave (d.1641)

Mary Knightley (d.1594) —M— Sir Thomas Barnardiston (d.1610)

Anne Barnardiston (d.1616) —M— Sir William Clopton (d.1619)

Sir Nathaniel Barnardiston (d.1653)

Anne Clopton (d.1641)

APPENDIX 3

THE CHILDREN OF SIMONDS D'EWES

Key

M Married

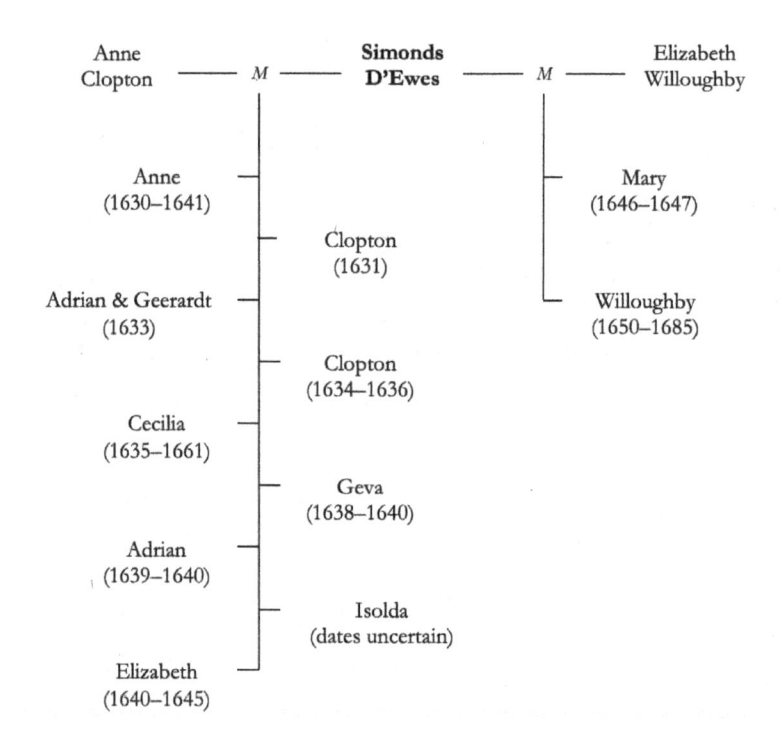

Anne Clopton —— *M* —— **Simonds D'Ewes** —— *M* —— Elizabeth Willoughby

Children of Anne Clopton and Simonds D'Ewes:
- Anne (1630–1641)
- Clopton (1631)
- Adrian & Geerardt (1633)
- Clopton (1634–1636)
- Cecilia (1635–1661)
- Geva (1638–1640)
- Adrian (1639–1640)
- Isolda (dates uncertain)
- Elizabeth (1640–1645)

Children of Simonds D'Ewes and Elizabeth Willoughby:
- Mary (1646–1647)
- Willoughby (1650–1685)

NOTES

Abbreviations

Autobiography – (Halliwell, 1845) The Autobiography and Correspondence of Sir Simonds D'Ewes, Bart., During the Reigns of James I and Charles I
BL (Harl.) MS – British Library (Harley) Manuscripts
CJ – Commons Journal
CSP – Calendar of State Papers
HMC – Historical Manuscripts Commission
MHS – Massachusetts Historical Society
PCCRP – Prerogative Court of Canterbury and Related Probate Jurisdictions

Introduction

1. John Bruce, 'The Long Parliament and Sir Simonds D'Ewes,' *The Edinburgh Review* 84, issue 169 (1846): p.84; John Forster, *Arrest of the Five Members by Charles the First* (London: John Murray, 1860), pp.219, 233.
2. J. Sears McGee, *An Industrious Mind: The Worlds of Sir Simonds D'Ewes* (Stanford: Stanford University Press, 2015), p.10.

Chapter 1: In the beginning

1. Joan Thirsk, *The Agrarian History of England and Wales*, Vol. 4 (Cambridge: Cambridge University Press, 1967), pp.64, 68, 70; Joyce Youings, 'Some Early Topographers of Devon and Cornwall,' in Mark Brayshay (ed.), *Topographical Writers in South-West England* (Exeter: University of Exeter Press, 1996), p.57.
2. James Halliwell (ed.), *Autobiography*, Vol. 1 (London: Richard Bentley, 1845), p.2; George P.R. Pulman, *The Book of the Axe* (Bath: Kingsmead Reprints, 1969), pp.550–1.
3. Halliwell, *Autobiography*, Vol. 1, pp.37, 41. Though this work has been criticised by some scholars in the field for containing inaccuracies and omissions, it nevertheless excels as a comprehensive source on D'Ewes for

those who do not have ready access to the original manuscripts in the British Library. Every care has been taken to ensure that the information in this book is historically accurate.

4. Ibid., p.117; PCCRP, *Will Registers*, PROB 11/159/401.
5. Anon., *A Catalogue of the Harleian Manuscripts, in the British Museum*, Vol. 3 (1808), p.101; Halliwell, *Autobiography*, Vol. 1, p.4.
6. Halliwell, *Autobiography*, Vol. 1, pp.5, 25.
7. Ibid., p.26.
8. Ibid., p.30.
9. Ibid., p.28.
10. Ibid., p.30.
11. Ibid., p.29.

Chapter 2: Out of Dorset

1. James Halliwell (ed.), *Autobiography*, Vol. 1 (London: Richard Bentley, 1845), p.32.
2. M.R. Postgate, 'Field Systems of East Anglia,' in Alan R.H. Baker and Robin A. Butlin (eds), *Studies of Field Systems in the British Isles* (Cambridge: Cambridge University Press, 1973), pp.285–6.
3. W.A. Copinger, *The Manors of Suffolk* (London: T. Fisher Unwin, 1905), pp.122, 123.
4. Halliwell, *Autobiography*, Vol. 1, p.38.
5. PCCRP, *Will Registers*, PROB 11/118/299.
6. G.W. Saunders and Charles Herbert Mayo (eds), *Notes & Queries for Somerset and Dorset*, Vol. 15 (Sherborne: J.C. and A.T. Sawtell, 1917), p.22.
7. Charles Henry Hopwood (ed.), *Middle Temple Records*, Vol. 2 (London: published by order of the Masters of the Bench, 1904), pp.541, 546, 551.

Chapter 3: Stowlangtoft

1. James Halliwell (ed.), *Autobiography*, Vol. 1 (London: Richard Bentley, 1845), p.62.
2. Ibid., pp.63–4.
3. Ibid., p.63.
4. BL MS 70518, ff. 144r-145r.
5. PCCRP, *Will Registers*, PROB 11/159/401; Anon., *A Catalogue of the Harleian Manuscripts, in the British Museum*, Vol. 1 (1808), pp.27, 228.
6. W.A. Copinger, *The Manors of Suffolk* (London: T. Fisher Unwin, 1905), p.364; Halliwell, *Autobiography*, Vol. 1, p.68.
7. Halliwell, *Autobiography*, Vol. 1, p.94.
8. Ibid., p.96.

9. 'History of Bury St Edmunds Abbey,' *English Heritage*, https://www.english-heritage.org.uk/visit/places/bury-st-edmunds-abbey/history/.
10. J. Deck, *A Guide to the Town, Abbey, and Antiquities of Bury St Edmunds* (Bury St Edmunds: W.T. Jackson, 1836), pp.32–3.

Chapter 4: A universal education

1. Willson Havelock Coates (ed.), *The Journal of Sir Simonds D'Ewes from the First Recess of the Long Parliament to the Withdrawal of King Charles from London* (New Haven: Yale University Press, 1942), p.53.
2. John Howard Marsden, *College Life in the Time of James the First* (London: John W. Parker and Son, 1851), p.6.
3. Ibid., p.11.
4. James Halliwell (ed.), *Autobiography*, Vol. 1 (London: Richard Bentley, 1845), p.110.
5. Ibid., p.118.
6. Marsden, *College Life*, pp.54–5.
7. Halliwell, *Autobiography*, Vol. 1, p.124.
8. Ibid., p.125.
9. Marsden, *College Life*, p.59.
10. Halliwell, *Autobiography*, Vol. 1, p.131.
11. Ibid., p.136; Ethel Williams, *Anne of Denmark: Wife of James VI of Scotland, James I of England* (London: Longman, 1971), p.201.
12. Halliwell, *Autobiography*, Vol. 1, p.134.
13. Samuel Clark, *The Lives of Sundry Eminent Persons in this Later Age* (London: Thomas Simmons, 1683), p.106.
14. Ibid., pp.107–8.
15. Ibid., p.111.

Chapter 5: The Road to the Temple

1. James Halliwell (ed.), *Autobiography*, Vol. 1 (London: Richard Bentley, 1845), p.140.
2. Ibid., p.142; J.T. Cliffe, *The Puritan Gentry: The Great Puritan Families of Early Stuart England* (London: Routledge & Kegan Paul, 1984), p.55.
3. Charles Henry Hopwood (ed.), *Middle Temple Records*, Vol. 2 (London: published by order of the Masters of the Bench, 1904), p.653.
4. Halliwell, *Autobiography*, Vol. 1, pp.147–8.
5. Anon., *A Catalogue of the Harleian Manuscripts, in the British Museum*, Vol. 1 (1808), p.29.
6. Hopwood, *Temple Records*, Vol. 2, p.545.
7. Ibid., pp.518, 580–1.
8. Ibid., p.657.

9. Anon., 'Courtship in the Time of King James the First,' *Blackwood's Edinburgh Magazine* 68, issue 417 (1850): p.142.
10. Anon., *Harleian Manuscripts*, Vol. 1, p.27; Anon., 'Courtship,' p.142.
11. Anon., 'Courtship,' p.143.
12. Hopwood, *Temple Records*, Vol. 2, p.659.
13. Ibid.
14. Ibid, p.803.

Chapter 6: Jemima Waldegrave

1. Anon., 'Courtship in the Time of King James the First,' *Blackwood's Edinburgh Magazine* 68, issue 417 (1850): pp.144–5.
2. Ibid., p.145.
3. John Nichols (ed.), *Extracts from the MS Journal of Sir Simonds D'Ewes* (London: J. Nichols, 1783), p.20.
4. James Halliwell (ed.), *Autobiography*, Vol. 1 (London: Richard Bentley, 1845), p.178.
5. Anon., 'Courtship,' p.147.
6. Ibid., pp.149, 150.
7. Ibid., pp.152, 154.
8. Charles Henry Hopwood (ed.), *Middle Temple Records*, Vol. 2 (London: published by order of the Masters of the Bench, 1904), p.667.
9. Halliwell, *Autobiography*, Vol. 1, pp.206–8.
10. Anon., *A Catalogue of the Harleian Manuscripts, in the British Museum*, Vol. 1 (1808), p.27; Halliwell, *Autobiography*, Vol. 1, p.212.

Chapter 7: City living

1. Gladys A. Harrison, 'The Diary of Sir Simonds D'Ewes, deciphered, for the period Jan. 1622–April 1624' (Master's dissertation, University of Minnesota, 1915), pp.24, 51, 52, 61.
2. James Halliwell (ed.), *Autobiography*, Vol. 1 (London: Richard Bentley, 1845), p.230.
3. PCCRP, *Will Registers*, PROB 11/159/401; Harrison, 'Diary,' p.249.
4. Harrison, 'Diary,' p.155; Halliwell, *Autobiography*, Vol. 1, p.232.
5. Halliwell, *Autobiography*, Vol. 1, p.235.
6. Harrison, 'Diary,' p.230.
7. Ibid., p.260; Paul S. Seaver, 'State Religion and Puritan Resistance in Early Seventeenth-Century England,' in James D. Tracy and Marguerite Ragnow (eds), *Religion and the Early Modern State: Views from China, Russia, and the West* (Cambridge: Cambridge University Press, 2004), p.236.
8. Anon., *A Catalogue of the Harleian Manuscripts, in the British Museum*, Vol. 1 (1808), p.27; Carol Rawcliffe, Richard George Wilson and Roger Virgoe

(eds), *Counties and Communities: Essays on East Anglian History: Presented to Hassell Smith* (Norwich: University of East Anglia, 1996), p.224.
9. Halliwell, *Autobiography*, Vol. 1, p.248.
10. Ibid., p.254.
11. Ibid., p.263.
12. Ibid., p.268.
13. HMC, *The Manuscripts of Henry Duncan Skrine: Salvetti Correspondence* (London: Her Majesty's Stationery Office, 1887), pp.15–6.
14. Ibid., p.16.
15. Ibid.
16. Ibid., p.17.
17. Ibid., pp.17, 21.
18. Halliwell, *Autobiography*, Vol. 1, pp.272–3, 279–80.
19. HMC, *Salvetti Correspondence*, p.44.
20. Halliwell, *Autobiography*, Vol. 1, p.292; Vol. 2, p.175.
21. John Nichols (ed.), *Extracts from the MS Journal of Sir Simonds D'Ewes* (London: J. Nichols, 1783), p.xiii.

Chapter 8: Anne Clopton

1. James Halliwell (ed.), *Autobiography*, Vol. 2 (London: Richard Bentley, 1845), p.164.
2. Ibid., Vol. 1, p.313; Vol. 2, p.188.
3. Ibid., Vol. 1, p.315.
4. Ibid., p.316.
5. Ibid., p.319.
6. London Metropolitan Archives, *London Church of England Parish Registers*, P69/Ann/A/002/Ms04509/001; Halliwell, *Autobiography*, Vol. 1, pp.322–3.
7. J.T. Cliffe, *The Puritan Gentry: The Great Puritan Families of Early Stuart England* (London: Routledge & Kegan Paul, 1984), p.130.

Chapter 9: Wolves

1. James Halliwell (ed.), *Autobiography*, Vol. 1 (London: Richard Bentley, 1845), pp.352, 355, 356.
2. Ibid., pp.358–9.
3. Ibid., p.359.
4. Ibid., pp.361–2.
5. Ibid., Vol. 2, p.196.
6. Ibid., Vol. 1, p.379.
7. Ibid., pp.391–2; H.R. Woudhuysen, *Sir Philip Sidney and the Circulation of Manuscripts, 1558–1640* (Oxford: Clarendon Press, 1996), p.128.
8. Halliwell, *Autobiography*, Vol. 1, p.402.

9. Ibid.; Kevin Sharpe, *The Personal Rule of Charles I* (New Haven: Yale University Press, 1992), pp.53–6.
10. Thomas Birch, *The Court and Times of Charles the First*, Vol. 2 (London: Henry Colburn, 1849), p.12.
11. Ibid.

Chapter 10: New lives and old

1. James Halliwell (ed.), *Autobiography*, Vol. 1 (London: Richard Bentley, 1845), p.418; Anon., *A Catalogue of the Harleian Manuscripts, in the British Museum*, Vol. 1 (1808), pp.25–6.
2. Halliwell, *Autobiography*, Vol. 1, pp.415, 420.
3. London Metropolitan Archives, *London Church of England Parish Registers*, P83/MRY1/1166.
4. Valerie Traub, *Thinking Sex with the Early Moderns* (Philadelphia: University of Pennsylvania Press, 2016), p.323; Halliwell, *Autobiography*, Vol. 2, p.216.
5. Halliwell, *Autobiography*, Vol. 1, p.438; John Nichols (ed.), *Extracts from the MS Journal of Sir Simonds D'Ewes* (London: J. Nichols, 1783), pp.70–1.
6. Halliwell, *Autobiography*, Vol. 2, p.5.
7. Ibid., pp.6, 8.
8. Thomas Birch, *The Court and Times of Charles the First*, Vol. 2 (London: Henry Colburn, 1849), p.100.
9. Halliwell, *Autobiography*, Vol. 2, p.22.
10. Ibid., p.26.
11. PCCRP, *Will Registers*, PROB 11/159/401.
12. Ibid.
13. Ibid.
14. Halliwell, *Autobiography*, Vol. 2, p.31.

Chapter 11: The Lavenham brass

1. James Halliwell (ed.), *Autobiography*, Vol. 2 (London: Richard Bentley, 1845), pp.41–2.
2. Ibid., pp.45–6.
3. H.R. Woudhuysen, *Sir Philip Sidney and the Circulation of Manuscripts, 1558–1640* (Oxford: Clarendon Press, 1996), p.127.
4. Halliwell, *Autobiography*, Vol. 2, p.71; J.T. Cliffe, *The Puritan Gentry: The Great Puritan Families of Early Stuart England* (London: Routledge & Kegan Paul, 1984), p.53.
5. Halliwell, *Autobiography*, Vol. 2, pp.78, 82.
6. John Nichols (ed.), *Extracts from the MS Journal of Sir Simonds D'Ewes* (London: J. Nichols, 1783), pp.71–2.
7. Halliwell, *Autobiography*, Vol. 2, p.89.
8. Ibid., pp.89–90.

Chapter 12: Laud

1. James Halliwell (ed.), *Autobiography*, Vol. 2 (London: Richard Bentley, 1845), pp.98, 103.
2. Ibid., p.111; Francis J. Bremer, *Puritanism: A Very Short Introduction* (Oxford: Oxford University Press, 2009), pp.14–5.
3. John Bruce (ed.), *CSP: 1634–1635* (London: Longman, Green, Longman, Roberts, and Green, 1864), p.263.
4. Ibid.
5. John Bruce (ed.), *CSP: 1635–1636* (London: Longmans, Green, Reader, and Dyer, 1866), p.124.
6. John Bruce (ed.), *CSP: 1635* (London: Longman, Green, Longman, Roberts, and Green, 1865), pp.394–5.
7. Tim Harris, *Rebellion: Britain's First Stuart Kings* (Oxford: Oxford University Press, 2014), pp.319, 320.
8. S.P. Salt, 'Sir Simonds D'Ewes and the Levying of Ship Money,' *The Historical Journal* 37 (1994): p.259; Allen B. Hinds (ed.), *CSP Relating to English Affairs in the Archives of Venice*, Vol. 23 (London: His Majesty's Stationery Office, 1921), p.443.
9. Halliwell, *Autobiography*, Vol. 2, p.104; Frank W. Jessup, *Background to the English Civil War* (Oxford: Pergamon Press, 1966), pp.19–20.
10. Randy Robertson, *Censorship and Conflict in Seventeenth-Century England: The Subtle Art of Division* (Philadelphia: University of Pennsylvania Press, 2009), p.3.
11. Pauline Gregg, *King Charles I* (Berkeley: University of California Press, 1984), pp.275–6; Wallace Notestein (ed.), *The Journal of Sir Simonds D'Ewes from the Beginning of the Long Parliament to the Opening of the Trial of the Earl of Strafford* (New Haven: Yale University Press, 1923), p.205.
12. Halliwell, *Autobiography*, Vol. 2, p.105.
13. Ibid., pp.107–8.
14. J.T. Cliffe, *The Puritan Gentry: The Great Puritan Families of Early Stuart England* (London: Routledge & Kegan Paul, 1984), p.106; Charles Henry Hopwood (ed.), *Middle Temple Records*, Vol. 2 (London: published by order of the Masters of the Bench, 1904), p.825.
15. Halliwell, *Autobiography*, Vol. 2, pp.122–3.
16. Patricia Crawford and Laura Gowing (eds), *Women's Worlds in Seventeenth-Century England* (London: Routledge, 2000), p.203.

Chapter 13: Ship money, the Elector Palatine and the New World

1. James Halliwell (ed.), *Autobiography*, Vol. 2 (London: Richard Bentley, 1845), pp.129–30.

2. William Palmer, *The Political Career of Oliver St John, 1637–1649* (London: Associated University Presses, 1993), p.24.
3. John Bruce (ed.), *CSP: 1636–1637* (London: Longmans, Green, Reader, and Dyer, 1867), p.344.
4. John Bruce (ed.), *CSP: 1635* (London: Longman, Green, Longman, Roberts, and Green, 1865), p.146; Halliwell, *Autobiography*, Vol. 2, p.132.
5. Pauline Gregg, *King Charles I* (Berkeley: University of California Press, 1984), pp.259–60.
6. Halliwell, *Autobiography*, Vol. 2, p.138.
7. PCCRP, *Will Registers*, PROB 11/314/242.
8. Halliwell, *Autobiography*, Vol. 2, pp.143–4.
9. Ibid., p.145.
10. Franklin M. Wright, 'A College First Proposed, 1633: Unpublished Letters of Apostle Eliot and William Hammond to Sir Simonds D'Ewes,' *Harvard Library Bulletin* 8, issue 3 (1954): p.261.
11. Ibid.
12. Ibid., p.274.
13. Halliwell, *Autobiography*, Vol. 2, p.146.
14. John Nichols (ed.), *Extracts from the MS Journal of Sir Simonds D'Ewes* (London: J. Nichols, 1783), p.74; Sara Warneke, *Images of the Educational Traveller in Early Modern England* (New York: E.J. Brill, 1995), p.184.

Chapter 14: Conflict at home, conflict afar

1. Ann Hughes, *The Causes of the English Civil War* (Basingstoke: Macmillan Press Ltd, 1998), p.32; R. Malcolm Smuts, *Political Culture, the State, & the Problem of Religious War in Britain & Ireland, 1578–1625* (Oxford: Oxford University Press, 2023), p.664.
2. John Nichols (ed.), *Extracts from the MS Journal of Sir Simonds D'Ewes* (London: J. Nichols, 1783), p.76.
3. John Nichols, *The History and Antiquities of the County of Leicester*, Vol. 2, Part 2 (London: J. Nichols, 1798), p.843; William Hamper (ed.), *The Life, Diary, and Correspondence of Sir William Dugdale* (London: Harding, Lepard, and Co., 1827), p.187.
4. Rick McIntyre (ed.), *War Against the Wolf: America's Campaign to Exterminate the Wolf* (Stillwater: Voyageur Press, 1995), pp.38–9.
5. S.P. Salt, 'Sir Simonds D'Ewes and the Levying of Ship Money,' *The Historical Journal* 37 (1994): p.266; William Douglas Hamilton (ed.), *CSP: 1639* (London: Longman & Co., 1873), p.248.
6. Ibid., p.250.
7. Henry Slingsby, *Original Memoirs Written During the Great Civil War* (Edinburgh: James Ballantyne & Co., 1806), p.28.
8. Patricia Crawford and Laura Gowing (eds), *Women's Worlds in Seventeenth-Century England* (London: Routledge, 2000), p.89.

9. Nichols, *MS Journal*, p.xvi.
10. William Douglas Hamilton (ed.), *CSP: 1639–1640* (London: Longman & Co., 1877), p.85; J.T. Cliffe, *The Puritan Gentry: The Great Puritan Families of Early Stuart England* (London: Routledge & Kegan Paul, 1984), p.212; Salt, 'Sir Simonds D'Ewes,' p.264.
11. Samuel Clark, *The Lives of Sundry Eminent Persons in this Later Age* (London: Thomas Simmons, 1683), p.108.
12. Vincent B. Redstone (ed.), *The Ship Money Returns for the County of Suffolk, 1639–40* (Ipswich: W.E. Harrison, 1904), p.ix.
13. Anon., *A Catalogue of the Harleian Manuscripts, in the British Museum*, Vol. 1 (1808), p.30.
14. William Douglas Hamilton (ed.), *CSP: 1640* (London: Longmans & Co., 1880), p.59.
15. Clark, *Lives*, p.109; Redstone, *Ship Money*, pp.24, 201.
16. Anon., *CJ*, Vol. 2 (London: The House of Commons, 1803), pp.9, 19.
17. Ibid., p.19.
18. Henry Ellis (ed.), *Original Letters of Eminent Literary Men* (London: Camden Society, 1843), pp.162–3; Hamilton, *CSP: 1640*, pp.269, 274.
19. Salt, 'Sir Simonds D'Ewes,' p.281; Anon., *Harleian Manuscripts*, Vol. 1, p.137.
20. John Rushworth, *Historical Collections*, Part 2, Vol. 2 (London: Thomas Newcombe, 1659), p.1245.
21. Slingsby, *Memoirs*, p.33.
22. William Douglas Hamilton (ed.), *CSP: 1640–1641* (London: Longman & Co, 1882), pp.38–9.
23. John Livingston, *A Brief Historical Relation of the Life of Mr John Livingston* (publisher unknown, 1727), p.24.
24. Ibid.
25. Nichols, *MS Journal*, p.80.

Chapter 15: The Long Parliament meets

1. James Halliwell (ed.), *Autobiography*, Vol. 2 (London: Richard Bentley, 1845), p.240.
2. Ibid., 243–4.
3. BL Harl. MS 286, f. 318v.
4. Thomas Carlyle, *Critical and Miscellaneous Essays*, Vol. 7 (London: Chapman and Hall, 1872), p.71.
5. Wallace Notestein (ed.), *The Journal of Sir Simonds D'Ewes from the Beginning of the Long Parliament to the Opening of the Trial of the Earl of Strafford* (New Haven: Yale University Press, 1923), p.1.
6. Ibid., p.120.
7. Halliwell, *Autobiography*, Vol. 2, pp.249–50.
8. Notestein, *Journal*, p.75; Halliwell, *Autobiography*, Vol. 2, p.252.
9. Halliwell, *Autobiography*, Vol. 2, p.254; Notestein, *Journal*, p.139.

10. Notestein, *Journal*, pp.162–3, 169.
11. Patricia Crawford and Laura Gowing (eds), *Women's Worlds in Seventeenth-Century England* (London: Routledge, 2000), p.193.

Chapter 16: Strafford

1. J.H. Hexter, 'The English Aristocracy, Its Crises, and the English Revolution, 1558–1660,' *Journal of British Studies* 8 (1968): p.68.
2. Wallace Notestein (ed.), *The Journal of Sir Simonds D'Ewes from the Beginning of the Long Parliament to the Opening of the Trial of the Earl of Strafford* (New Haven: Yale University Press, 1923), pp.234–5.
3. Simonds D'Ewes, *The Primitive Practise for Preserving Truth* (London: Henry Overton, 1645), no page number; J. Sears McGee, *An Industrious Mind: The Worlds of Sir Simonds D'Ewes* (Stanford: Stanford University Press, 2015), p.13.
4. MHS, *Collections of the Massachusetts Historical Society*, Vol. 7 (Boston: printed for the Society, 1865), p.9.
5. Notestein, *Journal*, pp.323–4.
6. Ibid., pp.324–5.
7. Ibid., p.340.
8. Ibid., p.407.
9. Ibid., pp.496–7.
10. Reginald F.D. Palgrave, 'The Story of the Death of Thomas, Earl of Strafford,' *Fraser's Magazine* 7, issue 40 (1873): pp.397, 400; Samuel R. Gardiner, *History of England from the Accession of James I to the Outbreak of the Civil War*, Vol. 9 (London: Longmans, Green, and Co., 1891), p.318; John Forster, *Historical and Biographical Essays*, Vol. 1 (London: John Murray, 1858), pp.253–4.
11. James Halliwell (ed.), *Autobiography*, Vol. 2 (London: Richard Bentley, 1845), p.268.
12. Maija Jansson (ed.), *Proceedings in the Opening Session of the Long Parliament*, Vol. 1 (Suffolk: University of Rochester Press, 2000), p.xxxvii.
13. Willson Havelock Coates (ed.), *The Journal of Sir Simonds D'Ewes from the First Recess of the Long Parliament to the Withdrawal of King Charles from London* (New Haven: Yale University Press, 1942), p.349.
14. Pauline Gregg, *King Charles I* (Berkeley: University of California Press, 1984), p.334.
15. Anon., *The truest relation of the Earle of Strafford's speech on the scaffold on Tower-hill, before he was beheaded* (London: s.n., 1641), pp.5, 6.

Chapter 17: The storm gathers

1. John Langton Sanford, *Studies and Illustrations of the Great Rebellion* (London: John W. Parker and Son, 1858), pp.373–5; W.A. Copinger, *The Manors of Suffolk* (London: T. Fisher Unwin, 1905), p.124.

2. William A. Shaw, *A History of the English Church During the Civil Wars and Under the Commonwealth*, Vol. 1 (London: Longmans, Green, and Co., 1900), p.82.
3. Barbara J. Shapiro, *Law Reform in Early Modern England: Crown, Parliament and the Press* (Oxford: Hart Publishing, 2019), p.97.
4. Simonds D'Ewes, *A speech delivered in the House of Commons* (London: s.n., 1641), p.4.
5. James Halliwell (ed.), *Autobiography*, Vol. 2 (London: Richard Bentley, 1845), p.271.
6. Ibid., p.273.
7. Ibid., p.275.
8. Ibid., p.279.
9. Ibid., pp.283–4.
10. Ibid., p.281.
11. Julius Hutchinson (ed.), *Memoirs of the Life of Colonel Hutchinson... Written by His Widow Lucy* (London: Henry G. Bohn, 1848), p.100.
12. Willson Havelock Coates (ed.), *The Journal of Sir Simonds D'Ewes from the First Recess of the Long Parliament to the Withdrawal of King Charles from London* (New Haven: Yale University Press, 1942), pp.6–7.
13. J.T. Cliffe, *The Puritan Gentry: The Great Puritan Families of Early Stuart England* (London: Routledge & Kegan Paul, 1984), p.226.
14. Sanford, *Studies and Illustrations*, p.415; William J. Bulman, *The Rise of Majority Rule in Early Modern Britain and Its Empire* (Cambridge: Cambridge University Press, 2021), p.113.
15. Bulman, *Majority Rule*, p.113; Anon., *CJ*, Vol. 2 (London: The House of Commons, 1803), p.330.
16. Sanford, *Studies and Illustrations*, pp.449–51.
17. Ibid.
18. Austin Woolrych, *Britain in Revolution: 1625–1660* (Oxford: Oxford University Press, 2002), p.212.
19. John Forster, *Arrest of the Five Members by Charles the First* (London: John Murray, 1860), pp.183, 184, 186.
20. Ibid., p.191.
21. Ibid., p.193.
22. Ibid., p.201.

Chapter 18: Brother against brother

1. Anon., *CJ*, Vol. 2 (London: The House of Commons, 1803), p.357.
2. Ibid.; Simonds D'Ewes, *Two speeches spoken by Sir Simonds D'Ewes* (London: Thomas Paybody, 1642), pp.5, 6.
3. J.T. Cliffe, *Puritans in Conflict: The Puritan Gentry During and After the Civil Wars* (London: Routledge, 1988), p.11.
4. John Langton Sanford, *Studies and Illustrations of the Great Rebellion* (London: John W. Parker and Son, 1858), p.474.

5. John Forster, *Arrest of the Five Members by Charles the First* (London: John Murray, 1860), p.228.
6. Ibid., pp.230–1.
7. Sanford, *Studies and Illustrations*, p.482.
8. Richard Holdsworth, *The people's happiness, a sermon preached in St Mary's in Cambridge* (Cambridge: Roger Daniel, 1642), no page number; Anon., *CJ*, Vol. 2, p.526.
9. Anon., *CJ*, Vol. 2, p.544.
10. Vernon F. Snow and Anne Steele Young (eds), *The Private Journals of the Long Parliament*, Vol. 3 (New Haven: Yale University Press, 1992), pp.43–4.
11. BL Harl. MS 286, f. 319r.
12. James Halliwell (ed.), *Autobiography*, Vol. 2 (London: Richard Bentley, 1845), p.290.
13. Ibid., p.292.
14. Charles Henry Hopwood (ed.), *Middle Temple Records*, Vol. 2 (London: published by order of the Masters of the Bench, 1904), pp.925–6.
15. Thomas Carlyle (ed.), *Oliver Cromwell's Letters and Speeches*, Vol. 1 (London: Chapman and Hall Limited, 1885), p.121; Anon., *CJ*, Vol. 2, p.688; Snow and Young, *Journals*, Vol. 3, pp.256–7.
16. Ronald Hutton, *The Royalist War Effort, 1642–1646*, 2nd edition (London: Routledge, 1999), p.22.
17. William Douglas Hamilton (ed.), *CSP: 1641–1643* (London: Her Majesty's Stationery Office, 1887), p.372.
18. Ibid.

Chapter 19: Edgehill

1. James Halliwell (ed.), *Autobiography*, Vol. 2 (London: Richard Bentley, 1845), p.296.
2. J.T. Cliffe, *Puritans in Conflict: The Puritan Gentry During and After the Civil Wars* (London: Routledge, 1988), p.28; Anon., *CJ*, Vol. 2 (London: The House of Commons, 1803), p.734.
3. Anon., *CJ*, Vol. 2, p.732; Samuel R. Gardiner, *History of the Great Civil War, 1642–1649*, Vol. 1 (London: Longmans, Green, and Co., 1901), pp.11–2.
4. John Bruce, 'The Long Parliament and Sir Simonds D'Ewes,' *The Edinburgh Review* 84, issue 169 (1846): p.95.
5. Ibid., p.96.
6. A.W., *The newest and truest, and most unpartiall relation of all the late occurrence which hath happened at Sherbourne-Castle, and thereabouts* (London: s.n., 1642), pp.5, 6.
7. Bruce, 'D'Ewes,' p.96.
8. Ibid., p.97.

9. J. Sears McGee, *An Industrious Mind: The Worlds of Sir Simonds D'Ewes* (Stanford: Stanford University Press, 2015), pp.379, 380; Bruce, 'D'Ewes,' pp.99–100.
10. Gardiner, *Great Civil War*, Vol. 1, p.30.
11. Bruce, 'D'Ewes,' p.100; Anon., *CJ*, Vol. 2, p.803.
12. John Rushworth (ed.), *Historical Collections*, Part 3, Vol. 2 (London: Richard Chiswell and Thomas Cockerill, 1692), pp.35–6.
13. Ibid., p.36.
14. Ibid., p.38; Nehemiah Wallington, *Historical Notices of Events Occurring Chiefly in the Reign of Charles I*, Vol. 2 (London: Richard Bentley, 1869), pp.115–6.
15. Margaret M. Verney (ed.), *Memoirs of the Verney Family During the Seventeenth Century*, Vol. 1 (London: Longmans, Green, and Co., 1904), p.272.
16. Matthew Sylvester (ed.), *Reliquiæ Baxterianæ: or, Mr Richard Baxter's Narrative of the Most Memorable Passages of His Life and Times* (London: T. Parkhurst, J. Robinson, J. Lawrence, and J. Dunton, 1696), p.43.

Chapter 20: An unhappy Christmas

1. Anon., *CJ*, Vol. 2 (London: The House of Commons, 1803), p.846.
2. James Halliwell (ed.), *Autobiography*, Vol. 2 (London: Richard Bentley, 1845), p.303.
3. Ruth Spalding, *The Improbable Puritan: A Life of Bulstrode Whitelocke, 1605–1675* (London: Faber & Faber, 1975), pp.86–7.
4. David Scott, 'Party politics in the Long Parliament, 1640–8,' in George Southcombe and Grant Tapsell (eds), *Revolutionary England, c. 1630–c. 1660: Essays for Clive Holmes* (London: Routledge, 2022), p.38; Charles Henry Hopwood (ed.), *Middle Temple Records*, Vol. 2 (London: published by order of the Masters of the Bench, 1904), p.928; J.T. Cliffe, *Puritans in Conflict: The Puritan Gentry During and After the Civil Wars* (London: Routledge, 1988), pp.37, 40.
5. Hopwood, *Temple Records*, Vol. 2, p.928.
6. G.N. Godwin, *The Civil War in Hampshire* (London: John and Edward Bumpus Ltd, 1904), p.47.
7. Anon., *CJ*, Vol. 2, p.896.

Chapter 21: Richard's farewell

1. Patricia Crawford and Laura Gowing (eds), *Women's Worlds in Seventeenth-Century England* (London: Routledge, 2000), p.250.
2. David Scott, 'Party politics in the Long Parliament, 1640–8,' in George Southcombe and Grant Tapsell (eds), *Revolutionary England, c. 1630–c. 1660: Essays for Clive Holmes* (London: Routledge, 2022), pp.40–1.
3. J.T. Cliffe, *Puritans in Conflict: The Puritan Gentry During and After the Civil Wars* (London: Routledge, 1988), p.89.

4. Anon., *CJ*, Vol. 3 (London: The House of Commons, 1803), p.47; Serena Jones, *No Armour But Courage: Colonel Sir George Lisle, 1615–1648* (Solihull: Helion & Company Limited, 2016), pp.100–1.
5. Jones, *No Armour*, p.94.
6. Clarendon, *The History of the Rebellion and Civil Wars in England* (Oxford: Oxford University Press, 1843), p.382.
7. Charles Coates, *The History and Antiquities of Reading* (London: J. Nichols and Son, 1802), p.32; Walter Scott (ed.), *Military Memoirs of the Great Civil War* (Edinburgh: Hurst, Robinson, and Co., 1822), pp.26–7.
8. Coates, *Reading*, p.35; Clarendon, *History*, p.386.
9. John Bruce, 'The Long Parliament and Sir Simonds D'Ewes,' *The Edinburgh Review* 84, issue 169 (1846): pp.100–1.
10. PCCRP, *Will Registers*, PROB 11/191/344.
11. Ibid., PROB 11/314/242.

Chapter 22: 'These miserable calamities and civil wars of England'

1. Edmund Ludlow, *Memoirs of Edmund Ludlow*, Vol. 1, 3rd edition (Edinburgh: Sands, A. Kincaid & A. Donaldson, 1751), pp.51–2.
2. Anon., *CJ*, Vol. 3 (London: The House of Commons, 1803), p.83.
3. Michelle Anne White, *Henrietta Maria and the English Civil Wars* (Aldershot: Ashgate Publishing Limited, 2006), p.83; Anon., *CJ*, Vol. 3, p.100.
4. Edward Vallance, *Revolutionary England and the National Covenant: State Oaths, Protestantism and the Political Nation, 1553–1682* (Woodbridge: The Boydell Press, 2005), p.56; Anon., *CJ*, Vol. 3, p.118; John Langton Sanford, *Studies and Illustrations of the Great Rebellion* (London: John W. Parker and Son, 1858), pp.566–7.
5. Samuel R. Gardiner, *History of the Great Civil War, 1642–1649*, Vol. 1 (London: Longmans, Green, and Co., 1901), pp.177–8.
6. J.T. Cliffe, *Puritans in Conflict: The Puritan Gentry During and After the Civil Wars* (London: Routledge, 1988), p.141.
7. Eliot Warburton, *Memoirs of Prince Rupert, and the Cavaliers*, Vol. 2 (London: Richard Bentley, 1849), p.244.
8. Ibid., p.245.
9. Ibid., p.251.
10. Ibid., p.255.
11. William Prynne, *A true and full relation of the prosecution, arraignment, tryall, and condemnation of Nathaniel Fiennes* (London: Michael Sparke, 1644), p.45; Andrew Hopper, *Turncoats & Renegades: Changing Sides During the English Civil Wars* (Oxford: Oxford University Press, 2012), p.183.
12. Gardiner, *Great Civil War*, Vol. 1, p.183.
13. Ibid., p.187.
14. Anon., *CJ*, Vol. 3, p.252.

15. T.V., *A True relation of the late battell neere Newbery* (London: John Wright, 1643), p.5.
16. Ian Gentles, *The English Revolution and the Wars in the Three Kingdoms, 1638–1652* (London: Routledge, 2007), p.459; John Miller, *A Brief History of the English Civil Wars: Roundheads, Cavaliers and the Execution of the King* (London: Constable & Robinson Ltd, 2009), p.103.
17. Anon., *CJ*, Vol. 3, p.298.
18. John Forster, *The Statesmen of the Commonwealth of England*, Vol. 2 (London: Longman, Orme, Brown, Green, & Longmans, 1840), p.295.

Chapter 23: Marston Moor

1. J.T. Cliffe, *Puritans in Conflict: The Puritan Gentry During and After the Civil Wars* (London: Routledge, 1988), p.67.
2. Anon., *CJ*, Vol. 3 (London: The House of Commons, 1803), p.415.
3. HMC, *Report on the Manuscripts of the Late Reginald Rawdon Hastings*, Vol. 2 (London: His Majesty's Stationery Office, 1930), pp.118–9.
4. HMC, *Calendar of the Manuscripts of the Marquis of Bath*, Vol. 1 (London: His Majesty's Stationery Office, 1904), p.29; Anon., *CJ*, Vol. 3, p.470.
5. Charles Sanford Terry, *The Life and Campaigns of Alexander Leslie, First Earl of Leven* (London: Longmans, Green, and Co., 1899), p.220.
6. Henry Slingsby, *Original Memoirs Written During the Great Civil War* (Edinburgh: James Ballantyne & Co., 1806), pp.45–6.
7. Blair Worden, *The English Civil Wars, 1640–1660* (London: Orion, 2009), pp.59–60.
8. John Langton Sanford, *Studies and Illustrations of the Great Rebellion* (London: John W. Parker and Son, 1858), p.615.
9. Frederic Harrison, *Oliver Cromwell* (London: Macmillan and Co., 1895), pp.76–7.
10. Sanford, *Studies and Illustrations*, p.599.
11. Ibid., p.606.
12. Peter Young, *Marston Moor 1644: The Campaign and the Battle* (Kineton: The Roundwood Press, 1970), pp.140–1; Terry, *Alexander Leslie*, pp.271–2.
13. Slingsby, *Memoirs*, p.51.

Chapter 24: The wrath of religion

1. William Palmer, *The Political Career of Oliver St John, 1637–1649* (London: Associated University Presses, 1993), p.84.
2. Anon., *An exact relation of the bloody and barbarous massacre at Bolton in the moors in Lancashire* (London: R.W., 1644), p.2.
3. Ibid., p.4.

4. William Douglas Hamilton (ed.), *CSP: 1644* (London: Her Majesty's Stationery Office, 1888), p.324.
5. James Halliwell (ed.), *Autobiography*, Vol. 2 (London: Richard Bentley, 1845), p.307.
6. Anon., *CJ*, Vol. 3 (London: The House of Commons, 1803), p.725.
7. Clive Holmes (ed.), *The Suffolk Committees for Scandalous Ministers, 1644–46* (Suffolk: Suffolk Records Society, 1970), p.106.
8. Anon., *CJ*, Vol. 3, p.634.
9. John R. MacCormack, *Revolutionary Politics in the Long Parliament* (Cambridge, Massachusetts: Harvard University Press, 1973), p.52.
10. William Douglas Hamilton (ed.), *CSP: 1644–1645* (London: Her Majesty's Stationery Office, 1890), p.228.
11. Peter Heylyn, *A briefe relation of the death and sufferings of the Most Reverend and renowned prelate, the L. Archbishop of Canterbury* (Oxford: s.n., 1645), pp.15, 23.
12. Ibid., p.26; Halliwell, *Autobiography*, Vol. 2, p.100.

Chapter 25: Naseby

1. Simonds D'Ewes, *The Primitive Practise for Preserving Truth* (London: Henry Overton, 1645), no page number.
2. R.N. Dore (ed.), *The Letter Books of Sir William Brereton*, Vol. 1 (Liverpool: Record Society of Lancashire and Cheshire, 1984), p.37.
3. Anon., *CJ*, Vol. 4 (London: The House of Commons, 1803), p.51; Austin Woolrych, *Battles of the English Civil War* (London: Phoenix Press, 2000), p.92.
4. Anon., *CJ*, Vol. 4, p.51.
5. Peter Gaunt, *The English Civil Wars, 1642–1651* (Oxford: Osprey Publishing, 2003), p.45; Anon., *CJ*, Vol. 4, p.98.
6. J.T. Cliffe, *Puritans in Conflict: The Puritan Gentry During and After the Civil Wars* (London: Routledge, 1988), p.90; John R. MacCormack, *Revolutionary Politics in the Long Parliament* (Cambridge, Massachusetts: Harvard University Press, 1973), pp.74–5.
7. Anon., *CJ*, Vol. 4, pp.85, 126.
8. MacCormack, *Revolutionary Politics*, p.75; Anon., *CJ*, Vol. 4, pp.169–70.
9. Clive Holmes (ed.), *The Suffolk Committees for Scandalous Ministers, 1644–46* (Suffolk: Suffolk Records Society, 1970), p.111.
10. John Rushworth (ed.), *Historical Collections*, Part 4, Vol. 1 (London: D. Brown et al., 1722), p.45.
11. Gaunt, *Civil Wars*, p.45.
12. Anon., *A more exact and perfect relation of the great victory (by God's providence) obtained by the Parliament's forces under command of Sir Tho. Fairfax in Naseby Field* (London: John Wright, 1645), pp.3–4.
13. Ibid., pp.4–5.

14. Matthew Sylvester (ed.), *Reliquiæ Baxterianæ: or, Mr Richard Baxter's Narrative of the Most Memorable Passages of His Life and Times* (London: T. Parkhurst, J. Robinson, J. Lawrence, and J. Dunton, 1696), p.50.
15. Charles Edward Long (ed.), *Diary of the Marches of the Royal Army* (London: Camden Society, 1859), p.180.
16. Ibid., pp.180–1.
17. Rushworth, *Historical Collections*, Part 4, Vol. 1, p.35.
18. Anon., *The manner how the prisoners are to be brought into the city of London, this present Saturday being the 21st day of June, 1645* (London: T.F. and J. Coe, 1645), p.1.
19. Anon., *CJ*, Vol. 4, p.182.
20. Ibid., p.264.

Chapter 26: 1646

1. Charles Henry Hopwood (ed.), *Middle Temple Records*, Vol. 2 (London: published by order of the Masters of the Bench, 1904), p.935.
2. Anne R. Larsen, *Anna Maria van Schurman, 'The Star of Utrecht': The Educational Vision and Reception of a Savante* (Routledge: Abingdon, 2016), pp.54, 59; Carol Pal, *Republic of Women: Rethinking the Republic of Letters in the Seventeenth Century* (Cambridge: Cambridge University Press, 2012), p.195.
3. Anna Maria van Schurman, *Opuscula Hebraea, Graeca, Latina, Gallica. Prosaica et Metrica.* (Leiden: Elzevir Press, 1648), pp.217–9; Larsen, *Anna Maria*, p.54; J. Sears McGee, *An Industrious Mind: The Worlds of Sir Simonds D'Ewes* (Stanford: Stanford University Press, 2015), p.429.
4. Anon., 'House of Lords Journal, Volume 8: 19 March 1646,' in *Journal of the House of Lords: Volume 8, 1645–1647* (London, 1767–1830), pp.220–1. British History Online http://www.british-history.ac.uk/lords-jrnl/vol8/pp220-221 [accessed 30 June 2023].
5. John Nichols (ed.), *Extracts from the MS Journal of Sir Simonds D'Ewes* (London: J. Nichols, 1783), pp.81–2.
6. Anon., *CJ*, Vol. 4 (London: The House of Commons, 1803), pp.537–8.
7. Hopwood, *Temple Records*, Vol. 2, p.939.
8. The Dean and Chapter of the Collegiate Church of Saint Peter in Westminster, *Registers and Books of St Margaret's Church, Westminster*, MA/01/01/006; McGee, *An Industrious Mind*, p.380.
9. James Halliwell (ed.), *Autobiography*, Vol. 2 (London: Richard Bentley, 1845), p.310.
10. Anon., *The Parliamentary History of England*, Vol. 3 (London: T.C. Hansard, 1808), p.515.
11. Anon., *CJ*, Vol. 4, p.712.
12. Ibid., Vol. 5, p.30.

Chapter 27: The king's escape

1. James Halliwell (ed.), *Autobiography*, Vol. 2 (London: Richard Bentley, 1845), pp.311–5; N. Denholm-Young and H.H.E. Craster, 'Roger Dodsworth (1585–1654) and His Circle,' in J.W. Houseman (ed.), *The Yorkshire Archaeological Journal*, Vol. 32 (Leeds: Yorkshire Archaeological Society, 1936), pp.15–6.
2. Anon., *CJ*, Vol. 5 (London: The House of Commons, 1803), pp.139, 189.
3. Various, *Notes and Queries*, 3rd series, Vol. 10 (London: The office of the Institute, 1866), p.33.
4. Susan Irvine (ed.), *The Anglo-Saxon Chronicle: A Collaborative Edition*, Vol. 7 (Cambridge: D.S. Brewer, 2004), pp.xv–xvi.
5. Henry Cary (ed.), *Memorials of the Great Civil War in England*, Vol. 1 (London: Henry Colburn, 1842), pp.233–4.
6. Ibid., p.235.
7. John Rushworth (ed.), *Historical Collections*, Part 4, Vol. 2 (London: Richard Chiswell and Thomas Cockerill, 1701), p.871.
8. Cary, *Memorials*, Vol. 1, p.359.
9. Anon., *Canterbury Christmas or, a true relation of the insurrection in Canterbury on Christmas day last* (London: Humphrey Harward, 1648), pp.1–2.
10. Ibid., p.3.

Chapter 28: Colchester falls

1. John R. MacCormack, *Revolutionary Politics in the Long Parliament* (Cambridge, Massachusetts: Harvard University Press, 1973), pp.251–2.
2. Anon., *CJ*, Vol. 5 (London: The House of Commons, 1803), pp.415–6.
3. Ibid., p.436.
4. Ibid., p.546.
5. Andrew Hopper, 'The Civil Wars,' in Carole Rawcliffe and Richard Wilson (eds), *Norwich since 1550* (London: Hambledon and London, 2004), pp.108–9.
6. John Rushworth (ed.), *Historical Collections*, Part 4, Vol. 2 (London: Richard Chiswell and Thomas Cockerill, 1701), p.1119.
7. W.A. Copinger, *The Manors of Suffolk* (London: T. Fisher Unwin, 1905), pp.124–5; Anon., *CJ*, Vol. 5, p.580.
8. Barbara Donagan, *War in England, 1642–1649* (Oxford: Oxford University Press, 2010), p.317; J.M. Russell, *The History of Maidstone* (Maidstone: W.S. Vivish, 1881), p.272.
9. George Hillier, *A Narrative of the Attempted Escapes of Charles the First from Carisbrooke Castle* (London: Richard Bentley, 1852), pp.167–8.
10. Ibid., p.168.

11. 'Charles I: A Royal Prisoner at Carisbrooke Castle,' *English Heritage*, https://www.english-heritage.org.uk/visit/places/carisbrooke-castle/history/charles-i-prisoner/; Hillier, *Narrative*, p.170.
12. Rushworth, *Historical Collections*, Part 4, Vol. 2, p.1242.
13. Donagan, *War in England*, pp.317–8.
14. Matthew Carter, *A most true and exact relation of that as honourable as unfortunate expedition of Kent, Essex, and Colchester* (London: s.n., 1650), pp.132, 133; Charles Carlton, *This Seat of Mars: War and the British Isles, 1485–1746* (New Haven: Yale University Press, 2011), p.139.
15. Carter, *Colchester*, p.140.
16. Ibid., pp.141–2.
17. Ibid., pp.164–5.
18. Rushworth, *Historical Collections*, Part 4, Vol. 2, p.1221.
19. Carter, *Colchester*, p.189.
20. Anon., 'Courtship in the Time of King James the First,' *Blackwood's Edinburgh Magazine* 68, issue 417 (1850): p.148.
21. Carter, *Colchester*, p.198.
22. Ibid., p.199.

Chapter 29: Purged

1. Anon., *CJ*, Vol. 6 (London: The House of Commons, 1803), p.49.
2. Henry W. Henfrey, 'King Charles the First's Collection of Coins,' in John Evans et al. (eds), *The Numismatic Chronicle and Journal of the Numismatic Society*, New Series, Vol. 14 (London: John Russell Smith, 1874), p.100.
3. John Rushworth (ed.), *Historical Collections*, Part 4, Vol. 2 (London: Richard Chiswell and Thomas Cockerill, 1701), p.1353.
4. Bulstrode Whitelocke, *Memorials of the English Affairs* (London: Nathaniel Ponder, 1682), p.354; David Underdown, *Pride's Purge: Politics in the Puritan Revolution* (London: George Allen & Unwin, 1985), p.147.
5. Rushworth, *Historical Collections*, Part 4, Vol. 2, p.1355.
6. Underdown, *Pride's Purge*, p.159.

Chapter 30: 'A happy hour'

1. William Hamper (ed.), *The Life, Diary, and Correspondence of Sir William Dugdale* (London: Harding, Lepard, and Co., 1827), p.218.
2. Ibid.
3. S. Isaacson, 'Notices of the Family of Stuteville, of Dalham Hall, Suffolk,' in Anon. (ed), *Transactions of the British Archaeological Association, at its Second Annual Congress, Held at Winchester* (London: Henry G. Bohn, 1846), p.322.

4. Anon., *CJ*, Vol. 6 (London: The House of Commons, 1803), p.126.
5. Rolf H. Bremmer Jr, 'The Reception of the Old English Version of Gregory the Great's *Dialogues* between the Conquest and the Close of the Nineteenth Century,' in Larissa Tracy and Geert H.M. Claassens (eds), *Medieval English and Dutch Literatures: The European Context* (Cambridge: D.S. Brewer, 2022), p.43; Rolf H. Bremmer Jr, '"Mine is Bigger than Yours": The Anglo-Saxon Collections of Johannes de Laet (1581–1649) and Sir Simonds D'Ewes (1602–1650),' in S.D. Hall T.N. (ed.), *Anglo-Saxon Books and Their Readers: Essays in Celebration of Helmut Gneuss's 'Handlist of Anglo-Saxon Manuscripts'* (Kalamazoo: Western Michigan University Press, 2008), p.156; Charles Richard Elrington (ed.), *The Whole Works of the Most Rev. James Ussher*, Vol. 16 (Dublin: Hodges, Smith, and Co., 1864), p.555.
6. Anon., *A Catalogue of the Harleian Manuscripts, in the British Museum*, Vol. 1 (1808), p.29; HMC, *Report on the Manuscripts of the Late Reginald Rawdon Hastings*, Vol. 2 (London: His Majesty's Stationery Office, 1930), p.139; W.A. Copinger, *The Manors of Suffolk* (London: T. Fisher Unwin, 1905), p.41.
7. Hamper, *Dugdale*, p.222.
8. Ibid., pp.221, 222, 223.
9. Isaacson, 'Stuteville,' p.322.
10. Ibid.
11. The Dean and Chapter of the Collegiate Church of Saint Peter in Westminster, *Registers and Books of St Margaret's Church, Westminster*, MA/01/01/006.

Epilogue: In the end

1. J. Sears McGee, *An Industrious Mind: The Worlds of Sir Simonds D'Ewes* (Stanford: Stanford University Press, 2015), p.431.
2. Anon., *CJ*, Vol. 6 (London: The House of Commons, 1803), p.400.
3. William Hamper (ed.), *The Life, Diary, and Correspondence of Sir William Dugdale* (London: Harding, Lepard, and Co., 1827), p.229.
4. Sophie van Romburgh, *'For My Worthy Friend Mr Franciscus Junius': An Edition of the Correspondence of Francis Junius F.F. (1591–1677)* (Leiden: Brill, 2004), pp.782, 785.
5. Hamper, *Dugdale*, p.236.
6. James Halliwell (ed.), *Autobiography*, Vol. 2 (London: Richard Bentley, 1845), pp.149–50.
7. Anon., *CJ*, Vol. 6, pp.421–2.

BIBLIOGRAPHY

Primary sources

A.W., *The newest and truest, and most unpartiall relation of all the late occurrence which hath happened at Sherbourne-Castle, and thereabouts* (London: s.n., 1642)

Anon., *A Catalogue of the Harleian Manuscripts, in the British Museum*, 2 vols (1808)

Anon., *A more exact and perfect relation of the great victory (by God's providence) obtained by the Parliament's forces under command of Sir Tho. Fairfax in Naseby Field* (London: John Wright, 1645)

Anon., *An exact relation of the bloody and barbarous massacre at Bolton in the moors in Lancashire* (London: R.W., 1644)

Anon., *Canterbury Christmas or, a true relation of the insurrection in Canterbury on Christmas day last* (London: Humphrey Harward, 1648)

Anon., *CJ*, 5 vols (London: The House of Commons, 1803)

Anon. 'House of Lords Journal, Volume 8: 19 March 1646.' In *Journal of the House of Lords: Volume 8, 1645–1647* (London, 1767–1830), pp.220–1. British History Online http://www.british-history.ac.uk/lords-jrnl/vol8/pp.220–1 [accessed 30 June 2023]

Anon., *The manner how the prisoners are to be brought into the city of London, this present Saturday being the 21st day of June, 1645* (London: T.F. and J. Coe, 1645)

Anon., *The truest relation of the Earle of Strafford's speech on the scaffold on Tower-hill, before he was beheaded* (London: s.n., 1641)

British Library, *BL (Harl.) MS* (Euston Road, London)

Bruce, John (ed.), *CSP: 1634–1635* (London: Longman, Green, Longman, Roberts, and Green, 1864)

Bruce, John (ed.), *CSP: 1635* (London: Longman, Green, Longman, Roberts, and Green, 1865)

Bruce, John (ed.), *CSP: 1635–1636* (London: Longman, Green, Reader, and Dyer, 1866)

Bruce, John (ed.), *CSP: 1636–1637* (London: Longman, Green, Reader, and Dyer, 1867)

Carlyle, Thomas (ed.), *Oliver Cromwell's Letters and Speeches*, Vol. 1 (London: Chapman and Hall Limited, 1885)

Carter, Matthew, *A most true and exact relation of that as honourable as unfortunate expedition of Kent, Essex, and Colchester* (London: s.n., 1650)

Cary, Henry (ed.), *Memorials of the Great Civil War in England*, Vol. 1 (London: Henry Colburn, 1842)

Clarendon, *The History of the Rebellion and Civil Wars in England* (Oxford: Oxford University Press, 1843)

Clark, Samuel, *The Lives of Sundry Eminent Persons in this Later Age* (London: Thomas Simmons, 1683)

Coates, Willson Havelock (ed.), *The Journal of Sir Simonds D'Ewes from the First Recess of the Long Parliament to the Withdrawal of King Charles from London* (New Haven: Yale University Press, 1942)

D'Ewes, Simonds, *A speech delivered in the House of Commons* (London: s.n., 1641)

D'Ewes, Simonds, *The Primitive Practise for Preserving Truth* (London: Henry Overton, 1645)

D'Ewes, Simonds, *Two speeches spoken by Sir Simonds D'Ewes* (London: Thomas Paybody, 1642)

Dore, R.N. (ed.), *The Letter Books of Sir William Brereton*, Vol. 1 (Liverpool: Record Society of Lancashire and Cheshire, 1984)

Ellis, Henry (ed.), *Original Letters of Eminent Literary Men* (London: Camden Society, 1843)

Elrington, Charles Richard (ed.), *The Whole Works of the Most Rev. James Ussher*, Vol. 16 (Dublin: Hodges, Smith, and Co., 1864)

Halliwell, James, *Autobiography*, 2 vols (London: Richard Bentley, 1845)

Hamilton, William Douglas (ed.), *CSP: 1639* (London: Longman & Co., 1873)

Hamilton, William Douglas (ed.), *CSP: 1639–1640* (London: Longman & Co., 1877)

Hamilton, William Douglas (ed.), *CSP: 1640* (London: Longman & Co., 1880)

Hamilton, William Douglas (ed.), *CSP: 1640–1641* (London: Longman & Co, 1882)

Hamilton, William Douglas (ed.), *CSP: 1641–1643* (London: Her Majesty's Stationery Office, 1887)

Hamilton, William Douglas (ed.), *CSP: 1644* (London: Her Majesty's Stationery Office, 1888)

Hamilton, William Douglas (ed.), *CSP: 1644–1645* (London: Her Majesty's Stationery Office, 1890)

Hamper, William (ed.), *The Life, Diary, and Correspondence of Sir William Dugdale* (London: Harding, Lepard, and Co., 1827)

Harrison, Gladys A., 'The Diary of Sir Simonds D'Ewes, deciphered, for the period Jan. 1622–April 1624' (Master's dissertation, University of Minnesota, 1915)

Henfrey, Henry W. 'King Charles the First's Collection of Coins.' In *The Numismatic Chronicle and Journal of the Numismatic Society*, New Series, Vol. 14, edited by John Evans et al., pp.100–4 (London: John Russell Smith, 1874)

Heylyn, Peter, *A briefe relation of the death and sufferings of the Most Reverend and renowned prelate, the L. Archbishop of Canterbury* (Oxford: s.n., 1645)

Hinds, Allen B. (ed.), *CSP Relating to English Affairs in the Archives of Venice*, Vol. 23 (London: His Majesty's Stationery Office, 1921)

Bibliography

HMC, *Calendar of the Manuscripts of the Marquis of Bath*, Vol. 1 (London: His Majesty's Stationery Office, 1904)

HMC, *Report on the Manuscripts of the Late Reginald Rawdon Hastings*, Vol. 2 (London: His Majesty's Stationery Office, 1930)

HMC, *The Manuscripts of Henry Duncan Skrine: Salvetti Correspondence* (London: Her Majesty's Stationery Office, 1887)

Holdsworth, Richard, *The people's happiness, a sermon preached in St Mary's in Cambridge* (Cambridge: Roger Daniel, 1642)

Holmes, Clive (ed.), *The Suffolk Committees for Scandalous Ministers, 1644–46* (Suffolk: Suffolk Records Society, 1970)

Hopwood, Charles Henry (ed.), *Middle Temple Records*, Vol. 2 (London: published by order of the Masters of the Bench, 1904)

Hutchinson, Julius (ed.), *Memoirs of the Life of Colonel Hutchinson... Written by His Widow Lucy* (London: Henry G. Bohn, 1848)

Jansson, Maija (ed.), *Proceedings in the Opening Session of the Long Parliament*, Vol. 1 (Suffolk: University of Rochester Press, 2000)

Livingston, John, *A Brief Historical Relation of the Life of Mr John Livingston* (publisher unknown, 1727)

London Metropolitan Archives, *London Church of England Parish Registers* (Northampton Road, London)

Long, Charles Edward (ed.), *Diary of the Marches of the Royal Army* (London: Camden Society, 1859)

Ludlow, Edmund, *Memoirs of Edmund Ludlow*, Vol. 1, 3rd edition (Edinburgh: Sands, A. Kincaid & A. Donaldson, 1751)

MHS, *Collections of the Massachusetts Historical Society*, Vol. 7 (Boston: printed for the Society, 1865)

Nichols, John (ed.), *Extracts from the MS Journal of Sir Simonds D'Ewes* (London: J. Nichols, 1783)

Notestein, Wallace (ed.), *The Journal of Sir Simonds D'Ewes from the Beginning of the Long Parliament to the Opening of the Trial of the Earl of Strafford* (New Haven: Yale University Press, 1923)

PCCRP, *Will Registers*, PROB 11, The National Archives (Kew, London)

Prynne, William, *A true and full relation of the prosecution, arraignment, tryall, and condemnation of Nathaniel Fiennes* (London: Michael Sparke, 1644)

Redstone, Vincent B. (ed.), *The Ship Money Returns for the County of Suffolk, 1639–40* (Ipswich: W.E. Harrison, 1904)

Rushworth, John (ed.), *Historical Collections*, Part 2, Vol. 2 (London: Thomas Newcombe, 1659)

Rushworth, John (ed.), *Historical Collections*, Part 3, Vol. 2 (London: Richard Chiswell and Thomas Cockerill, 1692)

Rushworth, John (ed.), *Historical Collections*, Part 4, Vol. 1 (London: D. Brown et al., 1722)

Rushworth, John (ed.), *Historical Collections*, Part 4, Vol. 2 (London: Richard Chiswell and Thomas Cockerill, 1701)

Schurman, Anna Maria van, *Opuscula Hebraea, Graeca, Latina, Gallica. Prosaica et Metrica.* (Leiden: Elzevir Press, 1648)

Scott, Walter (ed.), *Military Memoirs of the Great Civil War* (Edinburgh: Hurst, Robinson, and Co., 1822)

Slingsby, Henry, *Original Memoirs Written During the Great Civil War* (Edinburgh: James Ballantyne & Co., 1806)

Snow, Vernon F. and Anne Steele Young (eds), *The Private Journals of the Long Parliament*, Vol. 3 (New Haven: Yale University Press, 1992)

Sylvester, Matthew (ed.), *Reliquiæ Baxterianæ: or, Mr Richard Baxter's Narrative of the Most Memorable Passages of His Life and Times* (London: T. Parkhurst, J. Robinson, J. Lawrence, and J. Dunton, 1696)

T.V., *A True relation of the late battell neere Newbery* (London: John Wright, 1643)

The Dean and Chapter of the Collegiate Church of Saint Peter in Westminster, *Registers and Books of St Margaret's Church, Westminster* (Westminster, London)

Verney, Margaret M. (ed.), *Memoirs of the Verney Family During the Seventeenth Century*, Vol. 1 (London: Longmans, Green, and Co., 1904)

Wallington, Nehemiah, *Historical Notices of Events Occurring Chiefly in the Reign of Charles I*, Vol. 2 (London: Richard Bentley, 1869)

Whitelocke, Bulstrode, *Memorials of the English Affairs* (London: Nathaniel Ponder, 1682)

Selected secondary literature

Anon., 'Courtship in the Time of King James the First,' *Blackwood's Edinburgh Magazine* 68, issue 417 (1850): pp.141–159

Anon., *The Parliamentary History of England*, Vol. 3 (London: T.C. Hansard, 1808)

Birch, Thomas, *The Court and Times of Charles the First*, Vol. 2 (London: Henry Colburn, 1849)

Bremer, Francis J., *Puritanism: A Very Short Introduction* (Oxford: Oxford University Press, 2009)

Bremmer Jr, Rolf H. '"Mine is Bigger than Yours": The Anglo-Saxon Collections of Johannes de Laet (1581–1649) and Sir Simonds D'Ewes (1602–1650).' In *Anglo-Saxon Books and Their Readers: Essays in Celebration of Helmut Gneuss's 'Handlist of Anglo-Saxon Manuscripts'*, edited by S.D. Hall T.N., pp.136–174 (Kalamazoo: Western Michigan University Press, 2008)

Bremmer Jr, Rolf H. 'The Reception of the Old English Version of Gregory the Great's *Dialogues* between the Conquest and the Close of the Nineteenth Century.' In *Medieval English and Dutch Literatures: The European Context*, edited by Larissa Tracy and Geert H.M. Claassens, pp.29–52 (Cambridge: D.S. Brewer, 2022)

Bruce, John. 'Some Notes on Facts in the Biography of Sir Simonds D'Ewes.' In *The Archaeological Journal*, Vol. 26, edited by Anon., pp.323–338 (London: The office of the Institute, 1869)

Bibliography

Bruce, John, 'The Long Parliament and Sir Simonds D'Ewes,' *The Edinburgh Review* 84, issue 169 (1846): pp.76–102

Bulman, William J., *The Rise of Majority Rule in Early Modern Britain and Its Empire* (Cambridge: Cambridge University Press, 2021)

Carlton, Charles, *Going to the Wars: The Experience of the British Civil Wars, 1638–1651* (London: Routledge, 1992)

Carlton, Charles, *This Seat of Mars: War and the British Isles, 1485–1746* (New Haven: Yale University Press, 2011)

Carlyle, Thomas, *Critical and Miscellaneous Essays*, Vol. 7 (London: Chapman and Hall, 1872)

Cliffe, J.T., *Puritans in Conflict: The Puritan Gentry During and After the Civil Wars* (London: Routledge, 1988)

Cliffe, J.T., *The Puritan Gentry: The Great Puritan Families of Early Stuart England* (London: Routledge & Kegan Paul, 1984)

Coates, Charles, *The History and Antiquities of Reading* (London: J. Nichols and Son, 1802)

Copinger, W.A. *The Manors of Suffolk* (London: T. Fisher Unwin, 1905)

Crawford, Patricia and Laura Gowing (eds), *Women's Worlds in Seventeenth-Century England* (London: Routledge, 2000)

Deck, J., *A Guide to the Town, Abbey, and Antiquities of Bury St Edmunds* (Bury St Edmunds: W.T. Jackson, 1836)

Denholm-Young, N. and H.H.E. Craster. 'Roger Dodsworth (1585–1654) and His Circle.' In *The Yorkshire Archaeological Journal*, Vol. 32, edited by J.W. Houseman, pp.5–32 (Leeds: Yorkshire Archaeological Society, 1936)

Donagan, Barbara, *War in England, 1642–1649* (Oxford: Oxford University Press, 2010)

English Heritage, https://www.english-heritage.org.uk/

Forster, John, *Arrest of the Five Members by Charles the First* (London: John Murray, 1860)

Forster, John, *Historical and Biographical Essays*, Vol. 1 (London: John Murray, 1858)

Forster, John, *The Statesmen of the Commonwealth of England*, Vol. 2 (London: Longman, Orme, Brown, Green, & Longmans, 1840)

Gardiner, Samuel R., *History of England from the Accession of James I to the Outbreak of the Civil War*, Vol. 9 (London: Longmans, Green, and Co., 1891)

Gardiner, Samuel R., *History of the Great Civil War, 1642–1649*, Vol. 1 (London: Longmans, Green, and Co., 1901)

Gaunt, Peter, *The English Civil Wars, 1642–1651* (Oxford: Osprey Publishing, 2003)

Gentles, Ian, *The English Revolution and the Wars in the Three Kingdoms, 1638–1652* (London: Routledge, 2007)

Godwin, G.N., *The Civil War in Hampshire* (London: John and Edward Bumpus Ltd, 1904)

Gregg, Pauline, *King Charles I* (Berkeley: University of California Press, 1984)

Harris, Tim, *Rebellion: Britain's First Stuart Kings* (Oxford: Oxford University Press, 2014)

Harrison, Frederic, *Oliver Cromwell* (London: Macmillan and Co., 1895)
Hexter, J.H., 'The English Aristocracy, Its Crises, and the English Revolution, 1558–1660,' *Journal of British Studies* 8 (1968): pp.22–78
Hillier, George, *A Narrative of the Attempted Escapes of Charles the First from Carisbrooke Castle* (London: Richard Bentley, 1852)
Hopper, Andrew. 'The Civil Wars.' In *Norwich since 1550*, edited by Carole Rawcliffe and Richard Wilson, pp.89–116 (London: Hambledon and London, 2004)
Hopper, Andrew, *Turncoats & Renegades: Changing Sides During the English Civil Wars* (Oxford: Oxford University Press, 2012)
Hughes, Ann, *The Causes of the English Civil War* (Basingstoke: Macmillan Press Ltd, 1998)
Hutton, Ronald, *The Royalist War Effort, 1642–1646*, 2nd edition (London: Routledge, 1999)
Irvine, Susan (ed.), *The Anglo-Saxon Chronicle: A Collaborative Edition*, Vol. 7 (Cambridge: D.S. Brewer, 2004)
Isaacson, S. 'Notices of the Family of Stuteville, of Dalham Hall, Suffolk.' In *Transactions of the British Archaeological Association, at its Second Annual Congress, Held at Winchester*, edited by Anon., pp.317–325 (London: Henry G. Bohn, 1846)
Jessup, Frank W., *Background to the English Civil War* (Oxford: Pergamon Press, 1966)
Jones, Serena, *No Armour But Courage: Colonel Sir George Lisle, 1615–1648* (Solihull: Helion & Company Limited, 2016)
Larsen, Anne R., *Anna Maria van Schurman, 'The Star of Utrecht': The Educational Vision and Reception of a Savante* (Routledge: Abingdon, 2016)
Lockett, Mark and Michael Leach, 'The Search for a Lost Diary of Simonds D'Ewes (1602–50),' *Transactions of the Cambridge Bibliographical Society* 16 (2017): pp.161–180
MacCormack, John R., *Revolutionary Politics in the Long Parliament* (Cambridge, Massachusetts: Harvard University Press, 1973)
Marsden, John Howard, *College Life in the Time of James the First* (London: John W. Parker and Son, 1851)
McIntyre, Rick (ed.), *War Against the Wolf: America's Campaign to Exterminate the Wolf* (Stillwater: Voyageur Press, 1995)
Miller, John, *A Brief History of the English Civil Wars: Roundheads, Cavaliers and the Execution of the King* (London: Constable & Robinson Ltd, 2009)
Nichols, John, *The History and Antiquities of the County of Leicester*, Vol. 2, Part 2 (London: J. Nichols, 1798)
Pal, Carol, *Republic of Women: Rethinking the Republic of Letters in the Seventeenth Century* (Cambridge: Cambridge University Press, 2012)
Palgrave, Reginald F.D., 'The Story of the Death of Thomas, Earl of Strafford,' *Fraser's Magazine* 7, issue 40 (1873): pp.391–408
Palmer, William, *The Political Career of Oliver St John, 1637–1649* (London: Associated University Presses, 1993)

Postgate, M.R. 'Field Systems in East Anglia.' In *Studies of Field Systems in the British Isles*, edited by Alan R.H. Baker and Robin A. Butlin, pp.281–324 (Cambridge: Cambridge University Press, 1973)

Pulman, George P. R., *The Book of the Axe* (Bath: Kingsmead Reprints, 1969)

Rawcliffe, Carole, Richard George Wilson and Roger Virgoe (eds), *Counties and Communities: Essays on East Anglian History: Presented to Hassell Smith* (Norwich: University of East Anglia, 1996)

Robertson, Randy, *Censorship and Conflict in Seventeenth-Century England: The Subtle Art of Division* (Philadelphia: University of Pennsylvania Press, 2009)

Romburgh, Sophie van, *'For My Worthy Friend Mr Franciscus Junius': An Edition of the Correspondence of Francis Junius F.F. (1591–1677)* (Leiden: Brill, 2004)

Russell, J.M., *The History of Maidstone* (Maidstone: W.S. Vivish, 1881)

Salt, S.P., 'Sir Simonds D'Ewes and the Levying of Ship Money,' *The Historical Journal* 37 (1994): pp.253–287

Sanford, John Langton, *Studies and Illustrations of the Great Rebellion* (London: John W. Parker and Son, 1858)

Saunders, G.W. and Charles Herbert Mayo (eds), *Notes & Queries for Somerset and Dorset*, Vol. 15 (Sherborne: J.C. and A.T. Sawtell, 1917)

Scott, David. 'Party politics in the Long Parliament, 1640–8.' In *Revolutionary England, c. 1630–c. 1660: Essays for Clive Holmes*, edited by George Southcombe and Grant Tapsell, pp.32–54 (London: Routledge, 2022)

Sears McGee, J., *An Industrious Mind: The Worlds of Sir Simonds D'Ewes* (Stanford: Stanford University Press, 2015)

Seaver, Paul S. 'State Religion and Puritan Resistance in Early Seventeenth-Century England.' In *Religion and the Early Modern State: Views from China, Russia, and the West*, edited by James D. Tracy and Marguerite Ragnow, pp.207–252 (Cambridge: Cambridge University Press, 2004)

Shapiro, Barbara J., *Law Reform in Early Modern England: Crown, Parliament and the Press* (Oxford: Hart Publishing, 2019)

Sharpe, Kevin, *The Personal Rule of Charles I* (New Haven: Yale University Press, 1992)

Shaw, William A., *A History of the English Church During the Civil Wars and Under the Commonwealth*, Vol. 1 (London: Longmans, Green, and Co., 1900)

Smuts, R. Malcolm, *Political Culture, the State, & the Problem of Religious War in Britain & Ireland, 1578–1625* (Oxford: Oxford University Press, 2023)

Spalding, Ruth, *The Improbable Puritan: A Life of Bulstrode Whitelocke, 1605–1675* (London: Faber & Faber, 1975)

Terry, Charles Sanford, *The Life and Campaigns of Alexander Leslie, First Earl of Leven* (London: Longmans, Green, and Co., 1899)

Thirsk, Joan, *The Agrarian History of England and Wales*, Vol. 4 (Cambridge: Cambridge University Press, 1967)

Traub, Valerie, *Thinking Sex with the Early Moderns* (Philadelphia: University of Pennsylvania Press, 2016)

Underdown, David, *Pride's Purge: Politics in the Puritan Revolution* (London: George Allen & Unwin, 1985)

Vallance, Edward, *Revolutionary England and the National Covenant: State Oaths, Protestantism and the Political Nation, 1553–1682* (Woodbridge: The Boydell Press, 2005)

Various, *Notes and Queries*, 3rd series, Vol. 10 (London: The office of the Institute, 1866)

Warburton, Eliot, *Memoirs of Prince Rupert, and the Cavaliers*, Vol. 2 (London: Richard Bentley, 1849)

Warneke, Sara, *Images of the Educational Traveller in Early Modern England* (New York: E.J. Brill, 1995)

White, Michelle Anne, *Henrietta Maria and the English Civil Wars* (Aldershot: Ashgate Publishing Limited, 2006)

Williams, Ethel, *Anne of Denmark: Wife of James VI of Scotland, James I of England* (London: Longman, 1971)

Woolrych, Austin, *Battles of the English Civil War* (London: Phoenix Press, 2000)

Woolrych, Austin, *Britain in Revolution: 1625–1660* (Oxford: Oxford University Press, 2002)

Worden, Blair, *The English Civil Wars, 1640–1660* (London: Orion, 2009)

Woudhuysen, H.R., *Sir Philip Sidney and the Circulation of Manuscripts, 1558–1640* (Oxford: Clarendon Press, 1996)

Wright, Franklin M., 'A College First Proposed, 1633: Unpublished Letters of Apostle Eliot and William Hammond to Sir Simonds D'Ewes,' *Harvard Library Bulletin* 8, issue 3 (1954): 255–282

Youings, Joyce. 'Some Early Topographers of Devon and Cornwall.' In *Topographical Writers in South-West England*, edited by Mark Brayshay, pp.50–61 (Exeter: University of Exeter Press, 1996)

Young, Peter, *Marston Moor 1644: The Campaign and the Battle* (Kineton: The Roundwood Press, 1970)

INDEX

Abbot, George (archbishop), 37
Albury Lodge (Hertfordshire), 44, 135
Alington, Sir Giles (of Horseheath), 43
America, 66–7, 70, 83
Anna of Denmark (queen consort), 20
Antelminelli, Alessandro (Tuscan diplomat), 37–9, 98
Armine, Sir William (MP, d.1651), 105
Aston, Lady Anne (**sister-in-law**), 129
Aston, Sir Thomas (**brother-in-law**), 104, 129
Axminster (Devon), 2, 4, 11, 50

Barnardiston, Arthur, 40, 87, 146
Barnardiston, Dame Jane, xi, 74
Barnardiston, Sir Nathaniel, xi, 20, 22, 40, 41, 43, 57, 62, 72–3, 74, 79, 80, 161
 character of, 21
Barnardiston, Sir Thomas (**grandfather-in-law, d.1619**), 22, 40, 161
Bastwick, John (physician), 61
Baxter, Richard (theologian), 106, 133
Bishops' Wars:
 First Bishops' War, 70–2
 Second Bishops' War, 73, 75–7
Blandford Forum (Dorset), 7, 8
Bokenham, Wiseman (**brother-in-law**), 38
Bolton, storming of, 125
Bowes, Sir Thomas (**brother-in-law**), 42, 67, 137
Boxted Hall (Suffolk), 78
Brereton, Sir William, 129, 136
Bristol, 134
 storming of, 116–17

Brograve, Hannah (**aunt-in-law**), 44
Brooke Walden (Essex), 54
Burton, Henry (theologian), 61–2
Bury St Edmunds, xi, 14–15, 16, 20, 46, 56–7, 62, 63, 66, 143, 145
Bygrave, Lady Ann (**grandmother-in-law**), 40–2, 44, 82, 161

Cambridge, xi, 44, 66, 100, 109
 St Catharine's College, 56
 St John's College, xiv, 16–20, 22
 St Mary the Great, 98
Camden, William (antiquary), 39
Carisbrooke Castle, 142, 144, 146–7
Carter, George (Elmsett rector), 126, 131
Catholicism, 59, 83, 98, 119, 138
 at court, 38, 60
 contempt for, 60–1
 legislation against, 80, 114–15
Chardstock (Dorset/Devon), 2, 5–6, 9–10, 110, 159
Charles I of England, xv, 14, 20, 25, 29, 45, 55, 60, 65, 69, 70–1, 73, 78, 80, 83, 84, 85, 86, 88, 91–2, 96, 98, 100, 103, 106, 107, 112, 114, 115, 118, 119, 120, 126, 128, 132, 138–9, 140, 144–5, 146–7, 151–2, 153, 154
 accession of, 36–7
 attempted arrest of the five members, 92–3
 coronation of, 38–9
 Covenanters, surrenders to the, 136
 Hampton Court, escapes from, 142
 marriage to Henrietta Maria, 38

parliament, dissolves in 1629, 46–7
Short Parliament, dissolves the, 74–5
trial and execution of, 155
Charles Louis, Elector Palatine, xv, 65–6, 88, 93, 120
Clare Priory (Suffolk), 20, 40, 41
Clopton, Lady Anne (**first wife**), xiv, 13, 20, 40–2, 43–4, 50, 51, 52, 55, 56–7, 62, 63, 67, 72, 76, 78, 81, 82, 157, 160, 161, 162
death of, 89–90
Clopton, Sir William (**father-In-law**), 40, 62, 161
Colchester, 30, 102
siege of, 147–50
Copinger, Ambrose (rector), 54, 126
Corbet, Richard (bishop), 58
Cotton, Sir Robert (antiquary), 39, 45, 55
Coucher, Sir John (MP), 85–6
Court of Common Pleas, 40, 46, 87–8
Court of High Commission, 59–60
abolished, 88
Coxden (Dorset), xi, 2–6, 9–10, 11, 12, 50
Crew, John (future 1st Baron Crew of Stene), 44
Cromwell, Oliver, 83, 97, 100, 122, 129, 131, 132, 133, 136, 142, 144, 153, 159

Dalham Hall (Suffolk), 36
Danford, Richard (rector), 38, 53, 54, 58, 62, 90, 115, 126–7
Denton, Lady Elizabeth (**stepmother**), 33–4, 45, 52–4, 56, 58, 62, 89
Dering, Sir Edward (antiquary), 97, 102
Devereux, Robert, 3rd Earl of Essex, 100, 101, 103, 104, 106, 107, 110, 111, 112, 115, 117, 118, 130
Dodsworth, Roger (antiquary), 140, 156, 158
Dorchester (Dorset), 4–5

Dorset, xi, 4, 8, 10, 11, 12, 17, 110, 157
description of, 2
see also individual towns and properties
Downes, Andrew (professor of Greek), 22
Dugdale, William (antiquary), 70, 154, 155, 156, 158

Edgehill, battle of, 105–6
Elliot, William (**brother-in-law**), 29, 36, 57, 88, 91, 96–7, 107, 108
Elliot, William (**nephew**), 136
English Civil War, *see individual battles and sieges*
Ewes, Adrian D' (**great-grandfather**), 4, 160
Ewes, Adrian D' (**son, d.1640**), 72, 78, 162
death of, 75
Ewes, Adrian and Geerardt D' (**twin sons**), 63, 162
deaths of, 57
Ewes, Anne D' (**daughter**), 51, 56, 78, 162
death of, 88–9
Ewes, Cecilia D' (**daughter**), 63, 78, 135, 137, 157, 160, 162
Ewes, Cecilia D' (**mother**), 2, 3–5, 6, 8–9, 10, 11, 14, 31, 54, 63, 157, 160
description of, 3–4
illness and death of, 17
Ewes, Cecilia D' (**sister**), 9
death of, 26
Ewes, Clopton D' (**son, d.1631**), 57, 162
illness and death of, 55
Ewes, Clopton D' (**son, d.1636**), 62, 162
death of, 66, 67
illness of, 63
Ewes, Elizabeth D' (**daughter**), 81, 137, 162
death of, 135
Ewes, Elizabeth D' (**sister**), 4, 9, 53–4, 57, 62, 66, 110

192

Index

Ewes, Geva D' (**daughter**), 70, 162
   death of, 78
Ewes, Grace D' (**sister**), 9, 10, 38
Ewes, Isolda D' (**daughter**), 78, 135, 137, 157, 162
Ewes, Johanne D' (**sister**), 9, 10, 19, 29, 36, 54, 63, 108
   death of, 136
Ewes, Mary D' (**daughter**), 137, 162
   death of, 140–1
Ewes, Mary D' (**sister**), 9, 10, 42, 67, 137
Ewes, Paul D' (**brother**), xiv, 9, 50
Ewes, Paul D' (**father**), xiii, 2, 4–5, 8, 9, 10, 11, 13, 14, 16, 17, 19–20, 22, 29–30, 31, 32, 33–4, 35, 36, 41, 42, 43, 45, 47, 55, 56, 57, 58, 111, 126, 157, 160
   disagreements with Simonds, 18, 23, 25–6, 28, 31, 40
   illness and death of, 51–4
   marriage to Elizabeth Denton, 33
   purchases Stow Hall, 12
Ewes, Richard D' (**brother**), 9, 14, 26, 34, 50, 51, 58, 63, 108, 112, 114, 137
   death of, 110–11
   fathers a bastard child, 99–100
   relationship with Simonds, xvi, 55–6, 108, 110, 112–13, 157
   soldierly activities of, 75–6, 99, 101, 104, 107, 116, 155
   travels the continent, 67–8, 70
Ewes, Sir Simonds D':
   accidents involving, 4, 5, 6, 8, 13, 18–19, 44, 62
   ancestry of, 4, 43, 119, 160
   antiquarian pursuits of, 34, 35–6, 39, 45, 50, 56, 63, 70, 135, 140, 141, 151–2, 155, 156, 158
   baronetcy conferred on, 88
   birth of, 2
   births of the children of, 51, 55, 57, 62, 63, 70, 72, 78, 81, 137, 156
   burial of, 158–9
   Commons contributions of, 80, 81, 82, 83, 84, 87–8, 90, 91, 96, 97, 98–9, 100, 103, 104–5, 109, 110, 112, 115, 117, 120, 126, 127, 134, 136, 139, 144
   death of, 157–8
   duel organised by, 34–5
   education of, 5–6, 9, 10–11, 12, 14, 16–17, 18, 22, 23
   Elector Palatine, visits the, 65–6
   financial struggles of, 87, 146, 155
   illnesses of, 5, 6, 14, 20, 36
   knighted by Charles I, 42
   legacy of, 157
   Long Parliament, enters the, 79–80
   marriage negotiations of, 22–3, 28–31, 32, 38, 40–2, 102
   marriage to Lady Anne Clopton, 42
   marriage to Lady Elizabeth Willoughby, 104
   Middle Temple associations of, xiv, 10, 11, 22, 23, 24, 26, 33, 34, 44, 99–100, 108, 137
   New Model Army, views on, 130–1
   presents the Grand Remonstrance to Charles I, 91–2
   publications of, 50, 96, 129
   purged by Colonel Pride, 152–3
   religious activities of, 25–6, 35, 58, 69, 96–7, 115, 119, 126–7, 131
   religious beliefs of, xvi–xvii, 6, 21, 22, 35, 43, 45, 51, 58–9, 60, 73, 92, 127, 140, 157, 159
   ship money, views on, 64, 65, 78
   shrieval duties of, 72–3, 74, 75, 78–9
   Solemn League and Covenant, takes the, 119
   tonnage and poundage, views on, 80
   Vow and Covenant, takes the, 115
Ewes, Willoughby D' (**son**), 156, 157, 160, 162
executions, *see individuals*

Fairfax, Sir Thomas (parliamentary commander), 121, 122, 126, 130, 131–2, 134, 136, 137, 144, 146, 147, 148–9, 152
Fawley Court (Buckinghamshire), 108
Finch, Sir John (Speaker of the House of Commons), 46–7

Gerard, Sir Gilbert (MP), 105, 119
Goring, George, 1st Earl of Norwich, 146, 147, 148, 149
Grand Remonstrance, xv, 91–2, 97
Greyfriars Kirk (Edinburgh), 69

Hampden, John (MP), 88, 92
Hampton Court Palace, xv, 20, 91–2, 96, 142
Haselrig, Sir Arthur (MP), 85, 86, 92, 119
Henrietta Maria of France (queen consort), 38, 60, 61, 83, 115, 118
Hobart, Sir Henry (Lord Chief Justice of the Common Pleas), 23, 28
Hobart, Sir John, 102
Hobart, Lady Mary, 23, 28
Holdsworth, Richard (academic theologian), 16, 18, 22, 23, 35, 98, 142
Holles, Denzil (MP), 46, 92, 93, 105–6, 107, 119

Ipswich, 79
Ireton, Henry, 152
Isham, Justinian, 47
Ixworth Abbey (Suffolk), 58, 62, 81, 89

James I of England, 14, 29, 69
  death and funeral of, 36–8
Jermyn, Sir Thomas (Comptroller of the King's Household), 83
Jesson, William (MP), 103
Joachimi, Sir Albertus (ambassador), 39, 45, 75
Junius, Francis (Dutch scholar), 155, 158

Kedington (Suffolk), xi, 28, 74
Kedington Hall (Suffolk), 21, 41, 74
Kentwell Hall (Suffolk), 40, 50

Laet, Johannes de (Dutch geographer), 104, 155
Laud, William (archbishop), 35, 47, 59, 60, 61, 69, 74, 82, 84, 90, 141
  execution of, 128
  impeachment of, 81
  trial of, 127
Laudianism, 58–60, 71, 74, 81, 82–3, 90, 91
Lavenham (Suffolk), 9, 11, 34, 53, 57, 62, 87, 126, 159
  'baby brass' at the church at, 55
Lawford Hall (Essex), 28, 30, 31
Leicester, 131
  storming of, 133–4
Lenthall, William (Speaker of the House of Commons), 75, 80, 84, 87, 93, 100, 103, 105, 112, 118, 131, 136, 141, 142, 147, 153
Lisle, Sir George, 147, 148
  execution of, 150
London, 4–5, 6, 7, 8, 14, 19, 23, 25–6, 28, 29, 33–9, 42, 43, 45–6, 50, 56, 57, 58, 76, 78, 81, 86, 88, 96, 98, 99, 101, 105, 107, 108, 115, 118, 119, 122, 132, 136, 143, 150, 152, 157, 158
  Bishopsgate, 104
  Blackheath, 147
  Camberwell, 141
  Chancery Lane, 9–10, 11, 12, 25, 29, 31–2, 45, 52, 54
  Charing Cross, 25
  Fulham, 84
  Islington, 50, 51, 56, 104
  London Charterhouse, 34
  St Ann Blackfriars, 25
  St Faith under St Paul, 29, 33
  St Mary Axe, 12
  St Mary Woolchurch Haw, 91
  St Paul's Cathedral, 25, 122

Index

Stepney, 88–9
the Strand, 29, 37
Tothill Fields, 134
Westminster Abbey, 20, 25, 37, 38–9, 119
Whitehall, 14, 25, 29, 35, 38, 144, 155
Long Melford (Suffolk), 40, 50, 62
Lucas, Sir Charles, 147, 148–9
  execution of, 150
Lucas, Sir John, 102
Lunsford, Sir Thomas, 92, 111

Maidstone, battle of, 146, 147
Mansell, Sir Robert (MP), 87
Marston Moor, battle of, 121–4
Marten, Henry (MP), 104–5
Maurice, Prince Palatine of the Rhine, 116
Melcombe Horsey (Dorset), 5
Melford Hall (Suffolk), 62
Middle Temple (London), xiv, 3, 10, 11, 22–5, 26–7, 31, 33, 34, 42, 44, 56, 63, 99–100, 108, 135, 137
  Christmases at, 26–7, 108–9
Montagu, Edward, 2nd Earl of Manchester, 121, 123, 126, 130, 131
Much Bromley (Essex), 42, 67, 137

Naseby, battle of, 131–3
  aftermath of, 134
National Covenant, signed in Scotland, 69
New Model Army, 129–33, 134, 141, 142
Newburn, battle of, 76–7
  see also Second Bishops' War
Newbury, first battle of, 118
Newcastle, 71, 76–7, 138, 151
Newcastle Propositions, 138
Newenham, manor of (Essex), 43
Newmarket, xv, 36, 65–6, 120
Norwich, 82
  riots in, 143, 144–5

Oatlands Palace (Surrey), 107

Poley, Sir William (**brother-in-law**), 66, 74, 113
Potts, Sir John (of Mannington Hall), 102, 108
Pride, Colonel Thomas, 152–3
Pride's Purge, xv, 152–3, 154
Prynne, William (polemicist), 61–2
Puritanism, xvi–xvii, 6, 21, 22, 25, 45, 51, 59, 67, 73, 79, 82, 83, 90, 91, 92, 140, 142, 159
Pym, John (MP), 73–4, 81, 88, 91, 92–3, 96, 110, 115, 117–18
  death of, 119

Reading, 107
  siege of, xvi, 110–12, 115, 116
Risley (Derbyshire), 102, 104
Root and Branch Bill, 87–8
Rupert of the Rhine, 106, 107, 108, 111–12, 116, 118, 121–2, 123, 125, 132, 133
  his dog killed at Marston Moor, 123–4
  surrenders Bristol, 134
Rushworth, John, 93, 131, 132, 147

Sackville, Edward, 4th Earl of Dorset, 91
Savage, Thomas, 1st Viscount Savage, 62
Schurman, Anna Maria Van (Dutch scholar), 135
Selden, John (scholar), 144
Self-denying Ordinance, 130
Sherborne Castle (Dorset), 103
ship money, xiv, xv, 64–5, 73, 74, 75, 78, 80, 88
  condemned by the Commons, 81
Simonds, Joan (**grandmother**), 3, 6, 7, 8, 157
  death of, 9
  description of, 3

195

Simonds, Richard (**grandfather**), 3, 4, 5–7, 8, 157
   death of, 9–10
   description of, 3
Skinner, Dame Mary (of Lavenham), 9
Skinner, Sir Thomas (of Lavenham), 9
Slingsby, Sir Henry (royalist), 71, 76, 121, 124
Solemn League and Covenant, 119, 120, 121
Somner, William (antiquary), 155, 156, 157
St Albans, 134
St James's Palace, 144, 151,
St John, Sir Beauchamp (MP), 98
St John, Oliver (MP), 81, 119
Star Chamber, 33, 56, 61, 75
   abolished, 88
Starkey, Ralph (antiquary), 45
Stow Hall (Suffolk), 12–13, 14, 16, 17, 18, 20, 22, 23, 35–6, 39, 43–4, 47, 54, 56, 58, 62, 63, 65, 66, 76, 89, 105, 145, 153, 155
   description of, 13
   disputes over, 53
Stowlangtoft (Suffolk), 12, 14, 17, 20, 43–4, 53, 58, 62, 78, 82, 87, 90, 158, 159
   church at (St George's), xiii–xiv, 17, 35, 38, 50, 53, 54, 58, 66, 141, 158
   description of, xiii
   history of, 13, 35–6
Stuart, Elizabeth, Queen of Bohemia, 60
Stuteville, John, 89, 154, 156
Stuteville, Sir Martin, 36, 41, 45, 52
Suffolk, xiv, 23, 46, 79, 80, 82–3, 88, 105, 110, 115, 120, 126, 130, 131
   coastline of, 11, 14
   description of, 8–9

gentry of, 17, 21, 89
   see also individual towns and properties
Symonds, Richard (royalist soldier), 133–4

Theobalds (Hertfordshire), 36–7
Thou, Jacques Auguste de (French historian), 70
tonnage and poundage, 46–7, 73–4, 80
Tower of London, 34, 50, 84, 86, 92, 97, 127, 128, 156
Turnham Green, 107

Ussher, James, Archbishop of Armagh, 75, 155

Vaughan, Robert (antiquary), 155
Villiers, George, 1st Duke of Buckingham, 36

Waldegrave, Sir Edward, 28, 29–30
   death of, 32
Waldegrave, Lady Jemima, 28, 29–31, 32, 44, 149
Waller, Edmund (MP), 107, 115
Waller, Sir William (MP), 109, 117, 125–6, 130
Wardour Castle, 114
Warwick Castle, 137
Wells Hall (Suffolk), 4, 5, 8–9, 10, 23
Wentworth, Sir Thomas, 1st Earl of Strafford, 16, 83–6
   execution of, 86
Westminster Assembly of Divines, 114, 119, 134
Wheelocke, Abraham (linguist), 77
White, Richard (rector), 2, 5–6, 10
Willoughby, Lady Elizabeth (**second wife**), 102, 104, 105, 108, 129, 135, 136, 137, 141, 156, 158–9, 160, 162
Willoughby, Sir Henry (**father-in-law**), 102, 104

Winchester Cathedral, 109
Wren, Matthew (bishop), 82–3
Wriothesley, Henry, 3rd Earl of
 Southampton, 16, 18
Wriothesley, James (d.1624), 18

York, 98, 99, 124, 126, 151
 siege of, 121
Young, Patrick (Keeper of His
 Majesty's Libraries), 71,
 144, 151